Choice Notes
on
JOSHUA — 2 KINGS

F.B. Meyer Memorial Library

Devotional Commentary on Exodus

Choice Notes on Joshua to 2 Kings

Choice Notes on the Psalms

Devotional Commentary on Philippians

Choice Notes

on

JOSHUA — 2 KINGS

by
F.B. Meyer

Foreword by
J. Arnold Fair

KREGEL PUBLICATIONS
Grand Rapids, Michigan 49501

Library of Congress Cataloging in Publication Data

Meyer, F. B. (Frederick Brotherton), 1847-1929.
  Choice Notes on Joshua to 2nd Kings.

  Rev. ed. of "The Christian" Bible readings. 1895.
  Includes index.
  1. Bible. O.T. Former Prophets — Criticism, interpretation, etc.
I. Meyer, F. B. (Frederick Brotherton), 1847-1929. "Christian" Bible
readings. II Title.
BS1286.5M49 1984   222'.06   84-27869
ISBN 0-8254-3241-3

Printed in the United States of America

CONTENTS

Foreword by J. Arnold Fair. 7
Preface. 9
The Book of Joshua 11
The Book of Judges 40
The Book of Ruth. 71
The First Book of Samuel. 79
The Second Book of Samuel .116
The First Book of Kings 146
The Second Book of Kings 177
Index 215

Maps and Charts

Canaan, as Divided Among the Tribes 39
Judges of Israel 41
Prophecies Concerning Nations that Oppressed Israel
    in the Times of the Judges 70
Contemporary Kings of Israel and Judah 145
The Prophets in Chronological Order 176
Kings of Judah After Israel's Captivity 213

FOREWORD

This pleasure-to-read commentary was written for today's "on the move" society, both active layperson and busy pastor. You waste no time searching for the meaning of a passage. Dr. F.B. Meyer's notes are very clear. You will find this valued help to be plain, practical, precise, perceptive, and profitable for one interested in knowing what the Bible says.

The reading of this devotional commentary is interesting. As a pastor-teacher, F.B. Meyer carefully strives to make each passage clear. The teacher of God's Word will find a readied banquet of spiritual food prepared in plainness to present to his students. In typical Meyer style, the reader is inspired and uplifted, even while reading the jagged, jostling Judges. Oh, how we need this *plain* teaching today.

F.B. Meyer's many volumes are known for their penetrating *practicalness.* The application of timeless truth is made at every turn of these Old Testament events. At times, it seems Pastor Meyer has just stopped by to share these rich truths personally with you. This is of special help to one who is studying to help others. As one reads and rereads these old, but ever-fresh books, he will find the *practical* teachings taking root in his own life.

A busy pastor will greatly appreciate this commentary. Dr. Meyer lived in a day when men had time to get away and quietly think. It is this wondrous ability, to cut through the wordiness of exposition and present *precise* and concise concepts, that makes Meyer's writing so extremely valuable.

The useful charts and text combine to illustrate the *perceptive* wisdom of this author. It is with knifing pointedness that much truth is given. These are not the jottings of a young or middle-aged author, but of one who has matured in his walk with God.

All who use this commentary will find it *profitable.* Many are grateful to the publisher who had the foresight to keep this excellent help in print. May our blessed Lord, who guided F.B. Meyer in his writings, give you His understanding and spirit of wisdom, that you might have a deep and intimate knowledge of Him.

Dallas, Texas   J. ARNOLD FAIR

PREFACE

In these notes on the Books of the Old Testament, from JOSHUA to the SECOND BOOK OF KINGS, the primary aim has been to meet the needs of Sunday School teachers, and others who may not have access to larger commentaries. They contain, in a compendious form, the result of a considerable amount of investigation and thought.

Use has been made, in some parts freely, of the valuable notes, contributed to "The Christian," by Rev. H. E. Brooke and Rev. G. Wainwright, in connection with the Daily Readings. It has not been possible to acknowledge all these references; but it would have been foolish and needless not to have made use of them, and so preserved them. But all have been carefully reconsidered and revised.

Throughout *Choice Notes on Joshua to 2 Kings,* the spiritual significance and personal reference have been kept well in view; and it is hoped that this volume may become the companion not only of the teacher, or of the local preacher, but of Bible readers and students generally.

To open up the Divine Word, to excite interest in it, to indicate the line of thought of the sacred writers, to induce devout meditation, and to point the spiritual lessons that are strewn throughout the pages of the Holy Scriptures has been my simple aim.

F.B. MEYER

The Book of Joshua

INTRODUCTION

Though there are evident traces of the hand of an editing scribe, who was probably Ezra, or one of his associates, it is clear that the substance of this book was written when the memory of the events, which it records, were still recent. There is, therefore, no good reason for doubting that the book was written by Joshua, as the Jewish tradition alleges.

The book may be divided thus:

The entrance to Canaan (1-5)
The conquest of Canaan (6-12)
The distribution and partition (13-21)
The settlement and establishment of religion (22-24)

A division may also be made into two parts: 1 to 12, and 13-24.

The Book is full of helpful reading, as we hope to indicate in the notes that follow. The young servant and minister of Moses had absorbed much of the great leader's spirit. This qualified him to lead the people, and to be an eminent type of our Lord Jesus. His name is an equivalent for Jesus, and means *He shall save;* "Christ, as Joshua, is the Captain of our salvation, a leader and commander to the people, to tread Satan under their feet, to put them in possession of the heavenly Canaan, and to give them rest, which (it is said, Heb. 4:8) Joshua did not."

The Book of Joshua is to the Old Testament what the Acts of the Apostles is to the New. Moses and Joshua together cover the earthly and heavenly ministry of the Lord Jesus. In Him are united the functions of Moses, the Lawgiver, and of Joshua, the Commander and Leader. The Jericho of the Early Church was Jerusalem, which they compassed for *ten* days; at Pentecost, the walls of prejudice fell flat. Ananias

and Sapphira were the Achan of the first days. The successful victories of the Church at Samaria, Antioch, and
elsewhere, remind us of the progress of conquest under
Joshua. And the failure of the Church to go forward to the
conquest of the nations has a bitter parallel in the story of
Israel's apathy in driving out the Canaanites.

There is also much to be learned by the individual believer.
In the story of the inner life, there are close analogies between this book and the Epistle to the Ephesians. The Jordan
is the emblem of our death with Jesus, through which we
pass to the Canaan of the Heavenlies; in which we have to
war with the wicked spirits, who contest each foot of
progress. We must have our Gilgals of putting away all
filthiness of the flesh and spirit, and we shall also have our
days when the light of the sun lingers on our victorious path.

Joshua 1   AFTER MOSES, JOSHUA

1-9 *The Divine summons.* — The law, represented by Moses,
serves its purpose in revealing to us ourselves, and showing our impotence and sinfulness; but it cannot conduct us
into the land of promise and victory. Our Saviour Jesus,
whom Joshua typified, alone can do that work in and for us.
Joshua, who was a prince of the tribe of Ephraim, was born
in Egypt. After the Exodus, he became captain of the host,
and typifies the warrior-victor side of our Saviour's character
and work. He, with Caleb, brought back a good report of the
land, and magnified the faithfulness of God; and having been
found faithful in the smaller sphere, was promoted to the
wider one. To him the Divine summons came.

The land of rest and triumph is ours by deed of gift; yet
we must go up and possess it. We must claim it by putting
down the foot of faith. Though Hittites and their confederates — the evil habits of the old past — would make it
impossible for us to realize and enjoy God's provision; yet
as we go forward, we shall find that they cannot stand before
us. God is with us, and they cannot stand before Him. The
promise of verse **5** is for all Christians (Heb. 13:5, 6).

Note the great weapon of successful conflict — *the Word of God* **(7)**. The sword of the Spirit is the Word of God. In His conflict with Satan, Jesus said, repeatedly, "It is written." We should not only read, but meditate day and night. Obedience to the principles of the Bible is the key to prosperity in this life and the next.

10-11 *Prompt obedience.* — It was enough that God had spoken and promised. Nothing more was required. Joshua took immediate steps dictated by sanctified common-sense, to prepare the people for that great step in advance to which he knew the Spirit of God was calling them. "Three days" is constantly used in Scripture in connection with death and resurrection. Faith does not supersede preparation and precaution, but suggests them.

12-18 *The people's voice.* — It must have been very helpful to have God's voice corroborated by that of the people; especially by that section of them which naturally would not be enthusiastic about the campaign that would sever them for a time from wives, children, and property. If these were loyal, of course the rest would be. How hearty and reassuring the response of the two and a half tribes! Oh, to say as much to Christ as they said to Joshua in verse **16**!

Joshua 2   THE SCARLET LINE

1-8 *The hiding of the Spies.* — To "view the land" **(1)** was a hazardous enterprise, for the countenance of the Jews would certainly betray them; and it did. Scripture does not commend Rahab's dishonesty and lying. Her morality was very faulty, as judged by our standards. But alongside of it there was strong and evident faith, such as would ultimately bear the fruits of truth and transparency of speech. The brook would certainly clear itself.

The stalks of flax **(6)** were probably laid out on the flat roof to dry.

9-13 *Rahab's faith.* — Her case, Gentile though she was, is quoted as one of the typical instances of faith in the same category as Abraham's (Heb. 11:31). She believed, on the ground of the wonders wrought in Egypt, that Jehovah was the true God, and that He would give His people the land. Her faith showed itself in her works: in her efforts to secure the safety of the spies; in her love to her kindred; and in the safety guaranteed to all who sheltered under her scarlet cord. That she was sneered at for her infatuated belief is more than probable; but she wavered not. Her heart was full of the conception of the great God, and she was certain that He could do as He had said.

14-24 *The Covenant and its symbol.* — Rahab's trust in the promise of the spies and in the efficacy of the scarlet line bound around the window — the sign by which her house would be known in the day of Jericho's judgment — was a striking type of the faith that relies on the promises of salvation, and rests within the precious blood of Christ for salvation. Note the strict condition exacted by the spies (**19**) as to the extent of their responsibility: only those who were within the house were to be saved amid the general destruction of the people of Jericho. So the salvation of Jesus is only available for those who are found "in Him," and who have responded to His invitation to shelter under the cover of His atonement, and abide there. To be outside is to be in danger of certain destruction, though related to a Rahab. What encouragement and stimulus was given through Rahab's faith to the spies, and through them to Joshua and Israel! Thus may the least in the kingdom of God become a fount of supply and nourishment to the greatest.

Joshua 3   THE PASSAGE OF THE JORDAN

1-6 *Preparation for the passage.* — For three days the host remained in view of that swollen river. It was enough to appall them; unless like Abraham, they dared to look at it as only a foil to set forth God's glorious power (Rom. 4:19). Every means was adopted to impress on the people that the river was cleft, not for them, but for the Ark of the Lord. It was not only the emblem of the covenant; but the symbol of the visible presence of Christ, our Propitiatory. The space between the people and the Ark was not only to promote a sense of reverence, but to make the miracle more apparent to the whole host. Two thousand cubits would be equivalent to about one mile.

We must never go before Christ; but we must surely follow Him, though into the waters of death. The way of the inner life is through the grave. Each day God says to us, "Ye have not passed this way heretofore." What need then to follow Jesus! We must sanctify ourselves, if we would see the wonders of God's right hand.

7-13 *The last instructions.* — It is an anticipation of the New Testament references to the living Christ, to hear Joshua speak of the living God (**10**). He is with us, and will not fail to expel the sevenfold evils of our hearts, as well as the mighty spirits that possess men's hearts against the Gospel. What God was about to do was a pledge of what He would do beyond that. Every deliverance is a pledge that God will not fail or forsake his own. "Hereby ye shall know." ...The victory of the Resurrection is the guarantee of Christ's ultimate triumph over all. The future, and especially the dark river of death, may lie before us as a swollen stream; but our Priest is in front, and by His feet there will be a passage made.

14-17 *The miracle of the passage.* — The waters far up the stream were blocked, and probably formed themselves into a vast lake. The bed of the river became dry, and the remnant of the water hurried down to the Dead Sea. Some miles of dry channels were thus exposed to the passage of the host. The Priests stood still till *all* Israel had passed over (**17**). Not only the leaders, but the led. Not only the Levites and Priests, but the rank and file. Each one of the blood-bought is dear to God; and the waters of judgment shall not be loosed from their leash, till the entire body is saved to sin no more — *Miss Much-Afraid,* and *Mr. Fearing* equally with *Mr. Greatheart.*

Joshua 4   THE TWOFOLD MEMORIAL

This chapter records the erection by Divine command of a double memorial of Israel's passage of the Jordan.

1-8 *The memorial of resurrection.* — Twelve stones were brought up out of the Jordan, and erected in Gilgal (**20**). They would last, at least, for a generation, citing questions, which would give an opportunity for fathers to tell their children the story of the passage. Spiritually, this heap of stones sets forth our oneness with the true Joshua in His resurrection life. We need to be perpetually reminded of it. The memorial must be ever before the eye of the faith. There is no key to spiritual victory more sure than this. "If ye then be risen with Christ, seek . . ." (Col. 3:1).

9 *The memorial of death.* — In the river bed twelve stones were placed where the priests' feet had stood, to give visual demonstration that the people had really been in those oozy depths. Let us not forget the death that we deserved to die, and that Jesus suffered for us. Having died with Him, let us mortify our members which are upon the earth (Col. 3:5).

10-19 *The return of the waters.* — Evidently the presence of the ark was the one sufficient power by which those waters were restrained; for when the bearers regained the further bank, the stream flowed on as before (**18**). Is it not thus that the presence of the Saviour, whom the ark and the priesthood typified, arrests the avalanche of judgment incurred by our sins, and stays the penalty which was our just dessert? And, in addition, we are reminded that we should put Him between us and every threatening stroke of man or devil. Let Him stand between your heart and your dread. Nothing can hurt you, if you shelter yourself behind His living grace and power. But oh, how bitter will be the anguish of those, who, in rejecting Christ, have thrust away the only screen from the waters of death and judgment! It is suggested also that these are held back, only because God's people are yet passing through.

20-24 *Joshua's outlook.* — If we live to do God's will, He will magnify us, and give us the faith and love of men (**14**). Joshua was set on God's glory. His one desire was that all the peoples of the earth should recognize Him, and that His people might be true to Him (**24**).

Joshua 5   CIRCUMCISION RENEWED

1 *The terror of Canaan.* — Evidently the people of the land realized the supremacy of Jehovah, and the impending judgment on their sins. This made their long and strenuous resistance less justifiable. They knew that they were fighting against the Almighty.

2-9 *Circumcision.* — The men who at Kadesh (Num. 14) had come under God's judgment were all dead. During their lifetime it is thought that the covenant was practically abrogated or in abeyance. This seems the meaning of verse **6**. And hence the badge of the rite was discontinued. But now that they were about to face their foes, and go up to possess the land, it was needful that the entire people should stand in the covenant; and that there should be, at least symbolically, a putting away of all filthiness of the flesh and spirit. "The reproach of Egypt" (**9**), which the Lord rolled away, seems to refer to the taunts and reproaches uttered by the Egyptians, who practiced circumcision, against Israel for not performing this rite.

Israel crossed the Jordan in an uncircumcised condition, but the rite was immediately attended to. So, in God's purpose, all believers in Christ have passed from death into life; but it behooves us immediately to mortify our members which are upon the earth, and to put off the old man. It is impossible to enter into the Rest of God until we have put away all known filthiness of the flesh and spirit (Col.2:11).

10-12 *The keeping of the Passover.* — The circumcised soul may eat the Passover. When we are living up to our light, we may freely feed on Christ, who is alike the Paschal Lamb, the Manna, and the old corn of the land. He alone is the Bread of souls. The Passover had not been kept since the hosts left Sinai.

13-15 *The Captain of the Lord's host.* — This must have been our Lord, who thus anticipated His Incarnation. The hosts of which He spake must have been some angelic legion, which was being led into conflict against the wicked spirits that ruled the darkness of Canaan. God usually gave a special revelation of Himself, and a promise, before some great crisis of temptation or service.

Joshua 6   JERICHO TAKEN

1-16 *Its siege.* — The last three verses of the previous chapter belong to this. The first verse is parenthetic; and the Lord, who speaks to Joshua (**2**), is the real Commander. He gives instructions to Joshua, which Joshua transmits to the priests (**6**), and they to the people (**7**). They were to do as little as possible; but exert faith in God, who would do all. Jehovah, who dwells between the cherubim, was the mighty worker. His ark in its repeated circuit, His priests, His determination of the times to be silent or to shout, His appointment of the division of the spoil — all showed that the stress of the conflict was on God; while Israel only took what He gave (**2-21**).

A profound lesson is taught in the fall of Jericho, which may well help us in spiritual conflict. The battle is not ours, but God's. He performeth all things for us. To Him, things that are impossible with man are easily possible. The walls that resist our progress may be high to heaven, and manned by mighty foes; but they shall crumble before the assault of the heavenly legions, and we shall go forward and take.

17-20 *Its capture.* — The taking of the city was the occasion of making good to Rahab, and all found in her house, the covenant mercy that had been promised her. May we and all who bear our name be at last found within the shelter of the covenant of God's grace! But let us beware! Rahab, the Gentile sinner, was saved; but Achan, the child of Abraham, took of the forbidden thing, and perished.

21-27 *Its destruction.* — The utter destruction of Jericho and its people was in keeping with the stern sense of righteous retribution for sin, which was characteristic of those times. No doubt the evil of the city was very great, and would have infected Israel and the world. But the Son of Man came not to destroy men's lives, but to save. Let us remember that God did not legislate in advance of the dispensation to which these Israelites belonged.

The city was "accursed" (**26**), that is, "devoted to utter destruction" (*Wilson*). The curse upon the rebuilder was fulfilled in the reign of Ahab upon the family of Hiel, the Bethelite, who laid the foundation simultaneously with the death of his first-born, and set up the gates with that of his youngest son (1 Kings 16:34). But Jesus stayed there in the house of Zaccheus, and brought salvation into the house of the despised publican.

Joshua 7   THE SIN OF ACHAN

1-6 *Israel's defeat.* — Israel was now taught that victory is only possible where there are literal obedience and entire consecration. We cannot hope to overcome our foes or surmount the difficulties of life, unless we are living in unclouded fellowship with God. Asa was taught the same lesson (2 Chron. 15:2). The reverse coming on the people, flushed with victory, must have been very bitter; but the moral issues at stake were great enough to compensate God in giving them pain. Besides, in the nature of things, those spiritual allies, "the Lord's host," could not cooperate while known evil was harbored in Israel. Canaan was a gift to faith; and the maintenance of a strong spiritual life in Israel was peremptory. The gold and silver that Achan stole was consecrated to God (6:19), so that his sin was sacrilege as well as theft.

Ai (Gen. 12:8; 13:3) was a considerable town, two miles to the north of Jericho and east of Bethel, containing twelve thousand (8:25) people, but was smaller than Jericho; and the spies probably undervalued its power of resistance. The recent victory filled them with conceited confidence. They forgot that without God we are powerless against the smallest opposition; with God triumphant over the greatest.

7-9 *Joshua's confession.* — If Joshua had been living in closer fellowship with God, he would probably have been led to detect the presence of this evil in the midst of Israel; as Peter did that of Ananias and Sapphira. But he did the next best thing in prostrating himself in confession and prayer. His most potent plea with God was for the honor of God.

He had learned to view matters from the Divine standpoint during his association with Moses.

10-15 *The Divine summons.* — There are times when we should no longer remain on our faces, but we should arise to put away the sin, which is revealed as lying at the root of defeat, whether in the personal or collective life. "Get thee up." In detecting the sin, which has produced failure, we must be specific, casting lots among the several faculties of the inner life. Sin has a pedigree. You may always trace out its parentage: "Achan, the son of . . ." (Josh. 7:1). When sin has been judged, the valley of Achor (*trouble*) becomes a "door of hope," through which we pass to victory (Hos. 2:15).

16-26 *Deserved punishment.* — Achan's family had been privy to his crime. It could hardly have been otherwise, since the goods were buried in the common tent. All therefore shared in his fate. It was a terrible tragedy; but we must remember that God's dealings with the people were necessarily dictated by their moral condition and the notions of the age in which they lived.

Joshua 8   AI TAKEN

1-9 *The plan of battle.* — Now that evil had been put away, God could assure Israel of victory, and could speak of the city as already given into the hands of His people. When we are right with God, He often lets us see our victories in advance, and we have but to take what He holds before us. At the same time, His gift is contingent on our energetic action: "Arise, go up."

It is remarkable that the restriction as to appropriating the spoil, which had been in force in the case of Jericho, is here removed. There are certain great distinctions of right and wrong, which are, so to speak, asserted by conscience as fundamental. But, in some cases, God has announced a special code of rites and regulations — such as the Levitical code; and as in the case of Jericho, which, having been arbitrarily imposed, could be arbitrarily removed, when they had served their purpose. All this was an unexampled benefit, as a means of education and discipline.

10-29 *A successful issue.* — Under cover of night, thirty thousand men were sent to station themselves as an ambush; of these five thousand concealed themselves in the immediate neighborhood of that town. The chief magistrates of Israel accompanied him, that there might be an equal distribution of spoil between the combatants and the rest of Israel (Num. 31:27). "At a time appointed" (**14**) may refer to a concert between the people of Ai and those of Bethel, for the towns were contiguous and confederate. At the signal of the uplifted spear the ambush fired the city, and the forces under Joshua turned back on their pursuers.

30-35 *After the battle.* — After the fall of Ai, the war, for a time, was suspended. The Divine Hand restrained the Canaanites from interfering with the obedience of Israel to the Mosiac Code. The whole nation was marshalled at the mountains Ebal and Gerizim to hear the law recited; and that, from the one side and the other, the Amens could be uttered by the thunderous voices of the tribes. We learn from Deut. 27:13 that the curses were to be pronounced from Mount Ebal. It was appropriate therefore that the altar should be erected there (**30**).

This was one of the most impressive scenes that occurred during the occupation of Canaan. Jericho and Ai were heaps of blackened ruins; their kings and people utterly destroyed; their dependent villages mute with terror. And all through the land the rumor ran of the might of Israel's God.

We are taught by this gathering that a pause must be often put on the activities of life, that we may consider the claims of God, and repeat our adhesion to His holy law. Let us go further, and ask that, as the law was written of old on those mighty stones, so it may be engraven on the tablets of our hearts, freely yielded to the hand of God. Thus, though the law cannot be the means of our justification, it may become the rule of our conscience. And as we live in the power of the Holy Ghost, we shall find ourselves increasingly moulded to its lofty ideal (Heb. 8:10). "Christ has redeemed us from the curse of the law, being made a curse for us" (Gal. 3:13).

Joshua 9   A LEAGUE WITH GIBEON

1-2 *The alarm of Canaan.* — The presence of a common danger forced the nations of Canaan to lay aside their internecine strife, in order to combine for self-preservation. Would that the various sections of the visible Church might see their way to adopt a similar policy!

3-15 *The wiles of Gibeon.* — Gibeon is now known as El-Jib, and lies about five miles north of Jerusalem. Its name means "built on a hill." The Church of God has always more to dread from the wiles of the devil than from his open attacks. The supposed conversion of Constantine was more hostile to her than the ten persecutions of Rome. The world is ever seeking to enter the ranks of the Church, to dilute its spirituality. Appeal is made to our pity, our charity, our broadmindedness; but we shall make a profound mistake if we are swayed by these considerations, and so miss asking counsel of God (**14**). There is no reason to believe that, if Israel had asked counsel of God, the destruction of Gibeon would have been inevitable. Nowhere are Joshua and the princes actually blamed. Indeed, there was a measure of faith in the Gibeonites (**24**), as formerly in Rahab, which led to their seeking this league with Israel, even though through deceptive means.

16-27 *Hewers of wood and drawers of water.* — The faith of these people was so far rewarded that, while their deception was punished by the degradation to a servile condition, their lives were spared; and, to a certain degree, they were incorporated amongst Israel, and associated in the service of God's house. The oath was a sacred bond, which no considerations could override; and therefore the Gibeonites were spared. Violation of the covenant with them in after days was severely punished (2 Sam. 21:1). How much more will God be true to His covenant relationships with us, though we be unworthy and unbelieving (2 Tim. 2:13).

The Gibeonites were afterwards called Nethinim, *given* (1 Chron. 9:2; Ezra 2:43; 8:20); and were appropriated by the Levites to the service of the sanctuary. If, in the earlier part of your life, you have made some great mistake, or contracted an alliance that threatens to impede your course, do not sit down to despair; but get useful service out of your mistake. Let it minister to you in hewing the wood of your sacrifice and drawing water for your spiritual cleansing.

Joshua 10   "THE SUN STOOD STILL"

1-11 *The battle of the five kings.* — The five kings combined to smite Gibeon, because it had acted treacherously to the rest of the Canaanites in making peace with Joshua and the children of Israel. They did not dare to attack the intruders into Palestine; but they set on those of their own country who had made peace with them. Thus Satan and his servants oppose us; not only because evil ever hates the good, but because they desire in injuring us to injure Christ.

The honor of Israel was implicated in this attack on their confederates, and Joshua went immediately to their assistance. The deception that they had practiced upon him did not alienate his help. Before he started he was assured of victory (**8**); but this did not make him slothful or careless. "All the people of war, and all the mighty men of valor went up with him." So will Jesus aid us in hours of peril. He will not deal with us after our sins, and He will not slack His hand. He will come up to us quickly, and save and help us.

The Lord's interposition on the behalf of His people seems to have been in a terrific storm. The fugitives had crossed the high ridge of Upper Beth-horon, and were in full flight down the descent to Beth-horon the Nether, when one of those fearful tempests, which from time to time sweep over the hills of Palestine, broke on them. Hailstones in the East are often as large as walnuts, and bigger; and frequently destroy life. Notice the immunity of Israel, proving that the storm was due to Divine interposition.

12-14 *The sun and moon stand still.* — We are not called upon to understand or explain this miracle. The prolongation of daylight must have been attained by the introduction of laws of which we are ignorant; but which may be illustrated by the after-glow of sunset, and the optical refractions on the mountains. God has many methods of aiding those that trust Him, and His omnipotence can never be baffled.

15-27 *The fate of the allied kings.* — The cave at Makkedah would be a perpetual reminder to after generations of the wonderful victory which God gave His people. The details of the placing the feet on their necks, and of their doom, are given with great precision to show the completeness of the conquest. Thus shall it be at the end of the present age; for we are told that all the enemies of Christ shall be put under His feet (1 Cor. 15:25). We may, therefore, well appropriate the words of Joshua (**25**) as we look out on the mighty forces gathered against Christ and His Church.

28-43 *The subjugation of the remainder of Southern Palestine.* — Joshua's career was one of unbroken success, because the Lord went before him, delivering kings and cities, armies and peoples, into his hands. God fought for Israel. It was a war of utter extermination; and, terrible as this appears, it was probably the only way by which the infection of heathenish and abominable practices could be arrested. The iniquity of the Canaanites was full, all previous warnings had been disregarded; in mercy to the rest of the nations, and especially Israel, the plague-spot must be eradicated.

Joshua 11   THE CONQUEST OF THE NORTH

1-9 *The defeat of the Northern confederation.* — The scene is here removed to the Waters of Merom, in the north of Canaan. Jabin took the lead. But that name was, like Pharaoh, an hereditary title (Judg. 4:2). Hazor was the capital of the region. It was an uprising of the whole of the northern peoples to oppose the further progress of Israel. Amorite and Hittite, Perizzite and Jebusite, the Canaanites on the east and on the west, were summoned to the one supreme effort of resistance. The result was a vast concourse of men, horses, and chariots (**4**). Joshua's heart may well have failed him; but on the night before the battle, he was reassured by the Divine promise: "Be not afraid!" (**6**).

Under the cover of night, and perhaps after a forced march, Joshua fell suddenly on the vast host. The Septuagint compares his attack to the falling of a thunderbolt. The effect was immediate and complete. The host was immediately routed and dissolved. Some fled over the mountains to Zidon, others eastward to the plain of Mizpeh. The crippling of the horses was to disable them, and to remove from Israel the temptation of forming a great standing army (Deut. 17:16; Isa. 31:1).

10-15 *The subjugation of the North.* — Hazor was destroyed. The king was beheaded by the sword instead of being hanged on the gallows, because of his great position. The other cities, standing on their mounds (**13**) or eminences, were also destroyed. God's will was literally carried out (**15**). Oh to have a record like that given of this simple-minded soldier: "He left nothing undone!" It is only as we literally obey God that we can count on victory over heart-sins, or on success in Christian work.

16-23 *Rest from war.* — We do not know certainly how long the struggle lasted. The long time (**18**) seems to have been not less than five, or more probably seven, years (**14:10**). And it was only in the reign of David that the ancient inhabitants of Canaan were finally destroyed or merged with Israel. The Anakim, in the days of unbelief, had been Israel's special dread (Deut. 1:28). These were now exterminated with a few exceptions. So do formidable difficulties disappear when we come to them in the power of God. It was a pity that any were left, as they became sources of great weakness and danger; just as any failure in consecration or permission of heart-sins will bring with them inevitable failure and disappointment. Note that Joshua took the land, and then gave it to Israel; so Christ has received the fulness of the Spirit and all spiritual blessings as the trustee of those who believe. But we must claim and possess them by faith. Then at last there will be *rest* (**23**). We shall be satisfied with the abundance of grace which is ours in enjoyment as well as by right.

Joshua 12   ISRAEL'S VICTORIES

This chapter summarizes Israel's victories, so far at least as the names of the kings are concerned.

1-6 *The two kings on the Eastern bank of Jordan.* — Sihon and Og are often named in subsequent parts of the Old Testament, as though Israel's earliest victories over them had left an indelible impression on their minds (Ps. 136:19, 20).

From the river Arnon on the south to the range of Hermon on the north, lay the territory which Moses acquired for, and allotted to, the two tribes and a half. It was never closely incorporated with the history of the chosen people; and reminds us of those natural virtues in the personal character, which may be beautiful and attractive, but have never passed through the Jordan of fellowship with Christ in His death.

7-24 *The thirty-one kings on the Western bank.* — It seems strange in the light of subsequent history to find that one of these was the king of Jerusalem (**10**); and yet it was not till four hundred years had passed that the Jebusites were driven out by David (2 Sam. 5:6), so slack were the people of Israel to avail themselves of God's provision, and enter upon the results of Joshua's victories. In like manner, it is one thing to rejoice in the victory which our Joshua — the Lord Jesus — has won for us (Col. 2:15); it is another to follow it up, and claim its results.

Joshua 13   THE DIVISION OF THE COUNTRY

With this chapter we commence the second part of this book, which records in this and the following chapters the division of the conquered territory among the tribes. It is the Doomsday Book of the conquest.

1-6 *The land which remained unoccupied.* — Joshua was probably about one hundred years old, and since the partition of the land, and the settlement of the people fell, as part of his duty, it was needful that it should be pressed forward. The enumeration begins with the south-western district, and goes northward. It includes the whole of Philistia (**3**). Then it comprises the region of Upper Galilee at the extreme north

(**4, 5, 6**). These territories, though still in the occupation of the original inhabitants, were to be allotted to the tribes of Israel; and God would afterwards give them the complete possession and enjoyment. How significant the sentence, "There remaineth yet very much land to be possessed"! This is true of tracts of the Bible, seldom explored by ordinary Christians; of regions of experience, such as deliverance from the power of sin and dying with Christ; and of countries of the world, never yet trodden by the feet of the ambassadors of peace.

7-33 *A recapitulation of what Moses had allotted.* — There is a great sadness in the words, which so often recur in these chapters and in the Book of Judges, "Nevertheless the children of Israel drove not out . . ." It is all the more terrible, when we remember the reiterated promise of God that He would settle His people. They either did not believe that God meant what He said, or did not arouse themselves from their indolent apathy to claim and use His help. We must first *comprehend* so far as we may what we have in Christ, and then proceed to *apprehend* it by faith.

The remark about the tribe of Levi having no inheritance assigned to them (**14**), because of the sacrifices of God which were theirs, is not introduced to disparage Levi; but to enhance the honor done to them, since theirs was a possession which could not be injured by their failures and sins. "The Lord God of Israel was their inheritance" (**33**). Thus the Lord is the portion of His people. We are heirs of God. All that is in Him is there for us. Let us live near the altar, to minister to Him, and receive our portion from the fire. And let us be His worthy portion!

The sad end of Balaam recorded here (**22**) is the melancholy close of a perverted course. He was once God's mouth-piece. But he thought to divorce character from his prophetic functions. In the New Testament he is the type of the corrupt and apostate portion of the Christian ministry (2 Pet. 2:15; Jude 11). His special sin was theirs, as Jude puts it: "They cast themselves away for hire" (R.V., *marg.*).

Joshua 14   THE PORTION OF CALEB

1-5 *A summary of the position.* — The division of the land between the nine and a half tribes was by lot. This method was adopted to remove all cause of jealousy, or appearance of favoritism. The lot denoted God's choice (Prov. 16:33; and 18:18). It should be used only under His direct suggestion, and in dependence on His providence; and the absence of any mention of His enjoining it in Acts 1:26 will always make it doubtful whether Matthias was really chosen to occupy the place of Judas. How important it is that God should choose our inheritance for us! There is no such thing as fate or chance; all is under rule.

Verse **10** throws an important light on the chronology of the period. The promise referred to by Caleb was given in the second year after the Exodus (Num. 14:20-30). Consequently, forty-five years brings us to the seventh year after their entering Canaan, which shows that the occupation of the land — the subject of this book — took about seven years.

6-15 *Caleb's address and request.* — Notice how Caleb dwells on his old fellowship with Joshua in the spying of the land, and speaks of their faithless fellows as *brethren.* His genealogy is given (1 Chron. 4:13-15). His name, *Kenezite,* indicates that his ancestors had belonged to some tribe friendly to the Israelites, as Jethro and the Kenites (1 Chron. 11:8). In his request he went back to words spoken forty-five years before. How he must have lived on that promise! They that wait for God cannot be ashamed. The Anakim were a branch of the Rephaim, and were formidable both for their stature and war-like qualities (Num. 13:33; Deut. 2:10, 11).

In all simplicity Caleb recalls his consecration in wholly following God. He attributes his hale strength and preservation, his vigor in war and faith, his certain victory over the great and fenced cities, to the fact that he was living in abiding fellowship with the Almighty.

Hebron is assigned to him. The word means "fellowship," and denotes that blessed communion with God into which faith introduces the soul, and which is a condition of serenity and calm. The Apostle John might have dated his first epistle from Hebron. Its former name, "the city of Arba" (a famous Anakite), bore witness to God's faithfulness (Num. 14:8). Those that follow the Lord wholly enter the Land of Promise in unwaning energy, subdue their foes, and find a scene of blessed enjoyment in the strong-hold where some dreaded son of Anak had harbored.

Joshua 15   THE TRIBE OF JUDAH

1-12 *The border of Judah.* — By the aid of a map, the line of the border may be followed on the south from the Dead Sea to the Mediterranean; on the north through Gilgal and Kirjathjearim. It is to be noticed that it ran on the south side of Jerusalem (**8**); so that, strictly speaking, the city which was to play so important a part belonged at first, not to Judah, but to Benjamin (see also 18:16-28). God's choice of the city to put his name there, and of Judah to be the reigning tribe, together with David's conquest of Zion (2 Sam. 5:7), virtually brought it into the possession of Judah.

13-19 *The request of Achsah.* — Her pleading with Caleb that, in addition to his gift of a south land, he should give her further "springs of water," suggests that God's children should not be content with their inheritance in Christ, but should seek also the fulness of the Holy Spirit. Our heavenly standing in our Lord is comparatively valueless apart from the Spirit of wisdom and revelation in the knowledge of Him (Eph. 1:17). Caleb gave Achsah "upper and nether springs"; so God gives exceeding abundantly above all that we ask or think.

Kirjath means a fortress, and *Sepher* a book; it was the city of the book. Recent discoveries have proved that, probably through the influence of Egypt, the Hittites had obtained to a considerable degree of learning and civilization. Othniel was the son of Caleb's younger brother. Achsah had urged her husband to press his suit for himself; but as he shrank from this, she spoke herself, probably at the time when she was removing from her father's to her husband's dwelling-place.

21-63 *A catalog of Judah's cities.* — Ashdod and Gaza (**47**) were afterwards regarded as cities of the Philistines (Judg. 16:21; 1 Sam. 5:1). They had, however, no right to them, as they were clearly included in the territory of Israel. Let us beware of leaving strongholds of sin in our hearts; they will be the worst enemies of our peace and power. Alas for the record of verse **63**! But God was perfectly willing to do for the children of Judah what He did afterwards for David. But "they entered not in because of unbelief."

Joshua 16   THE TRIBE OF EPHRAIM

1-4 *With Manasseh.* — The two tribes which sprang from Joseph drew one lot between them (**1**), and, therefore, their territories were contiguous. The *Speaker's Commentary* says: "The territory allotted to these two powerful tribes comprises the central, and, in every way, the choicest part of Canaan, west of Jordan. The hills of this district, making up what is called Mount Ephraim (20:7), are less high, and far less barren than those of Judah; the water supply is much larger; and the very rich and fertile plains of Sharon and Esdraelon are left between the rocky fastnesses of Benjamin on the south, and the highlands of Galilee, belonging to Issachar, on the north." In the richness of this fair portion, we see a fulfillment of the blessings foretold by Jacob (Gen. 49:25), and by Moses (Deut. 33:16).

5-10 *Alone.* — The fact of several cities of Ephraim being situated in the territory of Manasseh probably arose from their own being inadequate to contain all their people. Manasseh, on the other hand, appears to have been recompensed at the expense of Issachar and Asher (17:11).

It is sad to learn that the children of Joseph took their inheritance (**4**), but that "Ephraim drove not out the Canaanites" (**10**). And the mention of Gezer in 10:33 and 12:12, as a city whose king and people were exterminated by Joshua, makes the failure yet more culpable. This sad lapse is referred to in Judges 1:29 and Psalm 78:9. In the latter passage, it is expressly said that Ephraim was well equipped, *yet* they turned back. How often have we turned back when opportunities lay open to us, and we were well equipped for them, and God was waiting to give us blessed successes! This sad record is abundantly true of our service and character.

Joshua 17   THE TRIBE OF MANASSEH

1-13 *The borders of the tribe.* — In the first verse the reference is to the half tribe which was settled to the east of Jordan; in the second, our attention is recalled to the west. As firstborn of Joseph, this great tribe was entitled to a double portion.

The daughters of Zelophehad *claimed* the portion which had been promised them (4). It was not enough that God had commanded Moses; the girls came to Joshua asking that their portion might be given according to promise (Num. 27:1). There is a clear necessity in all lives that we should put in our claims with God. We must ask and receive, that our joy may be full.

There is a melancholy emphasis on the words *could* and *would* in verse **12.** They are both emphatic in the original. The "could not" of unbelief gives an occasion to the "would" of the foe. The word "impossible" has no right in a Christian man's vocabulary. "All things are possible to him that believeth."

14-18 *The complaint of the children of Joseph.* — The greatness to which they referred seems to apply, not to their numbers — for according to the census of Num. 26, the two tribes united did not very far exceed that of Judah, and one half of Manasseh had already had their allotment on the other side of Jordan — but to their estimate of their position in Israel, by virtue of the special promises to Joseph. However, Joshua, himself an Ephraimite, exhorted them to show their greatness by their deeds. Moreover, their territory was amply large enough if only they would cut down the wood which covered the hills, and drive out the Canaanites, who, with iron chariots, held the valleys.

All around us there is an uncleared forest. If we are wanting opportunities for Christian usefulness, they are all around us. By faith and courage let us put the fences of occupation further back, and take in new portions of territory, as yet unheld. What a precious promise for the Christian worker is contained in verse **18**!

Joshua 18   THE TABERNACLE AT SHILOH

The first verse records an event of great importance, which engaged the attention of the entire people. The Tabernacle had remained at Gilgal; it must now be removed to Shiloh, a site selected by God Himself (Deut. 12:11; Ps. 78:60). It is supposed that the name Shiloh, which means *rest,* and which recalls the prophecy of the dying Jacob, was given at this time, because war was at an end. The honor of having God's dwelling-place within its border was probably given to Ephraim, as the tribe to which Joshua belonged.

2-10 *A further survey of the Land.* — As an inducement to the more speedy occupation of the land, a company of twenty-one was dispatched to search the land and bring Joshua an accurate report, on the receipt of which he would cast lots before the Lord. How many Christians may be accused of being slack to occupy their heritage in Christ! And to stir us up, God has been sending His commissioners first to see and then to report the greatness of our privileges in Jesus.

11-28 *The portion of Benjamin.* — The sixteenth verse clearly indicates that Jerusalem was included in the confines of Benjamin (**28**). But the Jebusite held possession till David's time (2 Sam. 5:6). The children of Benjamin dwell between the shoulders of God; let them, therefore, arise and win their Jerusalems for Him, in His strength, so that there may no more pass through them the uncircumcised and the unclean.

Joshua 19   THE DIVISION COMPLETED

The bulk of this chapter is occupied with a recital of the remaining tribes and their boundaries.

2 *Beersheba.* — This historic town fell within the confines of Simeon. It was the extreme point of the land; so that "from Dan to Beersheba" became an abbreviated expression for the entire country. Simeon's lot was taken out of that of Judah, which was too much for them (**9**).

47 *The border of Dan.* — The R.V. reads, "The border of the children of Dan went out beyond them," and thus introduces an account of the expedition of the Danite against Laish, which is more fully recorded in Judges 18. Dan first set up idolatry (Judg. 18:30); and its name disappears altogether from the list of the tribes in Revelation 7.

50 *Joshua's inheritance.* — The veteran leader had earned a good reward, and received it. Timnath-serah is also called Timnath-heres, "portion of the sun." Perhaps it lay especially towards the ripening rays of the sun. And in a spiritual sense, they who wholly follow the Lord inherit the light of His face, and walk in the light of His smile. Christian, when he stayed at the Palace Beautiful, slept in the chamber Peace, which looked toward the sun-rising.

Joshua 20   THE CITIES OF REFUGE

1-3 *For whom the Cities of Refuge were prepared.* — These arrangements were the carrying into effect of directions given in more detail in Numbers 35:9-34. In each passage, a careful distinction is drawn between deliberate murder and unintentional homicide. Those alone who had committed the latter were eligible for refuge.

4, 5 *How the fugitive was received.* — The fugitive told his story to the elders at the gate, and was admitted provisionally (**4**); but his case was afterwards fully investigated by the citizens of the city, as he stood before them for judgment. Note how clear a distinction was thus drawn between sins of ignorance and of presumption. The latter harden the heart and deaden the conscience, and are very grievous in the sight of God. Abide in Christ, and you will be held back from presumptuous faults, while you will be sheltered from the consequences of unpremeditated transgression.

6 *How long the fugitive might remain.* — He might dwell in the city until the death of the high-priest. The usual explanation being that "the atoning death of our Saviour cast its shadow beforehand on the statute-book of the law. The high-priest was pre-eminently a type of Christ; and thus the death of each high-priest pre-signified that death by which captive souls are freed, and the remembrance of sins made to cease" *(Speaker's Commentary).*

7-9 *Where the Cities were situated.* — If the map be carefully studied, it will be seen that they were so disposed as to give three on each side of Jordan, about equally distant from one another, and so within easy access from all parts of the land. For spiritual references, see Proverbs 18:10, and Hebrews 6:18.

Joshua 21   THE LEVITES' CITIES

1-40 *The Cities given by lot.* — After the cities of refuge had been provided, those that were to be set apart for the priests, members of the house of Aaron, and for the Levites, were next allotted, according to the Divine command to Moses (Num. 35:1-8). The Levites were divided into Kohathites, Gershonites, and Merarites. The family of Aaron, which constituted the priests, was drawn from the former of these bodies. The first lot was drawn by the Kohathites, and among them again the first lot was drawn by the house of Aaron. Forty-two cities in all were devoted to the Levites, and the six cities of refuge in addition. It is noteworthy that thirteen of these cities were by lot appointed to the priests in the tribes of Judah, Benjamin, and Simeon — the tribes nearest to Jerusalem, where their services would ultimately be required. A striking testimony to the whole disposing of the lot being of God (Prov. 16:33). He alone knew what city He would hereafter choose to put His name there (Deut. 12:5).

41 *Forty-and-eight Cities.* — As skeptics quibble at what seems to have been an excessive number of cities provided for Levites and priests, "it may be well to note that they were not the sole possessors of these towns; but simply received the number of dwelling-houses actually needed, with the pasture land required for their cattle, the rest of the space still belonging to the tribe" *(Keil).*

43-45. — The concluding verses represent the general state of things about the period of Joshua's death (see his words, 23:14). So far as God's promises went, there was no failure on his part to make them good. What failure there was arose entirely from their lack of faith and courage. "It is true the Canaanites were not all exterminated; but those who were left were become so powerless that they could neither attempt, not accomplish, anything against Israel, so long as the Israelites adhered faithfully to their God" *(Keil).*

How emphatically the chronicler ascribes all to God. "The Lord gave Israel all the land . . . the Lord gave them rest . . . the Lord delivered them." This is the secret of a successful and blessed life. Live near the springs of life, and learn to receive from the Divine fulness, grace upon grace.

Joshua 22   THE ALTAR OF WITNESS

1-9 *The two and one half tribes dismissed with Joshua's blessing.* — There was dignity and generous appreciation of services rendered, as Joshua dismissed the warriors to their possessions. Something like, "Well done, good and faithful servant," rings through his words. But he takes care to remind them repeatedly that the tenure of their land rested entirely on their obedience to God. The mention of Moses **(5)** as the one from whom they received their inheritance accords with Galatians 3:19, 20. But may it not account for their speedy dispossession of their territory, that they received it not as the gift of God's grace through Joshua, but on the condition of obedience through Moses? Their failure to observe the terms of the covenant nullified it.

10-20 *The altar, and the contention to which it led.* — The expressions seem to denote that this altar was erected on the eastern bank of the Jordan, within the limits of the two and a half tribes. It was "over against" the land of Canaan. Perhaps it was a facsimile of that at Shiloh.

The motive that prompted the two and one half tribes in the erection of this altar was good; they wished to identify themselves as of Israel, and to cement the union. But these ends would have been better secured, if they had obeyed God's command of assembling with the rest of Israel at the great annual festivals. The words, "and the children of Israel heard say" (**11**), show the mistake of acting on "hear-say" evidence. So serious an accusation should not have been given credence to, until every means of ascertaining its truth had been investigated. Christians should be equally careful of accepting or circulating charges against their brethren. The offer of Israel, however, was a noble one, that their brethren should dwell with themselves on the western bank of Jordan, rather than be led to a sin which might, as in the case of Achan, involve the whole nation in sin and trouble.

21-34 *The reply of the two and one half tribes.* — The spirited protest of the unjustly accused tribes is full of truth and dignity, and quickly dissipated the wrath of Israel (**22**). Though this wrath was too hasty, we cannot but admire the zeal of the people against what they assumed, however wrongly, to be a serious breach of God's commandments. Would that it had been maintained throughout their subsequent history! Then their peace had been as a river, and their righteousness as the waves of the sea. But the Lord's rule should always be followed. Before indulging even in righteous indignation, speak to your brother first, alone.

This altar, bearing witness to the unity of Israel, reminds us of the many attempts, made in all ages, to promote the unity of God's people by creeds or by confederations. But the true unity is already formed in the risen Christ, between Him and those who are one with Him. We are one in Him. The one need is that we should all manifest that unity (Ephesians 4:1-6).

Joshua 23   "CLEAVE UNTO THE LORD"

1-4 *A recital of the past.* — Joshua's anxious solicitude for the welfare of his people, after his death, has New Testament parallels in the anxieties of the Apostles Paul and Peter (Acts 20:29; 2 Pet. 1:13-15); but most of all in Christ's tender solicitude for His people (John 13-17). It must have been a memorable meeting between the aged leader and his veteran friends and officers. He still lays stress, as in earlier days, on what the Lord had done: "It is He that fought for you" (**3**); "The Lord your God shall thrust out" (**5**); "The Lord hath driven out" (**9**). Not one ray of glory is stolen for himself.

5-16 *Arguments for steadfastness.* — These may be in three aspects.

5 *Promises.* — If only they would cleave to God, He would give them possession of parts of the land still unconquered. God's blessing would secure a succession of easy victories. Our failure in Christian life to drive out our foes arises from our failure to cleave unto the Lord. A lack of consecration lies at the root of all failure in conflict. Cleaving to the Lord is equivalent to whole-hearted abiding in Jesus. He fights for His own.

11-13 *Threatenings.* — If they went back, either in idolatry or in intermarriage, God would withdraw His help and blessing. These words also have a message for ourselves. We are all tempted to ally ourselves with those who know not God. It is so easy to trust in an arm of flesh. But God will be no party to such alliances. We must come out from among them and be separate, and not touch the unclean thing, if we would be His sons and daughters. Or if we still cling to them, our hearts will have to be delivered, as was Israel, through terrible sufferings.

14-16 *Exhortations.* — These verses give a sad summary and compendium of Israel's after history. Their last great sin, for which they have been dispersed, is included in these sad words of foreboding fear. They cleaved to other nations. But in contrast to man's inconstancy and infidelity, notice the sublime testimony to the faithfulness of God. "Not one thing hath failed." We may appropriate this assurance to ourselves. When at last we review our life, we shall also be able to say that we have not been ashamed. "He abideth faithful." Our sins cannot annul the covenant.

The last two verses of the chapter disclose what must ever be the end of all man's attempts to keep the covenant of works. Our only hope is in the New Covenant of which Jeremiah 31:31 speaks. Jesus must stand in our behalf, fulfill the law, and secure its fulfillment in our hearts.

Joshua 24   "CHOOSE YE THIS DAY"

1 *The assembling of the Tribes.* — The previous chapter contained Joshua's own last words of warning to Israel; here he is God's mouthpiece to give His message to the people: "Thus saith the Lord God of Israel." Hence a great meeting of the representatives of Israel was convened at Shechem, where the covenant had been solemnly renewed (8:30, 35).

2-13 *God recapitulates His past mercies.* — From his opening words we gather that Abraham was called out from an idolatrous family (**2**); and from the closing words that the position of Israel was entirely due to the Divine favor and grace (**12**). How true is this of our inheritance in Jesus! We are indebted for all we are and have, to unbounded mercy.

14, 15 *Joshua's entreaty.* — During their sojourn in Egypt Israel had yielded to the fascinations of idolatry around them (**14**). This broke out again at Sinai. How often do the sins of our youth and the mistakes of our early training break out in disastrous harvests in later years! It is brave and right to profess our inalienable devotion to the cause of God, let others do as they will. "As for me and my house, we will serve the Lord." As the head of the household does, so the family.

16-24 *The professions of the people.* — The old impetuosity which flamed out at Sinai here repeats itself (**16**). The heart of man is so self-confident and so weak; it boasts so much, and fails so terribly. Joshua did well to discourage and test these proud vauntings; and to show the people that they could not of themselves, and in their own might, realize

God's ideal (Ps. 105:4). The Book of Judges is a bitter commentary on these lofty words.

25-28 *The Stone of Witness.* — What that memorial was to Israel, that the ordinances of the Lord's Supper and of Baptism are to the Church and to the world. We do well sometimes to review the vows we have taken on ourselves.

29-33 *Joshua's death.* — As long as Joshua and his contemporaries lived, their influence kept the nation in the old groove of obedience. Such was the influence of the Apostles on the early Church during the first century. Let us learn the value of personal testimony and influence. The bones of Joseph were at last deposited (Gen. 50:24-26). Take heart, O child of God! thou mayest have to wait; but His word is as certain as the alternation of day and night; as steadfast as the everlasting hills.

CANAAN, AS DIVIDED AMONG THE TRIBES

The Book of Judges

INTRODUCTION

Judges is the title given to this Book, from its containing the history of those non-regal rulers who governed the Hebrews from the time of Joshua to that of Eli, and whose functions in time of peace consisted chiefly in the administration of justice, although they occasionally led the people in their wars against their public enemies.

The date and authorship of this book are not precisely known. It is certain, however, that it preceded the second Book of Samuel (*cf.* 9:35 with 2 Sam. 11:21) as well as the conquest of Jerusalem by David (*cf.* 1:21 with 2 Sam. 5:6).

Its author was in all probability Samuel, the last of the judges (19:1—21:25), and the date of the first part of it (chapters 1-16) is fixed in the reign of Saul, while the five chapters at the close might not be written till after David's establishment as king in Israel (see 18:31).

It is a fragmentary history, being a collection of important facts and signal deliverances at different times and in various parts of the land, during the intermediate period between Joshua and the establishment of monarchy.

The inspired character of this Book is confirmed by allusions to it in many passages of Scripture (*cf.* 4:2, 6:14 with 1 Sam. 12:9-12, 9:53 with 2 Sam. 11:21; 7:25 with Ps. 88:11; 5:4-5 with Ps. 68:7, 8 (see also Acts 13:20; Heb. 11:32).

The book consists of three parts. Chapters 1—3:4 give the history of events immediately subsequent to the death of Joshua. Chapters 3—16 give the story of the Judges from Othniel to Samson. The last portion (17 to end) is a collection of narratives of what happened during a course of years when "there was no king in Israel."

Judges of Israel

Judges		Oppressors from whom delivered	References
1. Othniel	(of Judah)	King of Mesopotamia	Judges 3:9-11
2. Ehud	(of Benjamin)	King of Moab	—15-30
3. Shamgar		Philistines	—31
4. Deborah	(of Ephraim)		
Barak	(of Naphtali)	King of Hazor	4, 5
5. Gideon	(of Manasseh)	Midianites	6-8
6. Abimelech			
(Usurper)	(Son of Gideon)		9
7. Tola	(of Issachar)		10:1, 2
8. Jair	(a Gileadite)		—3—5
9. Jephthah	(a Gileadite)	Ammonites	11, 12
10. Ibzan	(of Bethlehem)		12:8
11. Elon	(of Zebulun)		—11
12. Abdon	(of Ephraim)		—13
13. Samson	(of Dan)	Philistines	13—16
14. Eli			1 Sam. 1—4
15. Samuel	(of Ephraim)	Philistines	7-25

NOTE: Samson and Eli are supposed to have judged Israel together, during twenty years — Samson in the southeast; and Eli in the northwest.

Judges 1   ENEMIES CAST OUT

Whether this book is taken to represent the disorders of the professing Church, or those darker ones which convulse the soul, this chapter is full of holy lessons and instruction. Israel began right by asking counsel of God, and by endeavoring to ascertain His plan (**1**). If only we would build according to God's pattern, seek the works He has prepared, and war in this spirit, we should be more successful and useful. And there is much beauty in the suggestion that the different tribes of the one Church should help each other in the war (**3**).

There should be more of this holy alliance between Christian brethren — Judah asking Simeon to go with him, and then going with Simeon (**3, 17**). We should beckon to our partners in the other ship (Luke 5:7) to come and help us; if we did, we should lose nothing. We cannot have more than what our boat can carry, and it is an additional pleasure if their boat is also full to the water's edge. When shall we learn that the success of one is the success of all (1 Cor. 12:26)? We must never fail to go up against our foes, though we know and are sure that our going up is useless, unless the Lord deliver.

4-11 *Judah's success.* — Judah was to be first, because the strongest tribe; strength is given for service. To whom much is given, of him much is required. And is it not true that the Lion of the tribe of Judah must ever lead the way? But our strength avails not unless God gives the victory. The fate of the tyrant Adonibezek was acknowledged by himself to be deserved (James 2:13; Rev. 13:10); at the same time it was a barbarous infliction, which shows how vast is the change wrought on the world by the Spirit of Jesus. It was impossible for God to lead men immediately into the gentle manner of the Gospel (Matt. 19:8).

12-15 *Caleb's portion.* — Twice over is this incident told (Josh.15:13-19). Thus does God love to emphasize the exploits of His people. Kirjath-sepher is "the city of books," and was perhaps the university town, for the records of the nations were kept there. Othniel afterwards became the first Judge

(3:9). The request of Caleb's daughter for "springs of water" was cheerfully granted. Our Father, like Caleb, loves His children to ask freely for what they want. He gives to all liberally, and upbraideth not.

But it is only the men, who, like Caleb, wholly follow the Lord, they who are entirely consecrated to His service, who are able to give a blessing to others. It is the privilege of those who have received the fulness and anointing of the Holy Ghost to open up that blessing to others, teaching them how to receive it. Alas for these repetitions of "could not" (**19, 21**). The strength of the "chariots of iron" seem to have unnerved Judah, who, in their own strength, were not able to subdue the people in the valleys; but the Lord could have done it for them, if only they had obeyed and trusted Him. It is not our strength or weakness that is in question, but our faith in God's ability.

19-36 *Failure.* — Among the failure of the tribes to drive out the inhabitants of the land, Joseph stands out as an exception — "the Lord was with them," or, as the Chaldee version puts it, "the Word of the Lord was their helper," *i.e.,* the Lord Himself, the true Captain of the host. But the people of the other tribes did not avail themselves of God's help. Either through unbelief or cowardice, or both, Israel failed to expel their foes, and settled down among them, laying up for themselves some very bitter experiences. Asher even submitted to the predominance of the Canaanites among whom it dwelt. Oh, how many of us shrink from the cross, and from waging war against inbred sin to the knife? And thus, when we had seemed to be free from Satan's slavery, we are brought again into his captivity. We must give no place to sin. We must pursue each evil with relentless severity. We must, by the grace of the Spirit, appropriate the cross of Christ as our lot and destiny, and mortify each unholy passion. We have only to avail ourselves of God's help, and all this is possible.

Judges 2   APOSTASY AND FAILURE

This was the first of many bitter remonstrances that were to come to Israel. "The messenger Jehovah" must be He of whom the prophet spoke (Mal. 3:1), the Word and Son of God.

1-3 *There is a recital of the true cause of their failure.* — It was due, not to any failure on God's part, but to a great failure on theirs. They had made a league with the people, and had not destroyed their idols. Was this guilty collusion due to any shame of their allegiance to an *unseen* God; or was it owing to their love of the sinful orgies which characterized the heathen festivities?

God's warning angels still come to men. Let us be on the outlook for them. But how bitter sometimes is their reproof? Have not we entered into covenant with forbidden things, avoiding His altar, and disobeying His voice. And this is the reason why we are hindered and injured by the thorn in our side and the snare for our foot (**3**). We, at least, may learn this solemn lesson, that the Church is no match for the world, so long as it is allied to the world; and that the way of separation is the only path of victory and safety.

6-9 *The death of Joshua.* — The former part of this paragraph is identical with Joshua 24:29. There was a parenthesis of twenty years of rest, before the great warrior was summoned to his rest. During that time he exerted a great repressive influence, which waned when his sun set; and another generation arose.

10-15 *The sins and sorrows of Israel.* — What a marvellous relapse was here! How the heart of man abhors the spirituality and purity of God (Jer. 2:11, 12). But those who turn from God lay themselves open to bitter sorrows. If your heart is not perfect with God, your best plans will be spoiled by spoilers, and you will be sold as a slave to the flesh.

In the light of verses **14** and **15** it cannot be too clearly or constantly repeated that failure in consecration and obedience always means defeat. When we follow other gods, and bow ourselves down to them, we can no longer stand against our enemies. Then the hand of the Lord is against us, and we become sore distressed. But even under such circumstances He does not forget His covenant. Though we believe not, He remaineth faithful, He cannot deny Himself. He therefore raises up judges, and saves us from the full measure of His wrath (**18**).

16-18 *God's compassion.* — How touching is the account of God's pity (**18**). Even though we have brought grave sorrows on ourselves by sin, yet will God interpose to avert the full brunt of penalty. Though we believe Him not, He remaineth faithful. He cannot deny Himself. God can always find or make deliverers in the most degenerate age of the Church; so we find here that He raised up judges which delivered His people.

19-23 *The madness of their apostasy.* — After a while God left the people to the results of their own choice, and, as they had permitted the Canaanites, they were allowed to suffer from them, and the discipline which refined them came through the results of the sin, from which they were to be set free.

Judges 3   THE FIRST JUDGES

We have here an *enumeration* of the nations of Canaan left to try Israel (**1-7**). They ought to have been destroyed; but, as the chosen people failed to fulfil the Divine purpose and command, they had to suffer the fret of perpetual conflict. Difficulty and temptation, though due to our own failure and sin, may be used for blessed purposes, overruled by the providence of God, to teach us priceless lessons. The presence of the Canaanites, due to the disobedience and unbelief of Israel, proved them and taught them to be strong in war, and revealed to them many a trait in the Divine character to which otherwise they had been oblivious. But what a lamentable record is here that they forgot God. Intermarriage with the sinful peoples around had the effect of infecting them with their vices and sins, and it became only too convenient to ignore and forget the all-holy God. Be not yoked with unbelievers.

8-11 *The first captivity and deliverance.* — It is a bitter record which here begins. The Holy Ghost says the Lord "sold them into the hands of the king of Mesopotamia" (**8**), who probably invaded the trans-Jordanic tribes which lay nearest to him; but it is also true that the people sold themselves. In their distress the people cried unto the Lord. Those who had called upon Baal and Ashtaroth in their mirth were glad enough to call on God in the day of their trouble. Let backsliders, and those that are reaping a bitter harvest from the results of their wrong-doing, take heart from the next record, that when the people cried, "the Lord raised them up a saviour." Twice that statement is made in this chapter. Othniel was specially anointed for his work (**10**), and it would be well, if we would distinguish between the grace of the Spirit within us for character, and upon us for work, and if we would claim each. This anointing may be ours (2 Cor. 1:21, 22; 1 John 2:27).

12-30 *Ehud's achievements* stand next. — Eglon was permitted by God to wax strong and to prevail against Israel. But again, when the people repented, deliverance came through a man who might not have been supposed most suited for the purpose. Throughout this book we shall have occasion to notice the kind of instruments which God selected for His work. All of them to be classed among the things that are not, but which bring to nought the things that are. Here a left-handed man (**21**). Let us take courage from this. Out of weakness He makes strong. To those that have no might He increases strength.

31 *Shamgar.* — When it is said (**30**) that the land had rest for eighty years, it probably refers to that part of Canaan which lay east of the Jordan, and had been oppressed by Moab; but the other side, which lay southwest, was infested by Philistines, against whom Shamgar was victor. Deborah afterwards told how far-spread their plunderings or robbery had been (v. 6). An ox-goad would be simply a piece of pointed iron from six feet to eight feet in length; but, though a formidable weapon, it would have failed to do this deed;

unless God had been mighty with its owner. What may not the weakest weapons do with God behind them!

Judges 4   JABIN AND SISERA

These chapters of the Judges are full of encouragement to such as are discouraged by repeated failures; those whose experience has been one long series of endeavors after a better life, interrupted and darkened by transgression and relapse. They have gone back to God so often with the same tale that they are almost ashamed to go any more. Let these take heart; His mercy endureth for ever. Their remorse, and yearning to be different, are a clear proof that He has not withdrawn His favor from them. Let them look again towards His holy temple (Jonah 2:4).

1-3 *Jabin's oppression.* — In this chapter Israel had again rebelled against God; and this time Jabin, King of Hazor, was the oppressor permitted to bring them to repentance. His city had been razed once (Josh. 11:1-14); but, through the inactivity of Israel, had been built again, and his kingdom partially re-established. He must have been a very formidable foe, and his tyranny was very bitter (**3**). Mighty oppression like that of Jabin and Sisera, is a type of vehement hatred of our spiritual foes, but it is the foil on which God displays the might of His deliverance.

4-9 *Deborah and Barak.* — *Deborah,* the heroine of her time, was the prime mover in their deliverance. She was a prophetess, living in communion with God, possessed of remarkable insight into His will, and able to communicate it in glowing words. She was full of patriotic ardor, which she infused into others.

Barak, the soldier. — How lamentable that Barak should have pinned his faith to a woman, instead of to the eternal God! If only he had said these words (**8**) to God, he might have achieved a more wonderful deliverance, and his rule established on a more settled basis. We must beware lest we imitate his fault, and trust more in those who are around us than in the living God. There cannot be failure in our faith without our suffering in some way the results.

10-16 *The defeat of Sisera's host.* — The tribes of Zebulun and Naphtali chiefly bore the brunt of this conflict, which set them free from the tyranny which had lain especially heavily upon the luxuriant plain of Esdraelon. How sweet it is to know when the Lord is going before us; though this does not make our best efforts superfluous (**14**). The Lord will ever defeat the foes of those who follow Him.

17-24 *Jael* was the heroine of the day. At first she doubtless intended to show true Eastern hospitality, and then was seized by the impulse of ridding the land of her adoption of the instrument of Jabin's authority. A tent-peg sufficed for the grim deed of vengeance. Those were wild days, matched by the Border wars of Scottish and British history; and through all a Divine purpose ran, which, though not condoning these deeds of violence, wrought through all for the people, beloved for their fathers' sakes.

Judges 5   DEBORAH'S SONG

One of the noblest songs in history, composed by Deborah herself (**7**). In this magnificent ode we are taught to ascribe all glory in our successes to God. The people made themselves free-will offerings in the day of God's power; and it is only when we do so that the mighty power of God can work through human means.

1-5 *Its opening notes are praise.* — Whatever merit was attaching to Barak and his army, the glory of victory was with God. Oh, how negligent we are in the high praises of God; and how much easier would prayer and trust be if mingled more constantly with thanksgiving. The kings of surrounding lands were plotting to destroy the chosen people, and they are bidden to hear what God had wrought, lest they meddle with them to their hurt.

6-8 *The distress of Israel.* — No trade on the highways; no safe travelling; no tillage of the country, because the villagers had fled to the towns; no administration of justice, because war had invaded the gates, where the courts were kept; no arms of defense. And all because they had chosen new gods (**8**).

We do well to remember our low estate, to see the hole of the pit from whence we have been taken; to set our former low estate clearly forth, that the deliverance of God may be the more manifest.

9-18 *The muster.* — The governors first made themselves freewill gifts, and the story of their devotion, and of the righteous acts of God, would long be rehearsed with thankfulness beside the village wells, no longer held by the foe. Oh, when will men speak of the glorious majesty of our God with the enthusiasm that they now expend on the words or acts of some favorite leader!

The songstress (**12**) summons Barak and herself to yet higher ascriptions of praise. He must be on fire who would make others glow. Reuben came not, because of conflicting opinions; Dan and Asher stayed by their ships and creeks; Meroz, though so near the field of battle, remained neutral, and was cursed.

The cooperation of God and man is clearly revealed throughout the Bible. We are His fellow-workers, "fellow-helpers with the truth." It is well worth our notice that some of the strongest denunciations in the Bible are against those that do nothing. It is a sin *not* to do, *not* to come against might to the help of the Lord. "Curse ye Meroz." O my soul, dost thou rightly fulfil all the opportunities of thy life? The virgins that slept without oil: the man that hid the talent: the nations that did it not to the least of the king's brethren; these are held up by Christ to the most terrible denunciations that His gentle lips could frame.

24-27 *Sisera's death* described in highly poetic phrase.

28-30 *The anxiety of the harem* to hear the news of the fight. What a contrast between their disappointment and the realized hopes of the Church when Jesus returns from the last great fight! The closing words beautifully harmonize with Matthew 13:43. The deliverance was decisive. "The land had rest forty years."

Judges 6   GIDEON

1-10 *Midianite oppression.* — Israel's sin brought suffering, and this time from an almost despicable quarter; because Midian had been severely punished, and almost annihilated when Israel passed through their land (Num. 31:7). The invaders seem to have possessed themselves of all the valleys, where there would be pasturage for their flocks, etc., forcing the Israelites up into the hills. Their sorrows again drove them to their knees, and they cried to the Lord. Alas! That God has so often to *drive* men to Himself.

Often enough have the hosts of Midianites visited us, and left us very low, leaving no green thing in cornfield or vineyard. It is then that the Lord's voice (**8-10**) is heard, reminding us that we have fallen, not by any failure on His part, but by our own iniquity. I brought out; I delivered; I drove them out; I said, but YE have not hearkened to my voice. The path of obedience is the only safe and prosperous one.

11-24 *The commission to Gideon* was given by an angel, who was evidently the Angel-Jehovah (**14**).

God sends angels of deliverance as well as prophets of remonstrance, and they come to the men who hide in the winepress, and are least in their own eyes, and meditate on the past mighty works of the Lord. See what a look of the Lord can do; it carries with it might and salvation (**14**). God always goes with those whom He sends, and though our foes be as swarms of locusts, they perish as one man, when smitten by the sword of the Lord and of Gideon. When faith is weak, God nurtures it by sign of wonder and by fire, tenderly providing materials on which faith can build; and the peace of God is breathed into the heart. What a sweet title! *Jehovah-shalom!* The Lord is our Peace. He sends Peace and He is Peace, like the calm of evening settling down upon the heart. When we have seen God face to face, we have no reason to fear man.

25-32 *The destruction of idols* must precede all successful and victorious work. Before we can be delivered from Midian, there must be an honest dealing with the idolatry of evil in the inner life. The altar of Baal must be thrown down, and replaced by the altar of God, and there must be the burnt-offering of entire surrender to His claims. We are first tested in the less before being called to the greater. It was because Gideon dared to obey God, as far as concerned his home and village, that the Spirit of the Lord "clothed itself with" him for wider service (**34**, R.V., *marg.*).

36-40 *God's condescension to allay his fears.* — We must not be always looking for signs. God generally guides us by our sanctified judgment. Yet there are indications sometimes afforded to those who walk close with Him (Acts 16:6-10).

Judges 7   "TRUMPETS AND PITCHERS"

This is one of the most searching chapters in the Old Testament. It is full of teaching to those among us who are full of their own plans and strength, and who can count on many great alliances to assist them. God will not give His glory to another, and He cannot give the Midianites into our hand so long as there is a likelihood of our laying claim to the results. Success in spiritual work must be denied us if it would tend to our vaunting ourselves. Hence it is that so many of God's most successful workers have had to pass through periods of humiliation at the river's brink.

3-8 *The test.* — Two methods were employed for thinning the army. First, the usual proclamation was made (Deut. 20:8). Then the way in which the soldiers drank was carefully observed. Those that threw themselves at full length were evidently apt to prefer their own comfort and refreshment to their soldierly self-denial, which prefers duty to pleasure; these were, therefore, dismissed. And the little body which remained was specially equipped; taking no more victuals than they could easily carry, because the campaign would be short in spite of the numbers of the foe. A good equipment for the Christian, — a light to shine, a trumpet to proclaim the victory of Jehovah; though at the best we are but earthen vessels (2 Cor. 4:6, 7). "God counts hearts, not heads" *(Rev. J. M'Neill).*

9-15 *Encouragement.* — What a graphic picture! The leader listening under the covert of the night, and worshipping on the spot, and returning with new courage to make his careful preparations. If a cake of barley-bread overthrew a tent, what may not *we* do, if our God use us? Oh, to be nothing, nothing! Not wheat, but barley!

16-25 *Victory.* — The preparations made by Gideon were of the rudest description possible, and totally inadequate to account for the marvelous result; but the terror produced by the crashing vessels, the flashing lights, the blowing of trumpets, filled Midian with panic, and they fled. There is nothing in us to make the tents of Midian collapse. It is only as God delivers Midian into our hands that any victory is possible. We shall do more execution against Satan's kingdom by blowing the Gospel trumpet, and by shining, even though we be broken in the attempt, than by our most splendid arguments. The two princes of Midian also fell. Oreb signifies a raven; Zeeb a wolf. This was "the day of Midian" (Isa. 9:4).

Judges 8   "RULE THOU OVER US"

1-3 *The benefit of a soft answer* is well illustrated in the opening verses. Those who are most reluctant to undertake difficult services are quickest to find fault with such as carry them through to success. When we are doing God's work, and especially if we are successful in doing it, there will always be plenty of critics. *Answer them kindly,* or do not answer them at all. Gideon ruled his spirit, and behaved with true magnanimity and meekness (Prov. 13:10; 15:1).

4-12 *The pursuit of noble ends amid discouragement.* — How little does the world understand the faintness which overtakes the Christian warrior, never losing sight of his high purpose, yet often sorely in need of sympathy and help, which is not always given. We, however, are not at liberty to imitate Gideon in his threats of vengeance, which he terribly realized (**13-17**).

18-21 *The infliction of deserved punishment.* — Gideon

constituted himself the avenger of the blood of his brethren. Those were two striking sentences uttered by the captive kings, which we do well to ponder (**18, 21**). We, who belong to the family of God, should see to it that we resemble the children of a king, that there is a royalty in our bearing worthy of our origin. A notable sentence is that which repeats an old proverb that a man's strength is the outcome of his inner self (**21**). Force proportioned to character!

22-23 *The refusal of a generous request.* — "Rule, because thou hast delivered." As the men of Israel spake to Gideon, we should speak to our Lord: Rule Thou over us, for Thou hast saved us. "Thou art worthy to take the book, for Thou wast slain, and hast redeemed us." My soul, thou hast been saved out of the hand of thy foes, now enthrone the Lord, who has saved thee. When shall the love of Jesus so inspire and melt our hearts, that we shall gladly give to Him all the jewels of life?

24-27 *The ephod* was a rich priestly garment. Gideon's may have been made in good faith, but it was turned to very evil uses. Thus evil is often wrought for want of thought, as well as from want of heart. What we do innocently may become a terrible snare to others, and it behooves us to consider each act, not only as it is in itself, but as it may affect others (2 Cor. 6:3).

The closing words of the chapter (**33-35**) are bitter. They remind us of the way in which the butler treated Joseph and our own treatment of the Lord.

Judges 9   ABIMELECH, THE USURPER

This record of anarchy and blood is a photograph of the unrest of the world for want of a true Leader and Prince. As all these incidents were leading towards the days of David and Solomon, so the great agony and sorrow of our times must portend the advent of the true King. It is when the kingdoms of the world are rent by tribulation and war that we may expect to see the reign of the Son of Man. "Lift up your heads, and rejoice, for your redemption draweth nigh."

1-6 *Abimelech's conspiracy.* — Disregarding his father's express declaration (8:23), Abimelech desired the chieftainship of the people. How strong is the lust of power which will make men do the most abominable crimes to gain their ends; wading through seas of blood. The men of Sechem aided and abetted Abimelech, and then made him king.

7-21 *Jotham's parable.* — Government over men costs a great deal, and many a man has had to buy it by renouncing ease and comfort and many other delights. The vilest are sometimes exalted (Ps. 12:8). What a contrast between trusting in the shade of a bramble and in the shade of the great rock (Isa. 32:2).

22-29 *The intrusion of discord.* — For only three short years did the usurper enjoy his ill-gotten place. Trouble soon broke out between him and his new subjects. Having combined to do wrong, they now divided against each other to their mutual destruction. Gaal was the son of Ebed, which means a slave, and was perhaps descended from Hamor (Gen. 34).

30-49 *The destruction of Shechem.* — How much evil one traitor, or rebel, may work in any fortress! The power of Satan against us is immensely increased by a traitorous heart within. The people trusted in the protection of their god, and were miserably disappointed. How different to our lot (Ps. 27:5; Prov. 18:10).

50-57 *The fate of Abimelech.* — Abimelech thought much less of his character with God before whose presence he was soon to appear than he did of his credit with man (**54**). This fact which he was so anxious to conceal is the one thing remembered of him (2 Sam. 11:21). Though wickedness may prosper for a time, yet is its end sure and terrible (Ps. 37).

Judges 10   "REBELLIOUS AND BROUGHT LOW"

1-5 *Times of quietness.* — God will not be always threshing. After storms have disturbed the atmosphere, there come times of clear shining and peace. Such parentheses of rest came to Israel under Tola and Jair, of whom there is little notable to record. How often it happens that we make much of the days of strife and sorrow, while we permit the days of uneventful calm and prosperity to pass almost without remark.

6-9 *Times of sin and suffering.* — Very woeful is this incessant story of backsliding. The whole land must have been infected with multiplied idolatries. As an inspired commentary on these verses, we should read Psalm 106:36-46. The sentences there are very pathetic, and well in accord with the sad record before us. "Many times did He deliver them, but they were rebellious in their counsel, and were brought low for their iniquity."

10-18 *Times of repentance.* — Truly pathetic is this scene! The cry of agony (**10**). There is hope when sinners cry to God with genuine contrition, and to such cries there is an immediate response. The answer of God may have come by Him, or by angels, but it was very just. This apparent refusal of help was only intended to bring them more utterly to their knees in self-abhorrence, humiliation, and prayer. It is at such times that we not only pray, but we put away the strange gods, and cast ourselves utterly and hopelessly at His feet. "We have sinned, do Thou unto us whatsoever seemeth good unto Thee" (**15**). We should read also Hosea 14, appropriating the prayer with which it begins; and then we shall hear the reply coming from those gracious lips, "I will heal their backslidings, I will love them freely, mine anger is turned away." How touching the thought that our miseries can grieve God (**16**), even when they are the result of sin. "His compassions fail not."

Judges 11   JEPHTHAH

1-3 *Jephthah had a very base origin.* — But men ought not to be reproached with their parentage, if their own character is sweet and noble. Let us so live as to cast a halo of light on our origin, however lowly. Is not this also an illustration of God's constant action (1 Cor. 1:27)?

4-11 *The terms of agreement.* — How often it has happened that in our extremity we, like the elders of Gilead, have turned to Him whom we refused. But there is only one condition on which the Lord will fight for us against our over-mastering foes. He must be our Head; we must put Him on the throne.

12-28 *The meeting.* — This was consistent with Deut. 20:10, 11. The land had not belonged to the Ammonites, but to the Amorites, from whom Israel had taken it at God's command; Ammon, therefore, had no claim to it whatever.

It is important that we should vindicate the cause we espouse, that those who oppose us may know that they are in conflict not with us alone, but with the eternal principles of God's righteousness. It is a great thing to be able to say, "I have not sinned against thee, but thou doest me wrong" **(27)**. Even if we do not wrong people by act, let us guard against speaking treacherously or unkindly.

29-40 *His vow.* — There was no need of such a vow to obtain God's favor. Our vows should not be made to win God's help, but as an expression of our gratitude and love. We do not need to bribe Him to do aught for us. Not the burnt-offering as an inducement for God to deliver, but God's deliverance an inducement to the burnt-offering. Whether or not Jephthah did really offer his child is not material to our present consideration, for it must have been as great an agony to shut her away from the cherished hope of an Oriental woman, as to see her consumed on a funeral pyre.

Judges 12   "SHIBBOLETH"

1-6 *Fratricidal strife.* — This is the worst of all. There is no war to be compared to civil war. Ephraim had contended thus with Gideon (Judg. 8:1). Pride lay at the root of all. They could not endure that there should be honor and glory from which they were excluded.

Men are very unreasonable; like these children of Ammon, they are reluctant to take up a difficult cause. Then they are annoyed not to share in the glory when it has passed out of its narrowness into a large place. This comes of calculating results, and considering what will make for name, or fame, or prosperity. No man can live happily or honorably who has one eye towards his own interests and the other towards God's.

Oh, for the single eye, the united heart; the devoted purpose fixed on doing the will of God! When once the soul elects to seek first the Kingdom of God and His righteousness, he is indifferent to human praise or blame, success or failure, as the world may deem it, and turns away from the heated faces and words of critics and opponents, saying, "I put my life in my hands, and the Lord delivered" (**3**).

The word "shibboleth" means *river.* Forty and two thousand is 2040. This scene had led to the use of shibboleth, to indicate the tests which Christians impose on each other, and by which they condemn those who differ from them in matters trivial as an *h,* while they ignore the great bonds of a common brotherhood (Rom. 14:19).

There are many among us who might pass as allies and brothers, but they cannot adjust to pronounce certain words which to us are as dear as life. They utter them, indeed, with their lips, but there is a certain dialect, a color, an indefinable defect which we can instantly detect, and which betrays the false professor. God help us to speak plainly!

8-15 *Some minor Judgeships succeed,* which call for very slight notice, and yet in these quiet days the people were able to recoup themselves for the grievous rages made in their prosperity during the preceding years. We all of us need quiet, growing days in our lives, in which, although we may not be winning conspicuous victories or making remarkable progress, we are righting ourselves, striking our roots deep, and repairing the mistakes of the past.

Judges 13   THE BIRTH OF SAMSON

Samson's story is very interesting. It teaches what can be wrought by one man who is right with God, and in whom God's Spirit dwells with mighty power. Probably he was not specially remarkable in his physique; his power was the result of faith.

3-7 *An angelic annunciation.* — This Angel was the Lord Himself, who is the Word of God, for His name is called Wonderful (**18,** *marg.*) and Jehovah (**19**). How careful should parents be to deny themselves of even lawful indulgences for the sake of their children, for what parents are, children are likely to become. If a mother has no other inducement to live a noble life, let her do so on behalf of her children. It is interesting to compare verse **5** with Matthew 2:23, Luke 1:15, 2:23, as connecting the letter and the spirit of the Nazarite vow.

8-23 *Manoah's prayer and its answer.* — Well would it be for father and mother often to use the words of Manoah, when he asks for guidance as to teaching the child, "What shall be the ordering of the child, and what shall be his work?" (**12**). God has a plan for every child, and parents should be fellow-workers with Him. He is not far away from any who seek Him or need His help. He does wondrously, and His nature ascends like the altar-flame (**20**).

The reasoning of Manoah's wife (**23**) was very wise, and one that would help us in many an hour of alarm. Let us not always fear that God means harm, but look back upon the past, the services which He has permitted us to render, the offerings He has received, and the things He has shown us. Would He have done all this, and then fail us? Would He have begun if he had not counted the cost, and foreseen that He was able to complete? There are no unfinished houses in the Eternal City; no incomplete busts in His workshops; no half-cut jewels in His crown. It is not God's nature to thwart yearnings that He has instilled, or to cancel hopes that He has excited. What He has told us is a guarantee of what He will yet do for us.

24, 25 *Samson's birth.* — Zorah (Samson's birthplace), and Eshtaol, a few miles distant, occupied positions of the Danite border. The plain in which they were situated was noted for its vineyards (15:5), and Samson's self-denial, as regards the produce of the vine, would early be put to the test. Here, in his own country, and in close proximity to the Philistines, he was trained for his future life-work, and from the first there were evident traces of the Divine blessing, and of the possession of the Divine Spirit (Isa. 44:3, 4).

Judges 14   SAMSON'S MARRIAGE FEAST

Samson is the type of a man who, guarding against ceremonial laxity, and so keeping the Nazarite vow intact, is at the same time extremely lax in his morals. Though he touched neither wine nor strong drink, and ate no unclean thing, he was carried by passion, like a leaf before the autumn wind.

1-4 *Samson's illicit love.* — As in so many other cases this great mistake lay at the root of much of the misery and sin of Samson's life. He had no right to allow his heart to go out towards any woman of an alien race (Deut. 7:3); but apparently it was quite enough for a woman to please him well, and he insisted that his father should get the Philistine woman to be his wife. How foolish is it to be ensnared by a pretty or a handsome face, unless we know something of the inner life also! God overruled the results, though that did not relieve Samson of blame (*comp.* verse 4 and Acts 2:23).

5-9 *Samson's first exploit.* — The rending of the lion was accomplished by Divine power (**6**), but the contact with the carcass rendered Samson unclean (Lev. 11:27), and when, later, he returned to fetch his wife, and found the carcass full of honey, he would not tell his parents the origin of the honey, lest they might have scrupled to partake of it. In these little acts of laxity, he was already laying the foundation of his fall. The borer-worm prepares the oak for its fall, long before it snaps before the northeast blast.

Not once or twice in our lives have we met with a close analogy to this old story; circumstances which have roared against us, threatening our lives, have finally yielded honey and meat. We think as we meet them that they will involve us in unmitigated disaster; but as we look back upon them in after years, we count them the sources of unutterable delight. Everything depends upon how we meet them. It is only they on whom the Spirit of the Lord comes mightily, to whom the strong yields sweetness.

10-20 *Samson's marriage-feast, and riddle.* — The proposal of riddles was a favorite Oriental pastime. It was the seventh day of the week, but the fourth of the feast (**14, 15**). The sheets (**12**) were the *hykes* still worn in the East. When, at the end of the seven day limit, the Philistines were unable to solve the riddle, they sought the aid of the bride, so that they should not become impoverished (**15,** marg.), by forfeiting the penalty. Their threats caused this Philistine girl to waver in her allegiance to Samson, and she worked until she had extracted from him the answer. Her efforts, however, to avoid the fate with which she was threatened (**15**) only obtained for her a temporary respite, as the identical punishment she dreaded was afterwards meted out to her and her people (15:6). How weak human love may be unless it is sanctified by the love of God! Even the love of a newly-married wife may fail, unless it is possessed by a stronger passion, and held true by a mightier hand than her own.

Let us never forget the sense in which Samson's riddle has been realized in the destruction of death by Christ (1 Tim. 1:10; 1 Cor. 15:54; Heb. 2:14, 15). Some of our bitterest foes yield us strength and sweetness beneath the gracious influences of the Holy Spirit.

Judges 15   "THE JAWBONE OF AN ASS"

In the roll-call of God's heroes, Samson is spoken of as a man of faith (Heb. 11:32). It is so strange to find him classed with David, and Moses, and Enoch, for as we look upon the deeds recited in this chapter, they seem to us altogether so stormy, and boisterous, and savage. We find it hard to think of him as being inspired by the same holy purpose as filled the hearts of the saints, and that the hand of faith was indeed there beneath the plated armor of the warrior. Truly, "God fulfils Himself in many ways." And yet it is comforting that God's children are clad in a very different guise, speak many dialects, and are not expected to live higher than according to the light they have.

Samson was a genial, good-natured, happy soul; full of joke and mirth (16:25); willing enough to forgive and forget; and so he made new advances to the woman who had so basely betrayed his confidence, but he found that she had become the wife of another (1, 2).

3-8 *His acts of vengeance were terrible.* — The destruction of the standing crops and the vineyards, with the "great slaughter" (8) of the Philistines proved that Samson was moved by anger in a very high degree. But there is a sense in which we may emulate Samson, who, when he had completed his act of vengeance, went down and dwelt in the cleft of the rock. There we are secure from the attempts of faithless friends and the assaults of bitter foes.

9-17 *Judah's treachery* was mean in the extreme. It shows to how low a pitch of servility those will come who yield meanly to a foreign despot's yoke. The men of Judah treated Samson, as in after years they treated Christ, whom they bound and delivered to the Gentiles. But as Samson could not be restrained by the ropes, so did the bands of death fall off the limbs of Christ, when raised from the dead on the third day in the might of the Holy Ghost (Acts 2:24).

If any should read these words who have been bound by strong ropes and rendered powerless to do God's work as aforetime, let them trust and not be afraid, for there is that in the mighty descent of the Holy Spirit which shall set them free.

The Philistines had not allowed any weapon to remain in the possession of the Israelites (1 Sam. 13:19-22), so that Samson was dependent upon the jaw-bone of an ass to avenge himself upon his enemies; but in the hand of God a little thing is sufficient to accomplish a great result. Often the "weak things" confound "the things that are mighty," and "the things that are not" bring to nought "the things that are."

18-20 *A lesson of dependence.* — Samson gloried too much in his own strength. It was in the moment of exultation

that this great thirst came, from which his right arm could
not save him. He was driven to plead that he might be
delivered for God's glory, lest the uncircumcised should
rejoice. So when flushed with success, we are often
reminded that it is not ours, but God's good gift. Many a well
of comfort opened to us might be called En-hakkore "the
fount of him that cried" (Ps. 34:6).

Judges 16   DELILAH

1-3 *A fatal snare* again entangled Samson. — How many
great men have been too weak to resist the wiles of the flesh.
Those who do great exploits for God must ever watch against
these. This story should remind us of the death of Christ.
In His weakness as He hung upon the Cross, the power of
hell compassed Him in, and anticipated an easy victory, but
He laid hold on the doors of death, the gate into the unseen,
and plucked them up, bars and posts and all, and put them
upon His shoulders and carried them up to the top of the
everlasting hills, which lie towards the city of Rest (Eph. 4:8).

4-20 *A third time Samson fell under the deadly fascination
of a woman.* — Nor did he escape this time so easily. By the
promise of great riches, the Philistine lords successfully
bribed Delilah to ascertain the secret of his strength. A true
woman uses her influence over those she loves, to augment
rather than to sap their strength; but Samson, to his own
undoing, sought love outside the limits set by religion.
Whenever men or women act thus they forfeit their purity,
and hand themselves over to the enemies of God, and of their
souls, for their destruction.

Licentiousness robs men of wit and courage (Prov. 7:26,
27). What a warning to us not to tamper with any secret
Delilah sin. Notice how Delilah tried again and again to
obtain Samson's secret, and how he dallied with her, until
at last he yielded. Let us learn that when temptation comes
to us, it is a mistake merely to evade it, or to parry attacks,
as if to throw the tempter off the scent. These lines of
defense are taken one after another, and the foe presses into

the citadel, which in turn must yield. Let us beware of scissors, even though apparent love holds them, as they steal over the locks while we are steeped in unconsciousness of the havoc that they make; lest our strength goes from us, and we become "like other men." There are hours in our life when, though we know it not, our strength departs. Oh, the horror of *he wist not* (**20**).

21-31 *Repentance and renewal.* — Alone in the prison-cell reflection did its work; and prayer again arose from Samson's heart; his hair began to grow again. Is not there an analogy to Peter's repentance with bitter tears, preparing for Pentecost? What pathos in that last petition (**28**; Ps. 74:18-23)! There is an encouragement here for backsliders to return to God that He may forgive and restore them, and peradventure use them again.

Judges 17   MICAH'S IDOLS

The incidents related in this book do not follow in strict chronological order. They are fragments of history, strung together to show the confusion and sin which arise in the absence of a properly constituted central authority (17:6; 18:1; 19:1).

It is probable that what is here related, and to the close of this book, took place before Samson's time, for the origin of the name given to the camp, mentioned in the time of Samson's youth (**13, 25,** *marg.*) is given in the narrative (18:12).

1-5 *Idol-making.* — A miserable home was this. The mother hoarding (1 Tim. 6:9); the son robbing. It is best not to do evil; but it is next best, when it is done, to undo it, so far as may be, by confession and restitution. This is what Micah did. The money had been their god; but it remained the mother's god, for she devoted less to the images than she had vowed.

The family might be outwardly religious and accustomed to speak familiarly of God, and yet was evidently eaten through with lying, deceit, and such-like sins. We should be very careful that with a form of godliness in our homes, we also have its power, and train our children in the nurture and admonition of the Lord. Here for the first time we meet the phrase which often recurs in the latter chapters of this book, "there was no king in Israel, every man did that which was right in his own eyes." It is always so when Christ is not on the throne; we do as we like, and perhaps are more careful than ever in the observance of a ceremonial and outward religion.

7-13 *Priest-making.* — Micah thought that the Lord would do him good, because he had made a house of gods, an ephod and teraphim, and had secured a Levite to be his priest. But this Levite had no right to the priesthood, or Micah to consecrate him. How little did Micah know that disobedience to the second commandment did him more harm in God's sight and in his own soul, than these externals could do him good. "Neither circumcision availeth anything, nor uncircumcision, but a new creation and faith that worketh by love" (Gal. 5:6). There is a strong tendency among men to manufacture their own priests, and to suppose that things must go well when they have their presence and blessing. But a religion which man invents will not suffice him in the sight of God, and will some day desert him, as we shall see. He alone is the true Priest of souls who has been set apart to the work by the hand of God Himself (Heb. 2:17).

Judges 18   A DISTANT COLONY

We learn from Joshua 19:47 that the "coast of the children of Dan went out too little for them," *i.e.,* was too straitened. Probably they had not developed to the full extent the resources of their possession. Joppa — at that time the only port in the land — was in their territory, but the business of the sea does not seem to have afforded sufficient scope for the energies of the people, and an emigration scheme was decided upon. An embassy of five were sent out to search the land, and they came to the extreme north to the country between the tribes of Asher and Naphtali, the companions of Dan in the desert march.

1-10 *The Danite scouts.* — There is in all hearts a longing desire to have a consciousness of God's goodspeed. The Italian bandit seeks a blessing on some proposed crime. And so it was with these five men.

We must not suppose, because there is no obstacle to our possession of that which we covet, but that our course is clear, that therefore God hath given it into our hand. Many a time have souls been allured to their doom because they have pursued an apparently open course. But we need also the assurance of God's counsel, seeking it, not at the hand of a man-made priest, but in communion with God Himself.

11-26 *Micah's spoliation.* — What folly on the part of the Danites to suppose that they could be helped by gods, who could not keep themselves from being stolen, or protect the house of their proprietor (Ps. 115:8). The priest had come to Micah for wealth and left him at the first opportunity of preferment. It is a test of the true priest that he does not seek promotion, or a larger income, but is content to minister, though to the house of one man, if that be the will of God. It is of the essence of priestcraft to catch at worldly advantages and emoluments. God's Priest alone never forsakes, and "ever lives to make intercession."

27-31 *The capture of Laish.* — There was no harm in seeking an enlarged territory, but we can only turn with a sense of horror from these acts of wholesale extermination. The conscience which is trained in the school of Christ becomes very tender and sensitive, and rightly so. But the considerations which weigh with us could not have been appreciated in those rude times.

The "captivity of the land" (**30**) was the Philistine invasion (1 Sam. 4). These people were the first among the tribes to establish idolatry. To their lasting discredit this took place while the house of God was in Shiloh (**31**). How easy it was for Jeroboam to establish in their city one of his golden calves (1 Kings 12:29), and how necessary is it that our emigrants and colonists should take true religion with them to their distant homes.

Judges 19   A TERRIBLE CRIME

This and the following chapters hold up the mirror to human nature, and reveal what is in the heart of man apart from the grace of God. The Bible not only tells us of the remedy, but reveals to us the deadliness of the disease. We might wonder why so much is said about the blood of the Son of God, if we had not been told of the depravity and blackness of men's hearts. We must not suppose that these were sinners apart from others. We have all one human heart, and the same tendencies are in us each. Man is horrified when these reveal themselves in their naked hideousness in the lives of others, but is inclined to justify them in himself. But God justly brands with the same guilt the thought and intention of the heart, which is only restrained from breaking into open sin by the conventionalities of good society.

If you are standing near Christ, with your hand locked in His, it will not harm you to look over the jutting precipice into these seething depths. But if it be not so with you, pass over this record until your soul has become pure with a purity which turns from sin to Christ, with the shame that filled His holy soul in the days of His flesh, and made Him stoop to the ground (John 8:6).

Many interesting lessons are taught of the manners of the times. Unhappily, drunkenness was already invading the homes of the people (5-9). The surprise at the withholding of hospitality shows how general it was to entertain strangers in those simple, old-world days (11-15). The conversation with the old man reminds us how often the most generous feelings reveal themselves in the most unlikely quarters (16-21). In the subsequent assault upon his house, he was prepared to make any sacrifice in order to save him whom he was sheltering under his roof. So careful of the honor of the home, so careless of the honor of woman. One of the divinest traits in the religion of Jesus Christ, is the sanctity with which He has invested womanhood.

We are reminded of a similar scene at the gates of Sodom; but there were no angels here to stay the deeds of violence. Alas! that the redeemed people of the Lord had sunk to so low a depth (1 Cor. 6:9, 10, 11).

This incident is spoken of afterwards as the beginning of Israel's corruption, and a pattern of much after sin (Hos. 9:9; 10:9).

Josephus places this narrative at the beginning of the Judges. Phinehas, the grandson of Aaron, was living while these events took place (20:28).

Judges 20   NATIONAL INDIGNATION

The Levite's appeal to Israel had an immediate effect. We are reminded of Saul's appeal (1 Sam. 11:7), and of the Fiery Cross in more recent times. Mizpeh had already become the rallying-place of the people (10:17).

3, 11 *A judicial inquiry was instituted,* which issued in the unanimous determination to avenge the tragedy which had filled all hearts with detestation (**11**).

Amid the horror of a battlefield, there is one redeeming feature in the brave devotion of men for their country. And amid the horrors of this chapter, there is at least evidence that the conscience of Israel was growing in their detestation of the crime we have considered, though we must remember that it is always easier to denounce sins in other people, and vow vengeance against them, than to exterminate them in ourselves. Would that each reader would appropriate the words of Israel, "We will not any of us go to his tent till we have put away this evil from Israel" (**10**).

12-14 *Benjamin refused the opportunity of disavowing the perpetrators of the crime.* — This made the whole tribe accessory to the deed, and therefore liable to the punishment.

17-29 *The double defeat.* — It is at first difficult to understand why, in so good a cause, and after asking God in all sincerity for guidance on two occasions, the children of Israel fled in battle before Benjamin. But we must notice that it was only on the evening of the second day, in answer to fasting and prayer, that God promised to deliver Benjamin into their hand. And we must remember that God was compelled to speak in language that they could understand, and to teach them, through scenes of blood and tears, that higher morality to which they were yet to come.

30-48 *The terrible victory.* — This was a fearful act of vengeance. Benjamin was practically exterminated (**47**).

One turns from this chapter with a sad consciousness that it is a leaf out of the chronicles of human history which has had, and is having, many counterparts. The story of the extermination of native races, the mowing down of tens of thousands by the introduction of spirits and of opium, may read as darkly in the annals of eternity. Well may creation travail, and the saints cry, Lord! how long!

Judges 21   RETURNING HOME

It is gratifying to find that after the stormy outburst of the previous chapter, there came a return of tender feeling, like rain after claps of thunder. Human tears, as they well forth for others, evidence underlying fountains in the strongest natures, and the existence of those tender feelings of compassion without which the race could not exist.

1-7 *Israel's lamentation for Benjamin.* — Those that act in haste repent at leisure. Already there were symptoms that a sweeter and purer spirit was about to rise up in Israel. This yearning after a lost tribe (**6**) indicated that a flame of love was beginning to burn amid the steam and smoke of the newly-kindled fire; and if only there be love there is a point of contact at which God can reveal Himself to men, for he who loves his brother will presently come on to know God who is Love, and the tears shed over Benjamin are similar in nature to those shed on the Mount of Olives, when *He* beheld the city and wept over it.

9-14 *The sack of Jabesh-Gilead.* — It would have been better to turn their attention to the Canaanites still in the land (19:11, 12). But we are all more disposed to criticize our brethren, than to join forces with them against a common foe.

15-23 *The scheme at the dances at Shiloh.* — What an indescribable admixture there is here of a recognized religious worship, and its desecration, keeping a vow in outward form, while violating its tenor and spirit.

We cannot admire the method adopted by Israel to preserve Benjamin from extinction. As in so many other cases, a vow made rashly in a moment of excitement would have been better honored in the breach than in the observance. One star at least shone in the black night; truth began to be revered, and they would not go back from their solemn pledge and vow. The morals of the people were evidently lamentably low, but the whole of their course of action is probably to be explained by the fact that they looked upon this war as having been an act of righteousness.

There was an air of satisfaction in the return of the people to their homes (24). But we need to correct our self-estimate by the balances of eternity. As, in those days there could not be settled prosperity or peace till the true King came, so it is now in the kingdom of our hearts.

Prophecies Concerning Nations
That Oppressed Israel in the Times of the Judges

AMMON

Prophecies — Jer. 49:2; Ezek. 25:2, 5, 7; Zeph. 2:9.

All this country, formerly so populous and flourishing, is now changed into a vast desert. The far greater part of the country is uninhabited, being abandoned to the wandering Arabs, and the towns and villages are in a state of total ruin.

MOAB

Prophecies — Num. 24:17; Isa. 16:2; Jer. 48:1, 2, 46; Zeph. 2:9.

The cities of Moab have now disappeared: the whole country abounds with ruins. The Arab herds now roam in freedom over the valleys and the plains, and the many vestiges of field enclosures form no obstruction; they wander undisturbed around the tents of their masters, over the face of the country. The language of Moab was akin to the Hebrew.

PHILISTIA

Prophecies — Jer. 47:5; Ezek. 25:16; Amos 1:8; Zech. 9:5.

The plain of Philistia was famed for its corn, vines, and olives. Though the land was allotted to Israel, it was never permanently occupied by them, although at various times the Philistines were subject to the Israelites. The speech of the people differed from the Jew's language. The nation was finally overthrown by Alexander the Great, and now "cottages for shepherds, and fields for flocks" partially scattered along the sea-coast, are the only substitutes for the populous cities which this once powerful realm possessed.

The Book of Ruth

INTRODUCTION

This brief history forms an appendix to the Book of Judges with which it is obviously connected by the Hebrew word translated "Now." The object of the writer is to sketch the descent of David; and the narrative was probably written after his accession to the kingship, when a public interest in his ancestry was aroused. It supplies the genealogy of David which is not given in the Books of Samuel, and is thought by many to have been written by Samuel; if so, it was in his later years, as internal evidences in the narrative (obsolete Chaldaisms in the speech of characters introduced, and a similarity of expression with parts of Samuel) tend to show that the narrator adopted existing records in writing his own. There is also the ceremony of "casting the shoe" (4:7), which is described as being the "custom (R.V.) in former times."

The events recorded in this Book cover a period of about ten years, which would most probably commence during the seven years of the Midianite oppression recorded in Judges 6:1, so that the interval between the events and this record of them appears to have been about a century and a half.

The personal history of the central character in the Book is a very attractive one. Here we have established the fact of a heathen woman being counted worthy of becoming an ancestress of the great Messiah; and taken in connection with the history of Pharez (4:18, and Genesis 38) this narrative foreshadows the world-wide character of Christ's work for us, and how the purposes of God reach over the limits of the chosen people to bless and enrich all individual souls that truly love and seek Him. Throughout the Bible there are traces that God's heart went out after the other sheep that were not of the Israelitish fold, and in this exquisite story we catch a glimpse of the weaving through faith into the spiritual family of Abraham those who naturally had neither part nor lot with him. There is also interesting dispensational truth in these chapters, showing how the Gentile Church may enter into that union with the true Bridegroom of souls.

This Book forms a pleasant contrast to the more stormy and terrible episodes which marked the national condition between the days of Joshua and those of Samuel. It is like a smiling dale enclosed in gaunt and forbidding hills; or an idyll amid the storm of a tragedy. And in those stirring times of foreign inroads and domestic struggles of famine, and deeds of violence and crime which caused Elimelech to leave his village, it is evident that there were many devout souls like Boaz, who, with greater faith in God, maintained the loftiest conditions of patriarchal piety; and many homes hidden in the valleys where humility, endurance, industry, and love dwelt in exquisite and pure beauty.

Ruth 1   THE RETURN FROM MOAB

In this chapter the names tell a story: Elimelech, *my God is King;* Naomi, *pleasant* or *comely.* They tell of a religious life, and of the beauty of the young bride led to her new village home. Mahlon, *great infirmity;* Chilion, *wasting away.* They attest the inroad of want and famine, with the natural result of weak constitutions and broken health.

1-5 *The emigration.* — Surely this was through want of faith. Elimelech denied his name. When parents move into worldly circles, away from the ordinances of God's house, with an eye to worldly gain, they must not be surprised if their children make worldly alliances. The expedition ended in disaster, and the death from which they fled overtook them in the land of their adoption.

Too often when famine lies hard upon us, we attempt to help ourselves by desperate expedients which exclude God. We leave the land of promise for Moab, but there we meet the fate we thought to avert. Children of the world are at liberty to do things which the child of God cannot indulge in without peril and loss, and yet the results of our mistakes and sins are often so transformed by the touch of God's hand as to yield the richest fruits of life. Mahlon and Chilion are buried in Moab, but from Moab Ruth arises to be better than seven sons.

6-10 *The return.* — Naomi's sorrows had broken the ties which held her to Moab. Such is the explanation of many of those calamities which happen to the children of God. They are away from home, and must be driven back.

11-18 *The separation.* — Born in the same village, possibly betrothed and married on the same day, bound up in the same family life, companions on the road to Bethlehem; there their fellowship ceased. The one went back to her gods and obscurity; the other forward to Jehovah's worship and an honorable connection with Jewish story (Luke 17:33).

There are crises in all lives like that on the high pass that led from Moab to Canaan, where one soul cannot resist the fascinations of people and gods, lying far down the valley, while the other, thrilled with heroic purpose and faith, chooses the unseen and unknown. Although Ruth was, as far as we can discover, moved by no other considerations than affection for Naomi, and a desire to become a worshipper with her of the true God, yet she was unconsciously moving forward to her great destiny — an ancestress of Messiah. "Verily there is a reward for the righteous."

19-22 *The welcome back.* — Naomi's deep sorrow moved the city. The "pleasantness" had been turned into "bitterness" in her absence; but the welcome back was sincere on the part of the villagers. Nothing can so support us in sorrow as human love and sympathy, and the consciousness that under all secondary causes there is the purpose and hand of the Almighty Himself, dealing with us. Thus the Marah springs of our bereavements are staunched and transformed. The cup which my Father hath given me, shall I not drink it? (John 18:11).

The time of the return to Bethlehem (the beginning of barley-harvest) was probably in the month of April.

Ruth 2   RUTH, THE GLEANER

Our first experiences when we have chosen Christ are not always sunny ones. We have to glean in the fields of strangers. Testing times like these develop our nobler qualities, and make it clear that we have chosen God for Himself, and not for the wages that He pays.

1-3 *Ruth, the gleaner.* — The noblest natures are noble in the simplest of things. Those who are faithful in least, approve themselves worthy of being promoted to be faithful in much. Imitate Ruth, by doing the thing that lies next to your hand, and you will be probably promoted to a wider sphere. We must die in little acts of self-denial before we can bring forth much fruit. It is not in seeking great things for ourselves, but in doing little acts of service for those near to us, that we commend ourselves for usefulness and blessedness.

Those who glean in the fields of the Land of Promise will have enough and to spare, will meet their great Kinsman, and will become prepared to enter upon the higher experience of that union with Him, of which marriage is a shadow. Glean on, oh my soul! and gather after the reapers among the sheaves! Beat out what you glean with patient care! Do not hesitate to bring forth and give to those who need to abide at home! The time will come when those fair fields of Bible truth shall become your own, by union with their owner.

4-17 *Boaz, the master.* — Would that language like this was more frequently heard in harvest fields and factories! The speech of the employed is generally an echo of that of the employer (**4**). We should beware, however, of degenerating into a formality which speaks God's name thoughtlessly. How much good might we do if we were more careful to notice those who serve us, and speak kindly to servant-girls. Little acts and words of kindness do not cost much, but they mean much to a lonely soul (Matt. 25:40). Note the significant synonym for trust (**12;** Ps. 63:7; Matt. 23:37).

Boaz (*strength*) the near kinsman, is a glimpse of Him who, centuries later, was born in this same Bethlehem, and who appeals to each who does the will of His Father, as brother, sister, or mother. He takes knowledge of strangers; He is quick to see every trait of natural grace, and all kindly actions done to the least that belong to Him; He provides bread and wine; He causes handfuls to be dropped on purpose; He screens from annoyance and harm; He comforts and speaks to the heart; He blesses, and the humble, stooping spirit is blessed forever.

18-23 *Naomi, the anxious mother.* — How gladdened were those aged eyes with ephah (between three and four pecks) of barley, and with the reserves from the mid-day meal. We ought to bring home from every service the reserves of what we have heard (**18**). Man's kindness will sometimes soften a hard and weary heart, and enable it again to believe in the love of God (**20**). An over-ruling Providence had guided the young stranger to the field of a kinsman, though she knew it not (**19**). God remembers the prayers of the dead long after they have been offered, and answers them by mysterious providences, which show the eternal permanence and steadfastness of His love (Isa. 54:8-10; Rom. 8:28).

Ruth 3   A NEAR KINSMAN

Home ought always to mean Rest (ver. **1;** and 1:9). We need rest, and there is no such home wherein to find it, as the heart of our Maker, who is also our Husband! True wedded love is Rest, and the heart which has learned its true relationship to the great Kinsman, Christ, is at rest, no toilsome work in barley fields; all He has is ours.

2-6 *Naomi's proposals.* — To our notions of propriety they seem rather extraordinary. But we must remember that Ruth had a legal claim on Boaz, to be taken as his wife, on supposition that he was the nearest kinsman (Deut. 25:5-10). There is a sense in which a defenseless soul has a claim on the Lord Jesus Christ; nor is there any posture for us better than to lie at his feet, waiting for Him to tell us what to do (**4**).

6-15 *The chivalry of Boaz.* — He would not take advantage of the poor Gentile girl who appealed to him; and until his rights were clearly established, the question of their marriage union must needs wait; in the meanwhile he took the greatest care of her character (**14**). Nor did he leave her to plead her own case with the other kinsman, of whose existence Naomi seems to have been unaware, but undertook to ascertain his position for them. There seems a slight touch of pleased vanity in his allusion to Ruth's preference for himself over the younger men (**10**), which is very natural and lifelike.

16-18 *Waiting.* — And so the two women sat still. It was a good attitude, and one which well befits us all, when we have done all we can, and must leave the issue (Ps. 62:1). It was a grand character for faithfulness that Naomi gave Boaz (**18**). But how similarly it befits our blessed Lord, our Kinsman indeed. Put all into His strong hands, and then sit still.

When once we have put our matters into the hands of Christ, we have no further need for worry or fear, but may sit still in assured trust. We may rest, because He will not rest till He has finished that with which we have entrusted Him, and has fulfilled the word on which He has caused us to hope (Isa. 52:1; 2 Tim. 1:12).

Ruth 4   THE BRIDE OF BOAZ

It was probably early morning (**3, 13**) when Boaz "went up to the gate" — the customary place of Eastern legal transactions; and there he waited till the other and nearer kinsman came. And in that total disregard of time and absence of hurry, which are so characteristic of Oriental life, they sat down to discuss their matter in public, before ten elders, or, as we might call them, magistrates or judges.

3-11 *A law court.* — The kinsman was willing to acquire the land (**4**), which, perhaps, had been mortgaged, in payment of debt; but he was not willing to marry Ruth, because a son, born of the union, might divert the succession of his own lands from his family (**6**); so he renounced his right of claim, and confirmed the act by the Jewish custom, in which, by the transference of his shoe, he transferred his proprietorship (Deut. 25:8, 9).

Our Boaz pleads our cause in the gate, and what the law could not do, in that it was unable to redeem, our great Kinsman has done. And as the transference of the shoe indicated the transference of authority and poverty, so has all right and power over us passed into the hands of Jesus, who alone has a supreme claim over us. We are His. His because of His near kinship; His because He has fulfilled the law and possessed Himself of all legal right to us; His because He has redeemed us.

11-13 *A wedding.* — It was a rare lot for the Gentile maiden to have her case taken in hand by Boaz, the wealthy landowner of Bethlehem. To be his wife, and to realize that his inheritance was hers — this must have sent a thrill of bliss through her heart. Now the gleaner need not wearily follow the reapers' footsteps; all these broad fields were hers, because she had become one with their owner. So, when we are married to that other, Christ, we no longer toilsomely work for redemption, but, being redeemed, we bring forth fruit unto God (Rom. 7:4). Redeemed, wedded, fruitful.

But, after all, this raising up of the poor out of the dust to sit with princes is not to be named in comparison with the still more surprising fact in which each believer who reads these lines has a share. That we, who were not a people, should become the people of the living God, is much; but that is not all. We have become the Bride of Christ, and are joint-heirs with Him of His unsearchable riches.

14-16 *A nursery.* — What ectasy filled that aged heart! God will not ever be threshing us, but will give joy where He caused sorrow (Luke 1:45). And so, if we will wait for the end of the Lord, we shall always find that He justifies His dealings with His people. At first His hand seems against us. But it is only on account of our unbelief and disobedience. When we return to Him, He begins to work our help and cure.

17-22 *A genealogy.* — Of this line came David; and also on these same fields angels chanted the birth of another greater than all, who had sprung from this Gentile girl. Race cannot exclude from the line of blessing. In Christ we all are one (Col. 3:11).

The First Book of Samuel

INTRODUCTION

There is no mention in this Book of its authorship; it seems, however, reasonable to suppose that it was the work of Samuel himself, so far as the events recorded came under his cognizance. But there are evident traces of additions by later hands; as, for instance, the notice of his death. It has been thought that Nathan and Gad may have been concerned in this work of editing and completing Samuel's work (1 Chron. 29:29).

In the second book of Maccabees, it is said of Nehemiah, that he founded a library, and gathered together the acts of the kings, and the prophets, and of David. It is, therefore, a very fair inference that the books of Samuel were included, because they deal so largely with the story of the first two kings of Israel; and the passage bears witness to the care with which the sacred documents were treated and the way in which inspired men constituted themselves the custodians and editors of those that had preceded them.

There are internal indications of the extreme antiquity of the first book of Samuel, which support the belief that he was its author; such as its rare allusions to the sacrificial and ceremonial institutions at Jerusalem; its pure and noble diction; and its geographical and other explanatory notes added evidently by a much later hand (as 1 Sam. 9:9).

The main theme of the book is the institution of the monarchy, and the introduction of David on the scene of Jewish history. As these were matters of vital interest and importance, they are treated with some detail; and much attention is drawn to the fact that Saul was the choice of a self-willed people, while David was the man after God's own heart.

1 Samuel 1   THE BIRTH OF SAMUEL

1-8 *The yearly journey to Shiloh.* — This annual journey was undertaken by pious Jews to "sacrifice unto the Lord of hosts," at the Tabernacle, or — in later times — the Temple. It was on one of these journeys that our Lord was found questioning the doctors (Luke 2:46).

9-18 *Hannah's request.* — The bitter grief of Hannah on account of her childlessness did for her what anguish should always do. It drove her to God. There she found her only resource. When the heart is nigh to breaking, what else can we do than pour out our complaint into that tender and compassionate ear which is ever open to our cry? No human love can really allay our anguish as God can; though it may afford welcome solace, as Elkanah's to his much-loved wife. We turn from it, as well as from the scene of feasting, in the bitterness of our soul. Then we offer our prayers and tears to God; and He inclines unto us and hears our cry, and brings us up out of the horrible pit, and from among the miry clay.

What a sweet specimen of *secret fellowship* is here (**13**)! Many were coming and going in the court of the Tabernacle. There was no place for private prayer. The broken heart had no opportunity of audible petition: "she spake in her heart." We may each do that when amid the crowds that sweep us along in their busy current. *And let us not grow weary;* "she continued praying before the Lord" (**12**). If there is abundance of complaint and urgent need, let there be abundance of supplication. The overcharged spirit will not need to defend its case with men if it has committed it to God. And when once the burden is rolled off on God, the peace of God fills the heart. We go away in assured faith, and eat, and our countenances are no more sad.

19-28 *Samuel's birth, and presentation to the Lord.* — The ever-faithful God remembered Hannah's low estate; and not only answered her prayer by the birth of Samuel, but gave her the additional delight of being the mother of a son who afterwards became so famous, and of such great service to his country. Hannah "called his name Samuel, because I have asked him of the Lord" (**20**). God never fails. What we have asked of God should be given to God, devoted to His service, and held as His trust. Alas, that so often the parents' "thanksgiving" should only be a formal acknowledgement of God's goodness! Surely it is not too much for a child of God to say of his offspring, "he is lent to the Lord as long as he lives" (**28**).

1 Samuel 2   ELI, THE PRIEST

1-10 *Hannah's song of thankfulness.* — Oh, those notes of ectasy, which were to start David and Mary and many others singing! So the song of a bird will set the whole woodland ringing with feathered minstrelsy. We remember not our anguish for joy. The time is not far away for you to take your harp from the willow, and draw from it such music as will penetrate many another soul with trust. *How full of the Lord this song is!* Throughout, the overflowing heart ascribes its rapture to the Rock of Ages. He saves: He is holy: He knows: He weighs: He kills and makes alive: He brings down to the grave, and brings up: poverty and wealth, depression and exaltation, the keeping of the feet and the communication of strength, are His, and He will vindicate those that trust Him.

It is very needful that we lay to heart the motto, "By strength shall no man prevail" (**9**). We have often tried by expediency or energy to get our way; but in vain! To rise up early and sit up late will not effect our purpose. But to yield to God, to learn His lessons, to be submissive and gentle, to pray and trust and wait — thus we prevail. The Lord gives strength, and position, and success. We conquer by yielding; we gain by giving; He giveth unto His beloved as they sleep; in quietness and confidence shall be our strength.

11-17 *Samuel and the sons of Eli.* — What a contrast between the sweet God-appointed child priest, and the priests of title and descent! On the one God's favor rested, giving him favor with man; but the others had already committed the sin concerning which it is impossible to utter the prayer of faith (**25**).

18-21 *Eli's blessing.* — God did more than Hannah had asked or thought, and three sons and two daughters were added to the pious household. So that it came to pass that the "abundance of grief" (chap. 1:16) was transformed into "abundantly satisfied with the fatness of thy house" (Ps. 36:8).

22-26 *Eli's reproof to his sons.* — As in many other cases, Eli had left until too late his protest against his sons' behavior. Early training might have saved him the additional sorrow of his old age; but "as the twig is bent, so the tree is inclined."

27-36 *The curse on Eli's house.* — What a terrible calamity for a father to anticipate! — the loss of his whole family at one fell stroke (**34**). The "faithful priest" (**35**) was Zadok, who at the command of Solomon superseded Abiathar in the priestly office, "to fulfil the word of the Lord" (1 Kings 2:27, 35). And do not the words still further anticipate the priesthood of our Lord?

1 Samuel 3   THE CALL OF SAMUEL

1-14 *The voice in the night.* — Sweet story memorable to childhood! How many dear children have learned from you to listen for the voice of God! You have filled many a young sleeper with dream of that "still small voice," and made the night shine even as the day. But thou hast a message for us all and ever. We may not as yet look for the open vision; but we may listen to the voice of God speaking within, in the temple of the heart. Many a time He calls us by our name;

and we think it to be the echo of our own consciousness, or the summons of a friend. We need the anointed ear, to become familiar with the tender accents of God's voice; as Mary was with Christ's, when He called her by her name. We must know the Lord, and then the Word of the Lord will be revealed to us.

Have we not lain on beds of laziness, long after that voice has bidden us awake? Have not our spirits been lulled into fatal stupor by some lethargy or opiate, so that we have been disobedient to the heavenly voice or vision? What wonder is it that other instruments are selected to do work which we might have done, and that others receive revelations of the will of God which we might have caught and transmitted? First we should say: "Here am I"; next: "Speak, Lord!"

15-18 *Samuel's narrative of the vision.* — The delicacy of Samuel in trying to spare Eli's feelings, and the old man's resignation, are very beautiful. What better can we say as we hear the heavy tidings that at times must needs be spoken? — "It is the Lord; let Him do what seemeth Him good" (**18**).

19-21 *Further revelations to Samuel.* — "Samuel grew, and the Lord was with him" (**19**); reminding us of our Saviour's youth when He "increased in wisdom and stature, and in favor of God and man" (Luke 2:52). In the view of the whole country "from Dan to Beersheba" (**20**), Samuel was established to be a prophet of the Lord; and God appeared to him again in Shiloh. This instance of a child being the voice of God to the nation, is instructive in showing us how the weak things are used by the Almighty to carry out His purposes on behalf of His people. He hides things from the wise and prudent, which He reveals to babes.

1 Samuel 4   THE ARK TAKEN

1-9 *Israel's defeat and folly.* — After the defeat at the hands of the Philistines at Eben-ezer, the Israelites fell into the terrible error of removing the ark of the Lord from the tabernacle into the midst of the camp.

They thought that the presence of the ark of God must bring deliverance. It was like the *fetish* of the savage, the charm of the ignorant. No ark, however sacred its associations, could undo the effect of Israel's departure from God, or cancel the result of disastrous sins in the family of Eli. It is thus that our evil hearts still seek to evade the consequences of their wrong-doing, and to escape the necessity of putting wrong right. We resort to prayer, to vows of consecration, to strenuous resolutions, to sacraments and rituals, to ceremonialism and priestcraft. But all to no avail. if we regard iniquity in our heart, the Lord does not hear our prayer. "To obey is better than sacrifice, and to hearken than the fat of rams." If you are in trouble, or constantly overcome by your sins, the Philistines of your soul, it will be well to go to the very root and cause of all in the departure of your soul from God.

10-18 *The death of Eli and his sons.* — Samuel's prophecy is here fulfilled to its bitter end; and the news of the extinction of the priestly family must have "made the ears to tingle," notwithstanding the national sorrow at the overwhelming disaster of the loss of the ark. As in this chapter of Israel's history, so in our own hearts, the sons of Eli must be discerned and judged and put away; and the soul must be true in its allegiance to that faithful Priest, who does according to that which is in God's heart and mind. Only so will the rites and ordinances of God's house be of any avail.

19-22 *Ichabod.* — The disaster to Eli's family extended to the home of Phinehas, and his wife in distress succumbed to the accumulated troubles which fell on that day. Her end was, as indeed was that of Eli, very tragic; but there is a beautiful touch, in the case of each, of devotion to the cause of God. Eli did not succumb till the messenger made mention of the capture of the ark; and the new-born babe could not rally the mother from her death-swoon, since she accounted that Israel's glory departed, when the sacred symbol of their faith had passed into the hands of their foes. In each case there was an absorption in the interests of the

cause of God, which is full of instruction. Let us look at all
things in the light of God's glory, and let our soul be on fire
with holy ardor for the success of the kingdom of Emmanuel.

1 Samuel 5   THE ARK IN DAGON'S TEMPLE

1-9 *The Ark in a heathen temple.* — The ark was a type of
Christ. He is the propitiatory that covers the law, and on
which, blood-besprinkled, the eyes of the cherubim are fixed.
It was proper and right that Dagon, the guardian deity of
Philistia, should do Him homage by falling flat on the ground
before the emblem of His presence. As the apostle says, the
heathens sacrifice to demons, and not to God. Behind Dagon
therefore there was some evil spirit, who through the hideous
idol dominated and possessed the inhabitants of Philistia.
And thus there was the obeisance of one emblem to another
in that old temple, the sign and seal of a yet mightier conflict,
which was in process between the Son of God, and the
prince of the power of the air. Already Satan was falling as
lightning from heaven, and there were portents and presages
of his being cast out.

While the children of Israel looked upon the ark as sure
to bring them deliverance, it failed them; but this was not
to be construed into any preference on the part of God for
the men of Philistia; for as soon as it came into their borders
it brought them terrible plagues. With the froward God shows
Himself froward. What we are toward God, determines the
aspect of His dealings with us.

No evil thing can stand against the entrance of the
Redeemer. It must fall down before Him, and be broken.
Those who cannot cast down Dagon before introducing the
ark, should introduce the ark, and Dagon will fall down by
himself. The idols He shall utterly abolish.

10-12 *Smitten with plague.* — The disaster to their idol
caused the Philistines to send the ark to Ekron. Here,
however, the hand of God and His jealousy for His honor
pursued the captors of the sacred ark. "The hand of God was
heavy" upon them, and great destruction was in their midst.

Death and painful disease, between them, devastated the
male population.

1 Samuel 6   THE ARK SENT BACK

1-18 *The return of the Ark.* — The story of the deliverance
from Egypt had spread the fame of God throughout all these
countries (4:8), and especially lived in the hearts of the
priests and diviners. They, at least, knew that "the Lord, He
is God." But, like all of us, by nature they were disposed to
think that He could be propitiated by gifts of gold, rather than
by the sacrifices of a broken heart. This making a golden
image (**5**) of the causes of their suffering, is similar to our
habit of dwelling upon the secondary causes of our sorrows,
rather than dealing with the heart-evil that may have
originated them.

God's power was evident in making these cows take a road
foreign to their maternal instincts (**12**); and whenever God's
hand is at work, it shows itself in accomplishing what is
above nature. There is no greater proof of the reality of the
Gospel story than that description of the Lord Jesus given
in the four Gospels; which is so unlike the national Jewish
conception; and there is no stronger evidence of the work
of God in the human heart than that it makes us act in direct
opposition to our natural impulses. The flesh may sometimes
yearn for the opposite, but as the cows lowed for their calves;
but the spirit abates not an hairbreadth in its steady course.
However weak the flesh, our true self wills only the will of
God.

It was a strange sight, that new cart with its burden, the
ark, and the gold trinkets — the oxen swayed by a power they
could not understand; yet similar spectacles are to be
witnessed every day, when new hearts yield themselves to
God to bear forward His cause. Heart and flesh fail; but God
is the strength of the heart, and His Spirit bears us forward
we know not how or where.

19-21 *The catastrophe at Beth-shemesh.* — This was a
priest's city (Josh. 21:16); and the providence of God so

directed the cattle in their journey, that the proper hands should be at the first point of the Israelites' border to receive the precious treasure. Curiosity, however, tempted some of the inhabitants to pry into the interior, and immediately the judgments of God fell upon them. An error seems to have crept into this passage in regard to the number of victims. Many scholars hold that the "thousands" have no rightful place in the text, but that threescore and ten men — *i.e.,* seventy — is the true reading, with which Josephus agrees. *Fausset* says that one twentieth, instead of as sometimes one tenth of the people, were slain. This would make the passage to read that "fifty in a thousand, even threescore and ten men." Whatever the punishment was, it sufficed to cause urgency in the request that the men of Kirjath-jearim would remove the ark from their midst.

1 Samuel 7   "EBEN-EZER"

1-12 *The repentance at Mizpeh.* — In its new resting-place the ark was under the special care of Eleazar; and it remained in the house of Abinadab until it was taken by David to the house of Obed-Edom, and thence to the tabernacle at Zion (2 Sam. 6:3, 4, 10, 11), nearly eighty years after. But the twenty years (**2**) of utter neglect of the ark and tabernacle were a grievous break in the history of the redeemed people; and during that time they were exposed to the incursions of the Philistines, before which Shiloh itself may have been demolished (Jer. 7:12, 14). Similar breaks in our holy fellowship and walk with God will lead to similar results. When the ark, representing the Lord Jesus, is not in its rightful place, there is for us also the invasion of tyrannous and cruel sins, which make havoc of the holy institutions and resolves of other and happier days.

When such has been the case, there must be the judging and putting away of the Baalim and Ashtaroth (**4**), representing the principle of self-energy and the hidden evil of our hearts. We must pour out our hearts in humble confession, as Samuel poured out the water on the ground

(**6**). And we must renew the entire consecration and devotion of ourselves to God, as symbolized in the whole burnt-offering that Samuel made (**9, 10**).

13-17 *The enemy turned back.* — We should expect at Eben-ezer that our enemies will be turned back. The act of faith in the erection of "the stone of help" (*marg.*) threw the preservation of the nation upon God.

> "And can He have taught us to trust in His name,
> And thus far have brought us to put us to shame?"

Not only did God answer the prayer of the people (**8**) for deliverance on this occasion, but during "all the days of Samuel" (**13**) was the hand of the Lord against the Philistine. "There was peace between Israel and the Amorites" (**14**). Probably the warfare waged by these hill-dwellers was much less severe than the fighting on the plains with the armed Philistine host. But God often removes minor troubles, when we are called to face greater ones; and for those who are faithful to Him, there is ultimately peace in their borders.

Samuel's yearly circuit was of help to keep the people from forgetting God. At his house in Ramah he "built an altar unto the Lord" (**17**). Let us see to it that in our journeys and dealings with men we take with us the holy influence of the "altar" at our home. Oh, to commence every day with God; and to keep the influence of that time with us throughout the hours of journeying and occupation!

1 Samuel 8   "WE WILL HAVE A KING"

1-3 *Samuel's sons misjudge the land.* — How little room there is for any of us to "cast the stone"! We shall often find the evil which we condemn in others as a hiding-place in our own hearts, where to our own gaze it is much less heinous than it is in the life of our neighbor. So in this chapter we find that the sin which Samuel had rebuked in Eli was repeated in his own family. "His sons walked not in his ways." We should be on the watch; for the power to detect and rebuke does not necessarily imply that we ourselves are guiltless. Judge yourselves, that ye be not judged. "Behold, the Judge standeth before the door."

4-9 *The request for a king.* — How this request must have pained Samuel! "Thy sons walk not in thy ways; now make us a king to judge us like the other nations" (**5**). Conscious that his sons were not guiltless, yet he must have desired to find a lesser change in the government of the country than the election of a chief. But he sought the Lord's face; and whenever the heart is overwhelmed with the prospect of some imminent change; when we are hemmed in with difficulty; when men rise up against us, and such as breathe out cruelty — then to roll the whole anxiety to the heart of Jesus, in the belief that He has made the case His own, is the clue to right judgment, and the secret of a peace that passeth understanding. The Lord will speak to us. Samuel went between the people of God, now telling all the words of the Lord unto the people, and again rehearsing all the words of the people in the ears of the Lord. In this he reminds us of the true arbiter of souls, who lays His hand upon both; and suggests how much we might do as the priests of God and intercessors for men.

10-18 *The description of the king.* — One would have thought that the people's desire for a king would cease upon Samuel's recital of the characteristics of the coming monarch. Forcible removal from their homes of the flower of the youth of the land; compulsory labor in the royal estate, workshop, and household; a tithing of vineyard, and oliveyard, and sheep for the support of the court — formed only a part of the lot of the people under the new *regime.*

19-22 *The people's persistence.* — Though the king, whom they sought, was to be a misfortune and a curse, the people persisted in their request; and it was granted according to a principle in the Divine government, that man gets what he importunately seeks, though it breeds leanness in his soul.

"And the Lord said to Samuel, hearken unto their voice and make them a king" (**22**). To what fatal loss, however, the people exposed themselves, when they exchanged the royalty of Jehovah for that of an earthly sovereign — the theocracy for a monarchy! O my soul, see to it that thou dost not forsake the fountain of living waters, for a cistern of thine own hewing!

1 Samuel 9   SAUL, THE SON OF KISH

1-10 *Saul's fruitless search.* — Saul, "a choice young man and goodly" (**2**) now first appears upon the scene. His search after his father's asses proving futile, he accepts his servant's suggestion to consult "the seer." Perhaps he resembled the young man whom Jesus loved (Mark 10:21). His father was certainly rich (**1**); and perhaps in consequence of this Saul was wayward, self-willed, and impetuous.

11-24 *Saul's opportune arrival.* — Coincidences are providences. The lost asses brought Saul in contact with Samuel. His ineffectual search for them, and his servant's knowledge of the habits of Samuel, brought them to the city at a most opportune moment; for the prophet had just come there for a special occasion (**12**). Indeed, they seem to have met him in the highway (**18**). But the inner history of all this is revealed in God's words to His servant: "Tomorrow about this time I will send thee a man, and thou shalt anoint him" (**16**). Let us trust God to find us the men we need to help us in His work. They may come to us on quite another errand, or even as though led to us by some mishap; but we shall hear His voice suddenly saying, as we encounter them, "Behold the man of whom I spake" (**17**).

The feast which Samuel had prepared was perhaps only ordinary Eastern hospitality; but the aged seer would doubtless be watching the young man to see if there was anything in his behavior inconsistent with the kingly office.

25-27 *Saul's favorable departure.* — Saul's future life was beginning to open to his view. After the seat of honor at the feast comes this private talk with the prophet. "They arose early" (**26**) and Samuel showed Saul the word of the Lord.

1 Samuel 10   SAUL ANOINTED KING

1-13 *The prophetic signs, and their fulfilment.* — After anointing Saul with oil (**1**), thereby consecrating him to the service of God, the prophet sketched the events which were to happen on that and successive days.

The circumstances of meeting the two men at Rachel's tomb, the finding of the asses, the offering of bread and wine by the three men at Bethel were known to Saul, therefore before he came to them; but in each case he was to act as the occasion suggested and seemed to demand. Thus our life-course lies open before God. We have been created unto good works, which He has before ordained, that we should walk in them. But instead of prying into the future, let us leave Him to unveil it as we come to it; and, above all, to enable us to act in each new instance as it becometh the Gospel. We are bidden to walk as Jesus walked; let us, therefore, ask Him to live in us and walk in us. When we seek the anointing of the Holy Ghost in the spring of the day, His sacred unction will remain with us, and will teach us all things, and we shall know what He would have us do. "God is with thee" (**7**), to guide, and keep, and prosper, with his blessed help and grace.

Often in life we meet bands of prophets, and we catch the holy fire from their hearts; and for a little we burn with holy enthusiasm. But "another heart" (**9**) is not enough; we need another's — that is, the will, and purpose, and indwelling power of the Lord Himself. It is not enough to possess Him, we must be possessed by Him. Not the Spirit mightily *on* us only, but mightily *in* us. Not gift alone, but grace.

17-27 *The choice at Mizpeh.* — It would have been well for the people in rejecting God's sovereignty (8:7, 8), to have chosen one for the new kingship who, at least, was free from the vices of Samuel's sons, and endowed with kingly qualities; but Saul could not rule others, because he did not rule his own spirit; and he could not rule himself, because he had not learned to obey. Only those can properly rule who have enthroned God as king of the inner man; and, as his after-life proved, this had not been the case with Saul. The people, instead of concerning themselves about the inner qualities, were only eager as to the royal bearing and stature

of their future monarch. They chose after their own heart,
and God gave them up.

1 Samuel 11   THE KINGDOM RENEWED

1-3 *Nahash the Ammonite.* — Had this fighting chieftain
heard of the request of the Israelites? (8:20). The election of
a king "to fight out battles" seems to have immediately
provoked this incursion from the desert. A wise people will
refrain from displaying a belligerent spirit, thereby inviting
attack.

4-11 *Prompt interposition and deliverance.* — Upon receipt
of the news at Gibeah, Saul's anger rose (**6**); and following
the procedure of the Levite at the same place (Judges 19),
sent round to all the tribes of Israel, using for the purpose
a yoke of oxen "hewn in pieces."

What the fiery cross did in olden times to arouse the
people of Scotland to resist the invader, was accomplished
by these pieces of slaughtered oxen. But there was also a
Divine compulsion laid on the hearts of the people. The Spirit
of God came on Saul (**6**), and the fear of the Lord fell on the
people (**7**). It is our duty to carry the summons of the Gospel
into all the world; but after all, we need the co-operation of
the Divine Spirit to stir and move the hearts of men. We may
plant or water, but God alone can give the increase. In these
latter days the Spirit of God is mightily at work, and the
immediate symptom of His operations is unity. "They came
out with one consent," or "as one man" (**7**, *marg.*).

United action was crowned with success; and the enemies
of the people were "scattered so that two of them were not
left together" (**11**).

12-15 *Thanksgiving after victory.* — When the battle had
closed, the people at the word of Samuel journeyed to Gilgal,
and there renewed the covenant with Saul, with sacrifices
and rejoicings (**15**). So much were the people charmed with
their victorious leader, that they wished to put to death those
who on his first election did not welcome him. But Saul
quashed the proposal, and treated the opposition of the few

with generous magnanimity. It is very beautiful to hear his ascription of all his success to God: "The Lord hath wrought salvation in Israel." But see how far we may go, and yet become castaways. This man, who spoke and acted thus, was yet to perish by his own hand on the field of Gilboa. Let us beware! We say again, it is not enough to have the Spirit on us; He must be in us.

1 Samuel 12   SAMUEL'S REPROOF

1-5 *A life of unchallenged integrity.* — Although Samuel lived for probably thirty years after, he was now old; and, the king having been appointed, felt that his official work was done. What a record the prophet had established for righteous dealing! No bribe had ever perverted his judgments, neither had any suffered at his hand from oppression, nor had he defrauded any (**3**). Let us so live that when our work is done we may be able to call God and man to witness that we have behaved ourselves holily, righteously, and unblamably; and that our hands are free from the blood of men.

6-15 *A review of the past.* — In the margin (**6**) the Lord is said to have *made* Moses and Aaron. It is He that hath made us; we are His workmanship, the work of His hands, and our Maker becomes our husband. Let us be more pliable beneath the touch of those hands that reach down from heaven to mold men; or, if we are conscious of having been marred in His hands, let us ask Him to make us again, and to send us as He sent Jerubbaal, and Bedan, and Jephthah, and Samuel.

This history of the past dealings of the Lord is full of wholesome instruction, especially when we see that forgetfulness of the Lord has always involved us in captivity and sorrow; while repentance and the putting away of sin have immediately brought about a turn in the tide of outward and inward prosperity.

16-25 *A faithful Creator.* — Samuel's review of the past was uttered to strengthen the people in the fear of the Lord, and to warn them that, if they were not faithful to Jehovah, king and people alike would perish. The prophet called unto the Lord for thunder and rain at the time of the wheat harvest, to convince the people of their wickedness in asking for a king. But, their perversity notwithstanding, God would remain faithful. So, too, in these later days, "the Lord will not forsake his people." What a precious word is this! Even though we believe not, yet He abideth faithful. He works for His great name's sake. Throughout the Bible we find that God must maintain the honor of His name, which involves His character and truth. "I had pity for my holy name" (Ezek. 36:21). Therefore with what certainty must prayer prevail which asks in His name! It is a blessed thing to fall back on the covenant, ordered in all things and sure, by which our God has bound Himself.

1 Samuel 13   SAUL'S RASH FOLLY

1-4 *The revolt against the Philistines.* — The oppressors of all Israel had deprived them of all the blacksmiths (**19**), so that the people were unarmed. This, however, did not prevent Jonathan (*Jehovah's gift*) from attacking a Philistine garrison at Geba (**3**). Jonathan was an expert and accurate archer; and *Fausset* suggest that it was the "picking off" of a prominent officer that roused the Philistines into a general movement against Israel.

5-7 *The distress of the people.* — The immense gathering of the strong Philistine nation on the borders of the land, had the immediate effect of causing a serious defection in the ranks of Jonathan's army; some retreating across the Jordan, and many others hiding themselves in the caves, thickets, and pits of the "sharp rocks" (14:4). The remaining part of the army with Saul at Gilgal "followed him trembling" (**7**).

Up to this point Saul's influence had steadily waxed; henceforth it began to wane. Does this not show that, even before the offering of sacrifice on which the sentence of rejection was pronounced, there had been a subtle declension which had spread to the people? How different this to the victorious march on Jabesh-Gilead! Already the Lord had departed from him. The lordly oak is rotted at the heart, long before the storm lays it low in the forest glade.

8-16 *Saul's rash sacrifice.* — This is the dividing-line in the history of Saul. He had been appointed king by God, "that he may save my people out of the hands of the Philistines" (9:16); and the seven days' wait at Gilgal was for the purpose of receiving Samuel's final instructions as to what should be done in the campaign, which, perhaps, had been anticipated by the prophet (10:8). Becoming impatient at Samuel's deferred arrival, Saul decided to offer the sacrifice, thereby bringing upon himself the loss of his kingdom (**14**).

Saul's disobedience was due to want of faith. He saw the people melting away from his side. He thought that something ought to be done, but he lacked that calm assurance and spirit of quiet waiting which faith always imparts. And so because Samuel did not come till late in the appointed period (though he arrived late, it expired), Saul took the matter into his own hands, and offered sacrifice. Ah, it is hard to wait for God on the mountain brow, while human counsellors urge action, and every moment's delay seems a lifetime, and the case is becoming desperately urgent. Let us then remember that the cause is as much to God as to us, but that He is waiting till He can interpose with most effect; let us not force ourselves and offer. In acting thus we shall show that we possess the temper which is an absolute prerequisite for the Divine service. God can only use those who trust Him absolutely; and He often tests them by long delay. The established life must be a life of faith. Nothing else can impart it. We must literally and at all costs keep the commandment of the Lord. To do otherwise is a folly and a sin.

1 Samuel 14   JONATHAN'S VALOR

1-18 *Jonathan's heroic exploit.* — As Jonathan had been the cause of the Philistine incursion, he determined, in the strength of the Lord, to overthrow the hosts of the enemy. His armor-bearer was with him with all his heart (**7**); and the favor of the Lord rested on the perilous enterprise. After receiving the sign from Heaven, they passed over, and in a small space (half-an-acre, ver. **14**) slew twenty men. Probably this was due to Jonathan's sharp-shooting; for we read, "they fell before Jonathan, and his armor-bearer slew after him" (**13**). An earthquake added to the terror of the Philistine hosts, who in their eagerness to escape seem to have worked their own destruction, "beating down one another" (**16**). The absence of Jonathan and his armor-bearer was only discovered by a numbering of the six hundred, consequent on the watchmen seeing the "melting away" (**16**) of the great host. The whole incident is a piece of Israelite chivalry. Two men against a garrison; but with them was a third, who wrought for them, though they were but few. The work that was done that day was due to the faith that brought Divine power on the scene. There is no restraint on God's part; would there were none on ours! Though the steep crags be filled with the forms of the foes of God and man, impurity, drink, passion, a very legion of devils, yet two may chase a garrison, and send a trembling throughout the host. Nay, it is not necessary that there should be two in human guise, though it is pleasant for Peter and John to be together; but if one lonely disciple is willing to act as armor-bearer to the Captain of the Lord's host, Christ and He will put ten-thousand to flight.

19-46 *Saul's command to the people.* — The hasty self-will of the king is shown here, and the unfortunate result of the command upon the people. The enforced abstinence from refreshing food during the day caused faintness during the rout; and at night the eating of the spoil "with the blood" (**32**), thereby breaking the command of the Mosaic law.

However well intended to prevent the loss of time, Saul's command was fatal. Time is not really lost when we stay to refresh ourselves with the honey that drops from the rocks. Though our work for God may seem to demand every minute, we should save time in the end if we remained to eat of the heavenly food. The mower saves time when he pauses to whet his scythe.

It is no great wonder that the people refused to allow Saul to carry into effect his sentence against Jonathan (**43, 44**). Gratitude prompted the feeling of the nation that he should not die, the people being in advance of the king as to the interpretation of the spirit of an oath. Such a rash oath as Saul's was honored more in its breach, than in a slavish obedience to its terms. Well had it been if Herod under like circumstances had been prevented by the people from carrying out his unwise oath, and thereby been saved from the eternal disgrace of causing the death of John the Baptist.

1 Samuel 15   SAUL REJECTED

1-9 *The expedition to Amalek.* — Saul's great army (**4**) was enabled to smite the whole nation to the Amalekites. The sparing of the Kenites (**6**), in view of the past kindness to the Israelites, was a touch of gratitude which would be acceptable to the weak, and ennobling to the strong. But Saul's second great error was committed here. The saving of the king and "the best of the sheep and oxen" was in direct violation of the explicit command to "utterly destroy" (**3**). Amelek is always the type of the flesh, which God will not spare; though we are all too prone to spare that which is good and prepossessing in its appearance. We do not always see as much evil in the religious self as in the vile and refuse self, which is the wreck of the wildest passions; but every form of the self-life is equally abominable to God, though it may have been kept for sacrifice and burnt-offering.

10-23 *Samuel's message.* — "It repenteth me that I have set up Saul to be king" (**11**). Such was the word of God to Samuel. The prophet sought Saul after spending a night in prayer, and found him surrounded by the evidences of his unfaithfulness. The king must have been willfully blind to his disobedience when he met the prophet with the words, "I have obeyed the voice of the Lord." Note too that he puts the blame upon the people for what had been saved: "*they* have brought them"; while he takes credit with them for "the rest" which "*we* have utterly destroyed."

Have we ever made God repent having given us a niche in His holy service? Have we turned back from following Him, and failed to perform His commandments? Or does the fact of others having done so make us cry all night? These words of Samuel indicate that a higher conception of the Divine will was beginning to pervade the leaders of Israel, and that they were coming to see that obedience and loyalty were more to God than rites and sacrifices. It is, however, a lesson that needs repeating always. We are all too prone to substitute the outward for the inward, the altar for the heart, the sweet incense for the fragrance of yielded life.

24-35 *Saul's remorse.* — The turning again of Saul was mingled with his pride; he wished to be honored before men (**30**), although he knew that God had rejected him. Samuel, after the rending of his garment (typifying the rending of the kingdom from Saul), joined in prayer with the king for the last time. Agag's death preceded the final farewell of the prophet. "Samuel came no more to see Saul" (**35**). From this moment Saul seems to have been shut off from all Divine approval and assistance. The words, "nevertheless he mourned for him," are extremely touching — sorrowing that the man should have so conducted himself as to lose the kingdom, and yet faithfully abiding by the commands of God that a new king should be anointed.

In Samuel's rebuke he seems to have foreshadowed Saul's later wanderings from God, specifying the heinous sin into which Saul afterwards fell. "For rebellion is as the sin of witchcraft" (**23**). Saul's experience with the witch of Endor was the inevitable outcome of the course to which he had committed himself.

1 Samuel 16   DAVID ANOINTED

1-13 *The call of David.* — We turn from the wreck of Saul to the idyllic beauty of David's life among the sheepcotes of Bethlehem.

Samuel had journeyed there with two objects: to sacrifice, and to anoint the new monarch. His judgment miscarried, as brother after brother passed, in stalwart manhood, before the prophet's eye; and he would have overlooked David, had not the Lord repeatedly stayed his hand. The prophet was so ready to think that the outer man was a true reflection of the inner. But it is the hidden man of the heart which is dear to God; humility, unselfishness, willingness to be unknown, unrecognized. Our God is constantly passing over the wise and prudent to reveal Himself to babes; and choosing the weak and base things of the world to bring to nought the things that are. Last of all, David was brought in from the care of the sheep.

Among his flocks, the boy had watched the heavens declaring the glory of God, and had known himself to be a sheep under God's shepherd care. He had been faithful in a very little, and was now called to a wider sphere; and as he stepped up to fill it, the Spirit of the Lord came mightily upon him. Every fresh summons is accompanied by a fresh anointing for those who look for it. Stormy indeed was to be the life into which the shepherd lad now stepped; but he was to be the minstrel of the world, and the education of circumstance was to add chords to his lyre, which would express with unique fulness and beauty the elegies of human life and experience, redounding in praise and worship towards God.

14-23 *Saul and David.* — When the evil spirit, permitted by the Lord, because Saul had shut his heart against his Holy Spirit, troubled the king, he sought relief in music. David had some fame in this direction, and this sufficed to obtain his introduction to court-life. Saul, apparently not knowing of the anointing at Bethlehem, "loved David greatly, and he became his armor-bearer" (**21**). The shepherd-lad, in no way embarrassed by his sudden transfer from sheepcote to palace, played so skillfully that Saul was refreshed (**23**). God was thus working in many threads to effect the pattern of His purpose toward Israel.

His purposes will ripen fast, Unfolding every hour.

1 Samuel 17   GOLIATH OF GATH

1-27 *Goliath's challenge.* — Yet another Philistine incursion! — and this time a giant champion, clad in brass, the strength of his armor being equal to his blatant impiety (**46**). David's journey to the camp on a visit to his three elder brothers (**13**) was the occasion of deliverance for the nation. Arriving at the scene of action, and leaving his carriage (*i.e.* baggage) in the hands of the keeper (**22**), he talked with his brothers. Upon hearing the Philistine challenge, he decided in God's strength to accept it.

28-39 *Discouragements in the conflict.* — The chilling words of Eliab were met by his young brother with the gentle question: "Is there not a cause for what I have done?" David had never conquered Goliath if he had not controlled himself. The words of David were reported to the king, who was glad to welcome a champion for his nation, even though he were a youth. David's recital of his deliverance from the lion and the bear, and his estimate of the Philistine to be "as one of them" caught Saul's ear, and he said, "Go, and the Lord be with thee." But why press upon David the use of the armor? "He assayed to go"; but it was not a part of God's plan that His chosen champion should use armor and sword.

40-54 *The victory.* — A sling and one small stone were the weapons of David as he drew near to the Philistine, and his faith in God got him the victory; so that the Philistine "fell upon his face to the earth." The fall of the champion was the signal for a general rout; and the Israelites pursued the flying hosts with a great slaughter.

Giants are found in every life — giant sins — as there are giants in every sphere of work. They stalk before us with sword, and spear, and javelin, and defy the hosts of God. It is not enough to have been redeemed by the Paschal Lamb. We shall be trodden down before them unless we have learned to go against them in the name of the Lord of Hosts. God has other armies than those which are reckoned by man; and if we live by faith in Him, those armies march unseen beside us, and win the victory which we think we win by our sling and stone.

The Angel of God fights beside each David-life that in faith refuses the armor of Saul. Give me the sling of a child-like faith, and the stones chosen, from the brook of Scripture, and no weapon that is formed against me shall prosper. We need more faith in the Living God, who saves not with sword and spear; a conviction which will come to us only when we understand that the battle is His — His to arrange, His to carry through, while we have but to do His bidding, to go or come. We are educated in the lonely conflict with lion and bear, for the greater arena with Philistine giant.

1 Samuel 18   DAVID AND JONATHAN

1-5 *The beginning of a memorable brotherhood.* — This knitting of soul is like the love between the Savior and His own. They have no claim on Him. There is not in them, as there was in David, a natural beauty, a chivalrous spirit, a great feat of bravery, to recommend them to the great Lover of souls. But it may be said of the Master, as of Jonathan, He loved them as His own soul. We may be glad that we are permitted to wear His robe, use His sword and bow, and bind His girdle on our loins for purity and strength. Beneath the inspiration of such a love, like David, we may well go out and prosper. Our outgoings for service must always be balanced by our incomings for fellowship.

6-9 *Jealousy.* — This is one of the worst temptations that can beset us. Some seem more susceptible to it than others. It arises in the most unexpected ways and times. When all around are possessed by a common joy, it steals in like a spectre and settles down on some heart, which it scourges with the whips of the Furies. Resist its first entrance! The Holy Spirit, infusing trust and love, is the only antidote against it. Walk carefully, O child of God; thou art being *eyed.*

10-16 *Hatred.* — The evil spirit is said to have come from God, in the bold language of Scripture, because He permitted it, and so constituted the laws of the human mind, that when a man gives himself up to any kind of sin, it always opens the door to Satan and to further and more desperate acts.

When we refuse God's Spirit, we surrender ourselves to the evil spirit. When we turn from God, we throw ourselves into the power of the devil. When men do not wish to retain God in their knowledge, He gives them up (Rom 1:28). What a contrast between the moody monarch and the beloved David, on whose heart, in those blessed days, the sun of human and Divine love shone so brightly! When God is with a man, He acts wisely, and strikes awe into the hearts of them that hate Him. If you have strong foes, be wary, and keep close to God.

17-30 *Murder.* — It was not the less murder, though none knew the murderous intent with which Saul lured David into danger. This secret thing is now proclaimed on the housetop of the world. "Murder will out." But how futile to enter into battle against the fixed purposes of God! Notice how repeatedly we are told that David behaved wisely (**5, 14, 30**). It is a great and holy art to walk carefully.

1 Samuel 19   DELIVERANCE FROM DANGER

1-8 *Jonathan's intercession.* — At the risk of losing all that earth could give him, the king's son espoused the cause of the young shepherd-ministrel-warrior. Nothing but love can give the clue to his interposition on David's behalf. But it is a greater marvel still that Jesus pleads for us at the right hand of God. In this case, however, He has not to overcome the hatred of God; but to vindicate His justice, in showing that a fit propitiation has been made for our sins.

8-17 *Prevenient Grace.* — The Psalmist composed Psalm 59 in memory of this incident. He depicts the emissaries of Saul as prowling around his house, while he within is hiding in God, His strength and high tower: sure that the God of his mercy will come between him and his foes. Twice he speaks of Him as the God of his mercy. How blest that frame of mind that can compose songs while tumult is all around!

18-24 *The savor of life to life, and of death to death.* — There was a great difference between David and Saul at Naioth — one of the prophetic schools maintained by

Samuel, as the means of evangelizing the nation. Between David and the band of young prophets there was a living sympathy, and he was one with them in the purity and simplicity of his life; but in the case of Saul there was only the passing wave of emotional enthusiasm. Brought for a moment within reach of the holy contagion, his soul became strongly moved by it, and he seemed to have become another man. But he was not a *new* man. The Spirit was *on* him, and not *in* him. He had the gifts, but not the grace; the blossom, but not the fruit. God save us from being as tares that resemble the wheat, but are ultimately burned!

1 Samuel 20   A TRUE FRIENDSHIP

This chapter gives a touching account of how much Jonathan was prepared to do for love's sake. And if a man would do so much, what will not God do, who loves us so infinitely?

1-10 *The ingenious proposal.* — There was a certain crookedness, a want of straightforwardness, in David's suggestions, which are not perfectly satisfactory. It seemed as if at this moment he stepped out of the light for a little. If we walk in God's light, we can count on His protection without resorting to subterfuge. How touching the dialogue between these two! yet how full of cheer for David to have a friend at court who could speak for him and declare the king's thoughts! And we may comfort ourselves with the memory that there is a link between us and the heavenly throne-room. We should be missed if our seat were empty. But there will be no gaps in the family circle — no children in the field who should be in the palace.

11-17 *The brotherly covenant.* — Jonathan had already a prevision of David's royalty, and that all his enemies would be cut off; but the love he had for his friend made jealousy impossible. His only agony just then was the dread of separation. There must have been moments when Jonathan saw clearly that the supremacy of David could only be secured at the cost of his own subordination; and there must have been other times, when he was tempted to relinquish all connection with his father and ally himself to David, that they two might face the world. But he obeyed the law of filial natural duty. He made this first, and then drank as deep draughts of joy from the cistern of human love as he might find opportunity for.

24-42 *Love braving hate and death.* — The development of sin is rapid and terrible. Violent as Saul had often been, his passion suddenly broke out in ungovernable rage; for it is the nature of evil to extend more and more, as fire in prairie-grass. Jonathan was grieved for David's sake (**34**) more than for his own. Thus love loses itself in the interests of the beloved.

How often are the arrows beyond us! Evil is determined against us, and we must be gone. But how often is the evil meant against us transformed to good; and we are like the young eaglets, driven forth from the nest, that we may learn to fly. How little did that lad know of the agony of those two hearts! Our nearest cannot guess how much trivial things may be affecting us. But God knows our sorrows, and writes the record of them in His heart.

1 Samuel 21   DAVID AT GATH

1-9 *David with Ahimelech.* — Nob is not certainly identified. It was in all probability a settlement of the priests in the neighborhood of the tabernacle and ark. The priest received David and his scanty escort with unsuspecting loyalty. Here, again, David resorted to deception. The vacillation from strict integrity, of which there were traces in the preceding chapter, is here more manifest. And his lie was destined to fill his heart with bitter anguish, and to dye his hands in the blood of a family of priests. He would never have yielded to it if his soul had been living in the heroic faith that breathes through his Psalms. Tell the truth! — trust God with the issue, and you will have nothing to regret. Transparency of speech and quietness of heart are one. In referring to this incident, our Lord does not refer to David's duplicity (Matt. 12:3, 4). Is it because when He forgives He forgets?

There are sayings here deserving attention. The business of our King requires haste (**8**); and there is no sword to be compared with the Word of God, with which our David defeated the tempter in the wilderness. Christ also taught from this incident that the great needs of our nature override ceremonial and arbitrary distinctions.

10-15 *David at Gath.* — How rapid is the deterioration of God's saints when once they begin to tread the downward road! The nobler their nature, the swifter and more headlong their descent. As David begins this chapter with lying, he ends it by feigning madness. This cannot be excused on the plea that the age invested madness with a halo of sanctity. It was certainly unworthy of his faith in God. How had the fine gold become dim, when he who had been anointed by the Spirit scrabbled (made marks, *marg.*) on the doors of the gates! Yet deep down his heart was filled with thoughts that were to fruit in two of his sweetest Psalms (34 and 56). He sought the Lord, and was heard. He cried, and was saved. he suffered; but not a bone was broken — not a good thing had failed.

1 Samuel 22   THE CAVE OF ADULLAM

1-5 *A realm within the realm.* — The cave of Adullam was situated in the valley of Elah, not far from the scene of David's conflict with Goliath. Saul's oppressions were causing disaffection among his people, and drove many to join their fortunes to his rival's. David's own family, sharing the royal hatred which he had incurred, resorted to him for safety. Gad the prophet was also among his followers. As in the case of Joseph, the despised brother became protector and leader. How true was David in his filial instincts! No doubt there was a natural tie with Moab, dating back to the days of Ruth the Moabitess.

During the present age Saul is on the throne, and the true King is in hiding. But around Him there is gathering in secret a host before which the kingdoms of this world will one day be subdued. His recruits are drawn from those who are in distress and debt — bitter of soul. And He sends none of them away. He sympathizes with their sorrows, pays their debts, and turns their bitterness to sweetness. Out of them He rears an army of mighty men, all of whom are welded to Him by indissoluble ties. What the world counts as its dregs and riff-raff, its ne'er-do-wells, Jesus transmutes into saints; and His true saints are all heroes.

6-19 *A harvest of blood.* — This was the foulest, blackest deed of which Saul had been guilty. It was the execution of Samuel's early prophecy (2:31-33); but this did not lessen Saul's guilt. Only jealousy, and a desire to attract sympathy where he had forfeited respect, could have led him to assert that either his people or his son was faithless. And even Doeg's story, corroborated by Ahimelech's frank avowal, gave no sufficient justification for so terrible an act of vengeance. What a commentary on James' statement, that "sin, when it is finished, bringeth forth death" (James 1:15). David predicts the fate of Doeg (*see* Psalm 52).

20-23 *A noble welcome.* — The fugitive priest was welcomed by the outlaw with words that we may assign to the lips of Jesus, as each soul comes over to Him from the kingdom of darkness (**23**). "Abide with Me" is equivalent to "Abide in Me." Because He lives, we live also. David's mind had evidently been uneasy about his sin, and he took sadly to heart the deed of blood.

1 Samuel 23   GREAT DELIVERANCES

This chapter reveals the way in which David constantly sought Divine protection and aid, and received it.

1-6 *His victory over the Philistines.* — It seemed absurd for six hundred men to attack a well-disciplined host. But there could be no doubt about the Lord's will in the matter. The Lord said, Go: and whenever He gives so clear a direction, He will give all needed strength and help. "I will deliver." Remember the name of the Lord (Psalm 20:7).

7-13 *The treachery of the Keilites.* — To Saul it seemed impossible that his prey should escape him; but he had not realized how much God was prepared to do for that soul which so implicitly trusted Him, and sought His guidance and help. David's enquiry of God is beautiful for its simple, childlike trust. It is thus that true hearts talk with their Father in heaven, and He answers them. Thus the fugitives took up again the wanderers' life amid the rocks and caves of Judah, little dreaming that their griefs and trials would live in all after-time in the music of the Psalms, which their leader may have recited to them around the campfires at night.

14-18 *The interview with Jonathan.* — Amid all outward strife God provides for us, as He did for David, some Jonathan — some brook of human love, some sweet friendship or brotherhod. Ah! this is the use of a friend: to strengthen our hands in God, to whisper words of hope, to enter into covenant with us. And this is what the best Friend does, who discovers us in the deepest, thickest woods, and whispers his *Fear not!* There is no soul so lonely or desolate with whom Jesus will not enter into covenant, and pour in the oil of His comfort and the wine of His love. Jonathan saw David's exaltation, but not his own death. How mercifully God veils the future! And His love made him content to be second, not first.

19-28 *The treachery of the Ziphites.* — It was base to attempt to curry favor with Saul at such a cost. It was an incident of extreme peril (**25, 26**). But God interposed at the critical moment by calling Saul's attention off. It is thus often in the fourth watch of the night that the Saviour comes — not too soon for testing; not too late for help.

1 Samuel 24   RECONCILIATION

1-8 *David's opportunity.* — En-gedi was on the western shore of the Dead Sea, midway between north and south. Here David and his men were in hiding. Psalm 63 tells something of the Psalmist's experiences in that region. There were large caves there, often used for sheltering cattle and sheep. Saul entered the very cave where David and his men were concealed. It was an opportunity that might never occur again for relieving himself of further trouble and realizing the Divine promise. But opportunity alone does not indicate God's will or our duty. Without doubt the kingdom was promised to David on the death of Saul. Even the king knew that. His life was accursed and a curse. It would have been natural for David to comply with the plausible advice of his followers, especially as Saul had come out to take his life. But to all such suggestions, which had in them the hiss of the serpent, David opposed the simple rule of right, and stayed his servants and himself. We must leave all vengeance with God (Rom. 12:19-21).

9-15 *David's pleading.* — When we compare the so-called imprecatory Psalms with this noble utterance, we feel that, whatever else they are, they are not the expression of any personal hostility. David's heart was very tender, and it smote him, even for cutting off Saul's skirt, lest it might seem like a personal insult (2 Sam. 10:4).

16-22 *David's triumph.* — Those touching words had made chords long silent vibrate again. Saul's better self for a moment came at their bidding; and his confession of sin vindicated David's character. But the change was only emotional — it did not arise from the will. There had been no alteration in his disposition. His goodness was like the early dew and the morning cloud. This was a double victory for David: first, over himself; and secondly, over his foe. It was a great foreshadowing of the law of Christ.

1 Samuel 25   NABAL'S FOLLY

There are two deaths recorded in this chapter. First, that of Samuel, who was much lamented, and with every reason. His godly life; his self-suppression at a time when there was every inducement to stand in the way of the great national revolution; and his marvellous power of intercessory prayer, were elements in a life of singular beauty and great usefulness to his nation. The second death recorded is that of Nabal, who, true to his name (**25**), died in his folly.

2-8 *David's application.* — With his men he had now gone further south, to the wilderness of Paran, the northern part of the desert, known as Et-Tih. Through this wilderness the Israelites had wandered. It was infested with wild wandering tribes; David therefore had rendered this great sheep-master conspicuous service in protecting his flocks, and, according to the usage of the desert, had some claim for compensation. To-day the Arab tribe, which guards the shepherd or caravan, or restrains itself from plundering, expects to be rewarded. Nabal's servants acknowledged this (**8, 15, 16**).

9-13 *Hot haste.* — The refusal was not only ungrateful, but rude and insulting; and it stirred David. It is striking to see how this man, who had borne patiently with Saul, is so suddenly and deeply moved by this rebuff. It shows that his self-restraint was due to the grace of God; and that naturally, or when left to himself, he was as volcanic as any.

14-31 *A woman's wit.* — Abigail was as full of tact and grace, as Nabal of surly doggedness; and she averted the impending blow by her swift and wise interposition. She also anticipated truly the great future in store for David, and appealed to him to avoid an act that would lie as a shadow on his memory. Oh to be bound up in the bundle of life with Christ! — one with Him in a union that death cannot dissolve!

32-44 *All ends well.* — David recognized that God had stayed his hand, and was thankful. Let us always give God time to speak to us. He withholds man from His purpose, and hides pride from him. And if we leave our cause with Him, we shall not only have reason to adore His prevenient grace, but shall see Him interposing to avenge all our wrongs.

1 Samuel 26   A RENEWED ATTACK

1-4 *Fresh treachery.* — For some reason the Ziphites were inplacable foes of David; and here again, as in chapter 23, they incite Saul against his rival. That the pursuit of David should again be taken up was the more disgraceful, after all Saul had said in confession and retraction.

5-16 *A brave act.* — There was a sturdy herosim among the mightier of David's army. They loved feats of hardy courage; and therefore the heart of Abishai rose to David's challenge. Would that there were more of this spirit in us still, to answer thus the appeals of Jesus, as from his throne He cries, Who will go down with Me? Again, as in a previous chapter, Abishai, when the two stand inside the royal barricade, suggests that opportunity indicates duty. But David would not hear of it for a moment. He vowed that he would not avail himself of any occasion, however tempting, to hasten the inevitable future. It must be God's act and in God's time. That dialogue over the sleeper is a picture of death, standing to threaten many a mortal; but the angel of long-suffering mercy pleads for a little respite, that there may be time to repent.

17-25 *The repentance of the world.* — Beneath the sudden emotion of deliverance from awful peril, Saul again breaks out in confession and contrition. David suggested that if there was any wrong between them, they should join in making a sacrifice and sealing forgiveness (**19**). The treacherous enemies, to whom David refers in the same breath, were probably led by Cush the Benjamite, mentioned in Psalm 7. David alleges that the effect of their treatment had been to alienate him from God's house and worship. How many may say the same of our influence as professing Christians? Let us be careful, lest we be a stumbling block to other souls. Saul's emotional outburst would soon subside again, leaving him even harder than before.

1 Samuel 27   LOSING HEART

1-7 *A fainting fit.* — There are times in all lives when we lose heart. We think we cannot suffer for a single moment longer, and we are strongly tempted to take a short cut to deliver ourselves. David had repeated assurances that he should be king, yet all suddenly he appears to have lost heart and hope; and, imagining that he would one day perish at the hand of Saul, went off to Achish. In doing so, he only involved himself in worse difficulties, as we shall presently see. How wonderful to find these contrasts in this man whom God loved! None could rise to sublimer expressions of trust, or sink to lower depths than he.

Let us beware of saying or thinking that we must perish by the hand of Saul. It need not be. It shall not be, if only we make God our strong tower. When once we look away from the promises of God and look at circumstances, we turn from the straight path into devious tracks, which lead to swamps and quagmires. If any tempted souls read these words, let them dare to trust God, though every appearance be against them. He will vindicate Himself and their faith. The wicked may spread himself in great power; but the righteous may not fret himself in any wise to do evil: for evildoers shall be cut off; but the meek shall inherit the earth, and delight themselves in abundance of peace.

8-12 *Unbelief leads to falsehood.* — When we once lose faith in God, there is no sin to which we do not become liable. David made raids (**8-10**, R.V.) against the enemies of Israel; but professed to have made them against his own people. He disarmed suspicion by this procedure, and made Achish think that the breach between his new servant and his nation was impassable. But, as we shall see, this duplicity wove a net around his feet that became every day more inextricable, till God delivered him from the consequences of his sin.

And yet 1 Chronicles 12 tells how God watched over His unworthy servant during his stay at Ziklag, and built up his power.

1 Samuel 28   THE WITCH OF ENDOR

This is the climax of Saul's sad and fateful story. The incident recorded in this chapter sealed his fate (1 Chron. 10:13, 14).

1-6 *Despair.* — When Samuel was alive, Saul made as though he could do without him; but when he was dead his heart cried out for one to be the medium of his soul's intercourse with God. He had often refused God's voice; and now God answered him not. Many a time he had sought for help; but he had done so without confessing or putting away the sins which had come between him and God. He regarded iniquity in his heart; and so the Lord hid his face from him. There is no doubt that if, even then, he had dealt truly with his sins in the sight of God, he would have found abundant pardon. "He who confesseth and forsaketh shall find mercy" (*See* Prov. 1:24-32).

7-15 *Witchcraft.* — Saul had put away from Israel the sin of witchcraft. That sin had even become as proverbial as idolatry (15:23) during his reign. But now he went back to it, as the dog to its vomit or the sow to its filth. The soul of man cannot be satisfied, except it hold fellowship with the unseen; and if not with God, then with the demons that rule the darkness of the world (Eph. 6:12). Spiritualism is the rebound of the heart from the negation of infidelity. It is a sign of an unbelieving age and a decaying faith, when spiritualistic phenomena are sought after in the place of God.

In the present case it is likely that Samuel was literally permitted to visit again the world that he had left, to give the last terrible warning to him over whose fate he had wept and prayed.

16-25 *Judgment.* — Even in this life men are sometimes summoned before the Throne of the Eternal, and hear their sentence spoken by that voice which warned them in vain. See how one failure, like Saul's disobedience with respect to Amalek, may determine our destiny. Saul is the Judas of the Old Testament. He thought there was no hope. His very attitude, full-length on the ground, reminds us of that awful scene in the field of Aceldama. Thus that goodly young man, whose life opened with such promise, fell toward the abyss.

1 Samuel 29   DAVID AND ACHISH

1-5 *A valid objection.* — The lords of the Philistines were perfectly justified in urging this objection against the presence of David and his followers in their camp, and such close proximity to their king. But surely that objection must have been an immense relief to David, who for the previous sixteen months had led Achish to suppose that, by his forays against his own people, he had put an impassable barrier between him and them; but who, of course, was as loyal to Israel as ever, and had indeed been spending that period in destroying the border tribes of the desert, who were more or less in alliance with Achish, but who lived by their plunder of Israelite homesteads and lands. When Achish proposed, in all good faith, to take David with him to the battle, it must have put him in a very anxious position, from which nothing but God's interposition could extricate him. So we often bring ourselves into positions of extreme difficulty by unbelief and deceit. God's deliverance came in the refusal of the Philistine lords to permit him to go with them into the battle. "What do these Christians do here?" is a question that may fairly be asked when the children of God go into worldly pleasure, or ally themselves with the enemies of God.

6-11 *A generous dismissal.* — There is something very striking and attractive in the words with which Achish dismissed David. And though David made as though he were hardly dealt with, his heart must have leaped up within him with thankfulness and joy. Thus does our God make crooked places straight, and rough places smooth. The stone is rolled away. The iron gate opens of its own accord.

1 Samuel 30   PURSUIT OF THE AMALEKITES

1-5 *Chastisement.* — It was an awful moment when David and his men reached the smoking embers of their city, and found not a trace of their wives, children, or possessions. It was what he and his men had often done without compunction in those border-wars; but this did not make it easier to bear. He had reached a very low point in his fortunes. Dismissed by Achish; conscious of insincerity to the man who trusted him as an angel of God; deprived of all his earthly goods; and exposed to the sudden hatred of his men — he had a bitter cup to drink!

6-8 *Quietness and confidence.* — He encouraged himself in God. His soul betook itself to the secret place of the Most high, and hid under the shadow of the Almighty. He was not afraid, though tens of thousands set themselves against him. There were two grounds for encouragement: 1st, that they had returned from Achish just at that very moment; 2nd, that God spoke to him yet, and bade him pursue. How self-possessed and calm his faith made him, that he was able to turn from the hubbub and wrath of his followers and enquire of God! But this is the secret of a blessed life.

9-21 *Victory.* — Evidently God led the expedition. That two hundred had to fall into the rear, unable to keep up with the rest in their furious pursuit, made no difference. The hand of Jehovah wrought for His restored and forgiven child. It reminds us of the pardoned Peter winning three thousand souls on the Day of Pentecost. Surely David must have seen that he need not fear what man could do against him, but only his own sin. Our Master does not treat His servants as the flesh (represented by Amalek) does its faithful devotees. He does not leave us when we fall sick, but nourishes and cherishes us.

22-32 *Generosity.* — How nobly does David stand out in contrast to the manners of his time! His decision as to the division of the stuff was wise and right, but far in advance of the men that followed him. He was also thankful for the opportunity of recompensing those who had been kind to him in his misfortunes. So our King does not forget those that stay by the stuff: mothers and nurses; those who care for others keeps them from active service in the church and world; or those who must remain at home, instead of serving in the foreign missionary field. All these shall share equally with those who have distinguished themselves in heroic deeds or martyr-pangs.

1 Samuel 31　DEATH OF SAUL

1-6 *Suicide.* — The battle was fought nearly on the ground where Gideon defeated Midian. The plain of Esdraelon has often been the scene of terrible battles, but never of one so disgraceful to Israel as this. Suicide came quickly in the wake of all the other sins that had gradually swept the ill-fated monarch onward to his doom. There is no telling to what lengths the smallest sins, if indulged against light and knowledge, may not conduct us. Jealousy of David had been like the letting-in of water; now the floods had come, which refused to be stemmed or turned aside. The suicide thinks less of the Judgment of eternity than of that of time; more of man than of God; rather of the ills of the body than of the fever of the soul. O my soul, see to it that thy one aim is so to prepare thyself to stand before the Judgment-seat of Christ, as to have a conscience void of offence toward God and man!

7-10 *After the battle.* — The Israelites fled in panic, while the Philistines took from them their cities and dwelt in them, ascribing their victory to their gods. But it could only be a short-lived triumph, as God had made a definite gift of the land to Israel by a covenant which Saul's sins could not annul.

11-13 *Befitting gratitude.* — The men of Jabesh-gilead give a beautiful example of gratitude. Saul had delivered them in the hour of their extremity, and they did not forget his kindness in that dark day of defeat and dishonor. So their deed has been made known to the world, and has shed its light over the ages. But Jesus redeemed us from a dreadful fate by His most precious blood. Let us be true to Him. He can never fall on the field of battle; but His followers seem sometimes to hesitate to follow Him there. Let us not flinch! — dying to live; suffering to reign; knowing the fellowship of His sufferings, to attain the glory of His resurrection. If they did it for the disgraced dead, what should not we do for the glorified Living!

The Second Book of Samuel

INTRODUCTION

This Book, of course, only bears its name because, in the Hebrew Bible, it is so closely connected with the preceding. The two books originally constituted one, and the present division was first made in the Septuagint, and adopted thence into the Vulgate, from which it passed into common use.

Obviously it was composed by some of the prophets in the days of David, perhaps by Nathan or Gad (1 Chron. 29:29). It is noticeable that the death of David is not actually recorded in the book, from which it is fair to infer that this account must have been as nearly as possible contemporaneous with his life and reign. The same conclusion is suggested by the lists of public functionaries.

This book is remarkable for the beautiful Odes or Songs which it contains; (1) The Song of the Bow; (2) The Lamentation over Abner; (3) A Song of David (22) that seems to partake of that gladness and lightsomeness of spirit which filled his heart in the earlier days of his reign; (4) The last words of David (23:2-7).

The period covered by this book would be almost forty years, from David's accession to the throne of Judah, to his death. His wars and victories; his extension of the border of Israel to the limits originally predicted to Abraham; his sins and chastisement and restoration — all these contribute their various lines to this fascinating picture.

2 Samuel 1   A SONG OF LAMENTATION

1-10 *Tidings from Gilboa.* — The Amalekite who came to David with the news of Saul's death (**1, 2**), invented a story in which he figured as giving the death-blow to Saul. It is impossible to reconcile his story with 1 Samuel 31. Probably he had followed the camp, that, after the battle he might plunder the slain; and, finding Saul's body and crown, was induced to make up his story, in the hope of winning David's favor. The crown would be a helmet, surrounded by a band of gold. Bracelets would be signs of royalty. It is remarkable, and more than a coincidence, that an Amalekite claimed to have slain Saul, who had spared his race (1 Sam. 15). If we spare the flesh, of which Amalek is always the type, it will not spare us. Mercy is ill-expended on that which is so deadly in its nature.

11-16 *David's magnanimity.* — The Amalekite thought that he understood human nature, but he had not gauged David's heart. Having given his message, he waits for his reward, which he gets, not as he expected, but as he deserved. Amid the lawlessness of an outlaw's life, the education of David's soul had been continually advancing. He would not condone the deed which injured the Lord's anointed; though it put a crown within his reach, and seemed to fulfil the promises of God. There was no doubt in his mind that God could fulfil His promise without the aid of sin, in himself or any one else. David's address to this man (**14**) corresponded with his own behavior on two former occasions, when he had spared Saul's life. This conception of God was far in advance of the notions of that age. Be sure that God will deliver you without your putting forth your hand to what conscience would condemn.

17-27 *The Song of the Bow.* — In verse **18**, the R.V. inserts for *the use* of the bow, *the song* of the bow. These verses were known as "the bow," either because of the occurrence of that word in verse **22,** or from the facts narrated in 1 Samuel 31:3. "The beauty of Israel" (**19**) is translated "Thy glory, O Israel" in R.V.**21,** "The shield of the mighty is defiled" (R.V., *marg.*); perhaps with blood and dust, as of one not anointed (R.V., *marg.*), *i.e.,* common soldier. **24,** David forgets all his sufferings at the hands of Saul, and speaks of him as he was in his best days. The grief is evidently so genuine, that we must admire the work of the Spirit of God, and remember it when we are dealing with expressions in the Psalms that seem full of personal denunciation.

2 Samuel 2   DAVID CROWNED KING

1-7 *A morning without clouds.* — David takes no further step at his own impulse, but waits before God, that He should direct him. This was a most blessed habit with David. He did nothing from his own origination. The language of his life was, "My soul, wait thou only upon God." His steps were ordered by the Lord, who delighted in his way. From how many blunders should we be saved; if we leaned less on our own understanding, and in all our ways acknowledged Him! There is no haste to them that wait on the Lord. They know that He will give, and abide His time. God is preparing deliverance for them, and them for it.

The first act of the new king was to send a conciliatory message to the man of Jabesh. To show kindness to Saul, was to show kindness to David. And he dexterously accosted them as his allies, asking them to supplement words with deeds, if occasion arose. The reign of David in Hebron, preceding by seven years his ascension to the throne of the entire realm, was a prefiguration of the reign of Jesus over His Church, as distinguished from His reign over the world. From Hebron the bands of mighty men went forth to war with Ish-bosheth, as the warriors of the Cross with the deadly evils around. But the end is not yet.

12-32 *The reign of Ish-bosheth.* — Joab was the son of David's sister, Zeruiah. Gibeon was near the frontier of Judah, David's new kingdom. This movement was intended as an attack on him, and to bring the whole kingdom back to Saul's family. **27,** Joab said that if Abner had not spoken as he did in the morning (**14**), there would have been no hostile encounter; and that he had simply repelled aggression. The chapter illustrates the distress of a divided heart. When a realm is torn with internal dissension there is no progress or power. Have you only surrendered part of your nature to God's appointed king? You will be the subject of perpetual anguish and conflict till He rules all (Isa. 9:6, 7).

2 Samuel 3   JOAB AND ABNER

1-5 *David's growing power.* — David represented the best traditions, and he expressed the noblest hopes of his people. And it was inevitable that God's purpose should be fulfilled in him and in his gradual rise to supreme power. Probably he was calm and confident, prepared to await the developing of the Divine purpose.

6-11 *Abner's quarrel with Ish-bosheth.* — The occasion was a woman, but it is marvellous how the passions of men are overruled to fulfil the counsels of God. Abner was "a prince and a great man," according to David's estimate (**38**); but his course was determined by ambition. He knew that David was God's appointed king, and that through him the Divine purpose was to be accomplished (**10**); and yet for his own advancement he set up Ish-bosheth, and maintained him by all the energy he possessed (**6**). It was a deliberate attempt to thwart and override God's declared purpose. Woe to him that striveth with his Maker! The attempt, of course, failed. And with his own hand he shattered the fabric he had taken so much trouble to rear.

Provoked by Ish-bosheth's remonstrance at his wedding with one of his father's wives, Abner suddenly turned against him, and tried to make the best terms with David for himself; but whether in fighting for Saul's house, or plotting against it, self-interest was his clue. They that seek their lives lose them; and Abner met his fate in direct connection with the measures he adopted for his personal safety. Those who knowingly go into conflict against God prepare for themselves swift destruction. No weapon that is formed against the Kingdom of Christ shall prosper.

12-21 *His overtures to David.* — David's wife, Michal, had been faithful to him on one memorable occasion, saving his life. Probably, however, he only claimed her now because he desired to remind the people of the close connection between himself and the house of Saul. "Now then do it" (**18**), is a soldier's call to decisive and prompt action. Let us be swift in acknowledging our Saviour as King. Benjamin was Saul's tribe, and therefore needed special management.

22-39 *His murder.* — Asahel's death needed no such avengement as this; and, in lifting his hand against his rival, Joab was probably moved more by jealousy than by a desire to righteously avenge the death of his brother. He was evidently a fierce, cruel, unscrupulous, and treacherous man, and troubled David more than he helped him. David had no partnership in the tragedy, and he made this abundantly clear. The spectacle of the king mourning over his new ally touched the heart of the people. Abner had not died as a felon who must needs be bound, but as a man who falleth before "the children of iniquity."

2 Samuel 4   ISH-BOSHETH

1-8 *The treacherous murder of Ish-bosheth.* — The death of Abner rendered the cause of Ish-bosheth hopeless. Two "captains of bands" expose themselves to lasting shame by this dark deed of murder. Their act is the more despicable, from their position near the person of their royal victim. Since Mephibosheth (**4**), the legal avenger of the crime, was incapable of acting, they were the more bold. The Septuagint has further light upon the circumstances attending the death. "And behold, the woman that kept the door of the house was winnowing wheat, and she slumbered and slept; and the brethren went privately into the house" (**6**, R.V., *marg.*).

9-12 *The deserved punishment of the murderers.* — David was careful to guard against the appearance of any partnership with these evildoers. He knew that true loyalty could only be founded on respect. Besides, God's name and character were closely involved with his own. Take heed to give men no cause against God by any doubtful act. The only time when we need to vindicate our character, should be when there is a risk of involving our Lord's; then we must take every measure to put ourselves beyond suspicion.

It was natural for David to allude to the living Lord, and His redeeming mercy (9). We too shall have reason to magnify that mercy so long as life and immortality endure. Whatever be the trial through which you may be passing, to be sure that, if you will be patient and trustful, and do not chafe nor worry nor allow yourself in any wise to do evil, the time will come when you will be able to look back on it, and be able to say with David, "The Lord redeemed my soul out of all adversity." Unwavering faith in God is the best preventative of sin. The man of faith can do no wrong, nor allow others to do it, for his advantage.

2 Samuel 5   THE CITY OF DAVID

1-5 *The Kingdom united under David.* — **1,** These tribes are enumerated in 1 Chronicles 12:23-40. **2,** The kingship of Jesus is based on His kinship, His achievements, and Divine promises. **3,** League, *i.e.,* covenant (R.V.). The Hebrew king was under certain defined conditions. **4,** Now the divided and distracted country was at rest — an emblem of the blessed rest that comes to those who give undivided allegiance, to Christ.

6-10 *The new capital.* — Though destined to so remarkable a history, Jerusalem had not been especially noticed in the foregoing history (Josh. 18:28). The Jebusites were in possession of the fort of Zion, which was surrounded on three sides by such deep ravines as to appear impregnable. Its inhabitants were so confident that they thought that the blind and lame would be sufficient for its defense (R.V., *marg.*). David hoped that the choice of captain might be decided for him by a display of personal valor on the part of one of his followers (**8**). **10**, How blessed and happy are they who rely wholly on God! When we have well learned the lessons of adversity, He makes us great. Our safety and victory are sure when the Lord, the God of hosts, is with us. What a history Jerusalem has had since then, and is yet to have.

11-16 *The established Kingdom.* — Tyre was a great trading city, on the sea-coast, to the north of Palestine. Its people were famous for their knowledge of arts and manufacture, and the working of metals (Ezek. 27, 28). It is a great matter when a man perceives, as David did (**12**), that he has been specially gifted and placed by God in order to pass on to others the results of his labors or gifts. All that we have is ours in trust for others — talents to be used for our King.

David had eighteen sons. The daughters, except Tamar, are not named.

17-25 *Victory over the Philistines.* — The growing prosperity of David's kingdom excited the fears of Israel's ancient enemies. Twice therefore they gathered their force against David in the valley of the giants, southwest of Jerusalem. By giving Jesus His rightful position as our King, we do not get free from conflict; but it is no longer within, it is from without. David did not trust in his new fortress, but in the Lord (**19**). What a contrast to Saul! All the glory of the successful campaign was given to God (**20**). David was equally dependent on the Lord on the second occasion (**23**). His previous success did not make him self-confident. He accepted God's plans, though they were quite different from the former ones. That stirring in the leaves (**24**) was like the sound of the feet of God's army, His angels, hurrying to fight against the Philistines, while David awaited the result. Oh, for the quick ear to detect the twelve legions of angels to our help!

2 Samuel 6   THE ARK BROUGHT TO ZION

1-10 *A right thing wrongly done.* — We have not heard of the ark since the Philistines sent it back to Kirjath (1 Sam.

7:1, 2). The nation must have been in a sad state of religious declension, that the symbol of God's presence should have been so neglected. The Tabernacle appears to have remained in Gibeon for some time after this (1 Chron. 16:39, 40). David's object in getting the ark to Jerusalem was to make that city the religious, as well as the political center of the nation. There is a mystery about the story, until it is carefully examined. It appears as though God were opposing David's purpose, and preventing its success. But He only opposed David's manner of action. And it was very important that the precise directions of the Levitical law should be again enforced.

The journey here noted was from Kirjath-jearim to the house of Abinadab, at a short distance from the town. The royal progress from Jerusalem is recorded in 1 Chronicles 13:1-6, verses which tell us that David "consulted with the captains of thousands and hundreds, and every leader." We are not told that he inquired of God in respect to the bringing up of the ark. Had he done so, the error into which he fell might have been avoided. There was a definite instruction in the Levitical law which had never been superseded; and David had no right to substitute the new cart (3) for the shoulders of living men (Num. 7:9; 1 Chron. 15:12-15). For *cornets* (5), R.V. reads *castanets.* Uzzah's rashness (7, *marg.*) was punished by death. The lesson was dearly bought; but it was very necessary. The Church, like the ark of God, needs no human hand to steady it.

11-15 *A successful renewal of the attempt.* — Obed-edom was a Levite, of the family of Kohath, to whom the care of the ark was entrusted by law; he is called *Gittite* because of the Levitical town of Gath-rimmon (Josh. 21:24, 25; 1 Chron. 6:24, 69). God paid well for the lodgment of His ark. None ever lose who devote themselves and their property for the furtherance of His cause. The ark, which was death to Uzzah, was blessing to Obed-edom. The difference lay in the characters of the two men. The sun that hardens clay melts wax.

Three months after the first attempt, the ark was carried up to the city of David with holy exultation and great enthusiasm (**14, 15**). And there was no accident, because David had carefully consulted God's word as to how the ark should be removed (1 Chron. 15:12-15).

16-23 *Michal.* — Michal's affections were now transferred to Phaltiel; and consequently she had no sympathy with David's behavior, which seemed to her to be extravagant and undignified. Psalm 65 is supposed to have been composed on this occasion. David had prepared a special tabernacle (**17**), probably on the model of that of Moses. **19,** "A cake of bread, and a portion of flesh, and a cake of raisins" (R.V.). However exciting and absorbing our public engagements, we must not forget the claims of family religion. Michal's speech (**20**) was beside the mark; for although David had put off his royal robes, he still had on his inner dress and the ephod. **21,** compare 2 Corinthians 5:13.

2 Samuel 7   GOD'S PROMISES TO DAVID

1-3 *David's desire.* — When David had rest, he spoke about building the Temple. It is out of the restful heart that the noblest projects proceed. Mary, who sat at the Master's feet, broke on His sacred person the alabaster box. The tranquil lake reflects more of the solemn beauty of the stars than the brawling stream. Evidently prosperity had not injured David; but he desired to consecrate all God's gifts to further service. Gratitude prompted him to make some return. How different he was from those whom Haggai reproved! (Hag. 1:4). Prosperity tests the sincerity of a man's devotion to God. It is not all men that can carry a full cup with a steady hand. Nathan evidently answered at the impulse of his own mind (**3**). It takes a lifetime before we learn to ask God before speaking or acting.

4-17 *God's reply.* — David's intention was good, and graciously accepted (1 Kings 8:18); but he was not the man, and that was not the time to build the Temple. War was not yet at an end. The sword could not yet be exchanged for the trowel. "Better a tent of God's appointing than a temple of his own inventing" (*Henry*). What a stream of blessed promises succeed! God is quick to notice the least desire to honor Him, and to reward it beyond all that we ask or think. **6,** God shares our wanderings. "Any of the tribes" (**7**) is rendered in R.V. (*marg.*) "any of the *Judges.*" **8,** A really great man is not ashamed of his origin, and knows that it is all the gift of his God. David must not build a house for God; but God will build a house for him (**11**). A son as successor, and a line of kings consummated in Jesus (Luke 1:31, 33). An everlasting covenant, which could not be broken by the sins of the following generations (**15**). They should be chastened, but not put utterly away.

18-29 *David's communion with God.* — It is well to have moments for holy reverie. When God has passed His word of promise, let us go in and sit before Him, to thank Him, to rejoice before Him, to contemplate His gracious promises, and to claim that He should fulfil them. God had spoken as men speak, binding Himself under similar pledges. It is by trusting to the Word that God speaks (**25**) that faith claims and appropriates Divine gifts. Whenever you have a promise brought to your heart, turn to God with these words. The true lover of God is above all things eager that He should be magnified (**26**) in his body, whether by life or death. God's revelations lead us to pray for things which otherwise we should not have dared to entertain.

2 Samuel 8   "FROM EGYPT TO THE EUPHRATES"

1 *War against Philistia.* — Metheg-ammah is Gath (1 Chron. 18:1). The meaning of the word is "bridle of the mother" (city); and what a bridle is in the management of a horse, that was Metheg to the land of Philistia. By subduing that metropolis, David had the whole land in his power.

2 *War against Moab.* — Eastern kings, when their enemies had made a peculiarly stubborn resistance, were in the habit of making them, when conquered, lie down on the ground, and then putting a certain part of them to death. Our version makes David keep one-third, other versions one-half alive. Jewish writers explain this unusual severity by saying that the Moabites had massacred David's parents and family whom he had entrusted to their safe keeping (*see* Balaam's prophecy, Num. 24:17).

3-8 *War against Zobah and Syria.* — David set about establishing the border of his kingdom at the river Euphrates in accordance with God's ancient promise (Gen. 15:18; Num. 24:17). *See* R.V. as to David's forces; 1 Chronicles 8:4 should also be referred to. The horses were of no service to David, as Israel was forbidden to use them; and they dare not leave them for their foes to use again.

9-12 *Submission of Hamath.* — Hamath was the chief city of a kingdom lying north of Palestine and west of Zobah. The king, delivered through David of a dangerous neighbor, sent his son with valuable presents to David, congratulating him on his victories, and soliciting his alliance and protection.

13-18 *War with Syria and Edom.* — The Syrians, as afterwards (2 Kings 16:6), were allied with Edom. It was a great confederacy to quell David's growing power. Victory was gained through the bravery and skill of Abishai and Joab (1 Chron. 18:12; Ps. 40 title).

Thus the Hebrew people became occupants of a vast extent of country, extending from the frontier of Egypt to the Euphrates, and realizing God's original promise to Abraham (Gen. 15). The woodlands of Gilead, the pasture-lands of Bashan, the harbors on the Red Sea, the caravan roads of the Euphrates, Arabia, and Egypt, were now within Hebrew territory.

6, 14 *The source of victory.* — Victory over the Lord's foes and ours is a gift to be claimed by faith. Do not doubt whether or not you shall succeed. Go forward, and the strongest opposition shall break in pieces; only be sure to devote the spoils to God. Is there not a hint, in the dedication of the spoils of Gentile peoples to the Temple, of the part which the Gentiles should have in the body of Christ?

15-18 *David's home administration.* — While extending his dominions abroad, he was not neglectful of the kingdom at home. The recorder kept the chronicles of the kingdom. The scribe would be the Secretary of State. The names of Abiathar and Ahimelech have been transposed. On the massacre of the priests of Nob, Saul conferred the priesthood on Zadok, of the family of Eleazar (1 Chron. 6:50), while David acknowledged Abiathar, of Ithamar's family, who fled to him. The two exercised a joint-ministry when David became sole monarch. Abiathar officiated at Jerusalem, and Zadok at Gibeon (1 Chron. 16:39). *Cherethites,* etc. - these were David's body-guard. Perhaps archers and slingers, or headsmen and couriers. It is probable they were foreign mercenaries, who had gathered around David during his sojourn in Philistia (1 Sam. 30:14, 16; Zeph. 2:5)

2 Samuel 9   MEPHIBOSHETH

David's kindness to Mephibosheth is a beautiful incident in his history, and strikingly illustrates the grace of our Lord Jesus.

It was unexpected and unsought. — The young prince was spending a retired life with one of the great families of the trans-Jordanic region. The thought of becoming an inmate of David's palace never occurred to him; and his great nervousness needed David's most careful reassurances. "What is thy servant, that thou shouldest look upon such a dead dog as I am?" "Behold, what manner of love the Father hath bestowed upon us, that we should be called the sons of God." "Depart from me, for I am a sinful man, O Lord."

3, 13 *It was unlikely.* — He was lame. This sad infirmity dated from his birth (4:4). We, too, are lame in our powers of spiritual obedience. We cannot do anything to merit the Divine regard.

It was not without good reason. — Probably Mephibosheth knew nothing of the covenant into which David and Jonathan had entered so long before (1 Sam. 20:14-16). But to David it was sacred; and even the unlovable son was dear to him for his father's sake. For a similar reason does God look on us. We are loved in Him in whom we have been chosen. God will ever be mindful of His covenant with His well-beloved Son.

It admitted him into the royal circle. — Though consciously unworthy, he received again Saul's family estate (**7**), was admitted to the royal table, and treated as one of the king's sons (**11**); he had, in Ziba and his household, a retinue worthy of a prince (**10**). All was due to the unmerited favor of the king; and is a type of all those spiritual blessings with which the God and Father of our Lord Jesus Christ has blessed us in heavenly places in Him (Eph. 1:3).

2 Samuel 10   THE AMMONITES

1-5 *Hanun's insult to David.* — Nahash, Hanun's father, had shown kindness to David. A Jewish tradition says that he sheltered one of David's brothers when the king of Moab killed his parents. Courtesy is a part of true piety (**2**). Beware of foolish counsellors (**3**, and 1 Kings 12:10, 11). The shaving of the beard (**4**) was the grossest insult that could be offered to an Oriental, who deems the beard the badge of the dignity of manhood. Through the ambassadors David and his kingdom were insulted. Thus do men insult God through their treatment of His faithful servants.

6-19 *The judgment which followed.* — Two wars are described (**6-14, 15-19**). Beth-rehob (**6**, Judg. 18:28) lay beneath Lebanon; Zoba (8:3) lay between Hamath and Syria; Maacah (Deut. 3:14) was toward the south, near to Bashan; Tob is to the east of Gilead. The battle took place at Medeba; the native troops covering the city, and the Syrians in the fields (1 Chron. 19:7-9). **8-11,** The armies were so arranged that a successful attack on either would leave the rear of Israel's army exposed. So Joab, with characteristic decision, determines to attack both. He mentions two possibilities, but never seems to think that both he and Abishai will be defeated. Let us never anticipate anything but victory in fighting God's battles. **16,** Hadarezer had been able to recuperate his energies after his defeat (8:3); now, alarmed at David's growing power, and being an ally of Hanun, he raised an army, not only in Syria, but in Mesopotamia. Shobach, his general, invaded David's kingdom as far as Helam, a border town of eastern Manasseh; but David, crossing the Jordan, surprised and defeated him.

The spirit of the New Testament is distinguished from the Old in its refusal to avenge insult or injury. These may be left to God. At the same time, the Divine purpose was served in punishing the crimes of these heathen nations, and in strengthening the Hebrew people. There is a judgment of nations, as well as of individuals (Matt. 25:32).

2 Samuel 11   DAVID'S SIN

1-5 *The story of David's sin.* — **1,** It began in sloth. The brunt of the war described in the previous chapter had fallen rather on Syria; now vengeance must be taken on Ammon. There are times when we are summoned to do God's bidding against His foes. If, then, we refuse, and linger in self-indulgence, we expose ourselves to terrific assaults of our great adversary. Idleness is the devil's opportunity. "The devil tempts all men; but idle men tempt the devil." David had just risen from his mid-day siesta when he was tempted. Temptation entered through the look (2). So Eve (Gen. 3:6); and Achan (Josh. 7:21). Well may we put our eyes into the Lord's keeping! How often temptation enters through them! Whatever be our attainments in the Divine life, we are never beyond the peril of falling into sin, which will blacken our record, and bring sorrow on all our days. The more intimate you are with God, and honored in His service, the more virulent the devil's hate, and his attempt to cast you down from your excellency (James 1:14, 15).

6-27 *What it led to.* — One sin never abides alone. If it be immediately confessed, it need lead to no more; but sin hardens the heart, and makes repentance difficult. Perhaps Uriah's suspicions were aroused by his sudden recall and the king's manner. To send food from the royal table is one of the greatest compliments that an eastern king can pay

(8). But Uriah did not fall into the trap, or go to his house; and his self-restraint **(9)** made David's self-indulgence appear the more guilty. In the warm spring weather the porters and guards would sleep in the long corridors of the palace. Uriah's drunkenness **(13)** was more David's sin than his own. "Sober David is worse than drunken Uriah" (*Bishop Hall*). **14-27,** There can be no excuse for such conduct. That the victim should carry the instructions for his own death; that other lives should be sacrificed as well as Uriah's; that Joab should be admitted into the plot; that the marriage should be so hurriedly consummated — all this was as bad as possible.

When we have sinned, we are more eager to conceal it before men than confess it before God. So soon as the sin was committed, David sought to obliterate its traces from the eyes of men; but Psalm 32 tells us that he "kept silence" towards God for long — probably about twelve months. Is it not remarkable that the Bible should tell this story of one of its chief saints, the "man after God's heart?" It is related for our warning; as well as to show how inexorably just He is, as well as merciful (1 Cor. 10:11, 12).

2 Samuel 12   CONFESSION AND FORGIVENESS

1-12 *The Divine indictment.* — During the period that followed his sin, David remained unrepentant (Psalm 32:3, 4). Conscience did not let him alone; but he did not return to God till the Good Shepherd sought His wandering sheep. But God could not forgive him till he had confessed. "He restoreth." Nathan's parable **(1-5)** put David off his guard. It supposes the same sin committed by someone else. We are more apt at judging others than ourselves. Let us sometimes look at ourselves as we should at other people, and judge our own actions by the standard we should apply to them. The application **(7-9)** was as bold as the parable was skillful. God often brings some incident of fiction or of real life before us, concerning which we have no difficulty in forming a judgment; and, when we have given the verdict, the Spirit turns our sword to divide between our soul and spirit. **8,** The mercies of God to David had been so conspicuous that his sin was more aggravated. **10-12,** Chastisement foretold. We are chastened that we may not be condemned with the world. The natural results of sin will follow inevitably, though God will transform them into blessing.

13, 14 *The penitent's confession.* — This was brief, but truly sincere. It is amplified in Psalm 51. He came to himself, and instantly he was forgiven and restored. There was no interval between the broken sob and the Divine response. "Many," says Augustine, "are disposed to fall like David; but not, like David, to rise again. The fall of David has been recorded, that those who have not fallen may be kept from falling, and that those who have fallen may rise again."

15-23 *The beginning of chastisement.* — The death of the child had been foretold (**14**); but with fasting and tears, David besought the Lord. Those who bend over dying children can understand something of David's anguish. Yet such may be comforted by the certainty that the Good Shepherd has gathered the lambs to His arms, and that parents shall go to them — *i.e.,* they will recognize and be recognized. **25,** The name Jedidiah (*beloved of the Lord*) given to this child indicates that David recognized his birth as an assurance that God had forgiven him. It is remarkable that Bathsheba should be chosen for the mother of Israel's greatest monarch, and a type of Christ. But such is the completeness of God's forgiveness.

26-31 *The capture of Rabbah.* — The siege had taken two years. It was the city of waters, as the Jabbok flowed around the lower town. **31,** David set the captives to work at saws, and axes, and in the brick kiln. An example of enforced labor. (*See* R.V., *marg.*). Confession is the basis of victory.

2 Samuel 13   SIN AND SORROW

"Whatsoever a man soweth that shall he also reap." David had sinned against the family, and through his own family troubles he suffered to the end of his life. God may forgive;

but the natural results of sin follow, though He may transform them into fires for our purification.

1-14 *Amnon's sin.* — The evil passion would probably have subsided had it not been for Jonadab's advice. He did not deserve to be called "friend." Such friends have ruined many young men. By laying stress on the word *sister,* Ammon disarmed David's suspicions. The appetite of a sick man needed gratifying; and the cakes were probably a kind of fancy bread which the eastern women take pride in making.

Awful as these chapters of the Bible are, they are necessary. It would be no mirror held to man's heart if it omitted records like this. To the child, they mean nothing; but they warn the simple. Better learn of our perils by such terrible examples than by drifting into them.

15-22 *Tamar.* — She was expelled from Amnon's house, as though she had been the aggressor. Unholy love often turns to violent hate. Shame, remorse, gluttony, fear, all combined to make Amnon treat her with this sudden revulsion of feeling. This is the invariable experience of the sinner. When he has his desire, he loathes himself and it. **19,** Tamar (*the palm,* tall and slender) was clothed in embroidered garments, only worn by those of highest rank. It is probable that she had been driven out without her vail, and therefore sought to hide her face with her hands. Absalom was Tamar's own brother. They had the same mother, Maacah, daughter of the king of Geshur.

23-39 *Absalom.* — He brooded over his revenge for two years, then struck the fatal blow. It was an awful tragedy. If David had dared to punish Amnon, it might have been averted. But David's own hands were not clean. It is an awful thing for a saint of God to fall into sin; here was Tamar ruined; the firstborn murdered; and Absalom branded as a murderer and banished.

2 Samuel 14   THE WOMAN OF TEKOAH

1-20 *The woman of Tekoah.* — Joab was shrewed enough to see that the king longed for Absalom, and had probably ends of his own to serve by the prodigal's return; and endeavored to bring David to consent by the parable put into the lips of this woman. Tekoah was a village about twelve miles south of Jerusalem. "She posed as a mourner, and said by way of parable that which in plain terms would have sounded too harshly; while she lamentably stated the loss and danger of her son, she showed David his own; and while she moved his compassion, she won him to pity on himself, and a favorable sentence on Absalom" (*Bishop Hall*). **13, 14,** She ran a parallel between God's treatment of the banished, and man's; and urged David to devise means for the return of his banished son. But she made a profound mistake. God's means involve the vindication of His holy law, and the confession of sin. But in the case of Absalom there was neither the one nor the other. He came back merely to gratify David's weak indulgent love, and this led to the evils that followed. Some seem to think that God can welcome His Absaloms back, just because He wills to do so. If He did, there would be revolt right through the universe.

21-24 *Absalom's return.* — This refusal to see Absalom was unwise. David faltered in his policy. Evidently he was conscious of acting unwisely and unjustly; and this prevented decisiveness, which, in such cases, is always the best policy.

25-33 *Joab's barleyfield.* — Beauty of body is often a snare, and hides a pit of corruption within. Josephus says Absalom cut his luxuriant hair once every eight days. The weight of the yearly cutting, by the king's shekel, would be about three pounds. It was galling to Absalom's pride to be shut out of the king's court, and avoided by men like Joab. Too often we are content to live without seeing the King's face. We should be more concerned about this. Sometimes God has to set our barleyfields on fire, as it were, to bring us to Himself.

2 Samuel 15   ABSALOM'S REBELLION

1-12 *Absalom's treachery.* — He had just received his father's kiss of reconciliation (14:33). And this is the first use he makes of favor so justly forfeited, and now restored. By slandering his father, and by insinuating speeches, he ingratiated himself with the people. When ambition prompts us, we can be courteous and pleasant. See how self may seem to expel self; when in reality it is but entering deeper into our heart. In verse **7**, read *four* for forty (*see* R.V. *marg.*).

Under the mask of religion, Absalom still further matured his plans. Hebron was his native place (3:2), and a city of the priests (Josh. 21:11), in addition to its sacred historic associations. Ahithophel was David's counsellor (**12**), but followed Absalom in his rebellion. This defection was probably due to the fact that Ahithophel was grandfather to Bathsheba. This may also explain Ahithophel's hatred to David, expressed in 18:2.

13-29 *David's flight.* — Was it that his courage forsook him; or that he could not bear to take arms against his son; or that he would bow beneath the hand of God? Whatever the cause, David's character never appears to better advantage than under this trial. The pruning was sharp, but it led to greater fruitfulness. Psalms 3, 4, 26, 28 and probably 62 belong to this period. **15,** This is the attitude we should maintain towards our King. **19,** Ittai seems to have been David's associate since his sojourn in Gath. His words are very noble. They remind us of John 12:26; 1 Thessalonians 5:10; and Philippians 1:20. It is thus that loyal hearts should address Christ. **25,** David did not believe, as the men of Israel in the days of Samuel, that the ark was a *fetish* which carried with it the assurance of victory and the presence of God. Apart from ark or tabernacle he could seek and find God. In dark and sad days we cannot do better than appropriate these noble words, "Behold, here am I; let Him do to me as seemeth good unto Him."

30-37 *Days of testing.* — Trouble shows us the real value of those who have professed the utmost attachment. **30,** We are reminded of another procession, led this way by David's Son (Matt. 26). The covered head and bared foot were signs of intense grief. How David's sins must have come back on him during that ascent! Yet God was in his thoughts. There was the exclamatory prayer and worship (**31, 32**). Faith in God is not inconsistent with making wise preparations for our defense. We have no right to call for the supernatural till we have done our part.

2 Samuel 16   SHIMEI'S CURSE

1-4 *Ziba's deception.* — It was a crafty plot. There may have been a shadow of truth in it. But we should put Ziba's statement beside chap. 19:24. In any case David was rash and premature in answering so hastily (**4**). Let us always hear both sides before we act or speak. How different is man to God! He will never be unmindful of His covenant, and though we prove ourselves unworthy, He will not alter the word that has gone forth from His lips.

5-14 *Shimei's curse.* — As a Benjamite, Shimei had never been really true to David, and now his real character appeared. Separated from David and his party by a deep ravine, he went along the hill opposite, casting stones and cursing. This, in the hearing of all his followers, must have been hard for David to bear. David was guiltless of the blood of Saul; but his heart accused him of other sins, and he was still. When men speak against us, let us look beyond them to the permission of God (**10**). Let us not avenge ourselves, but rather give place unto wrath. Vengeance is God's prerogative. He will repay. **14**, After temptation, and in the midst of sorrow, God provides refreshment. No difficulty without its arbor of ease! No wound without its palliative! No desert without its water-spring.

15-23 *Absalom in Jerusalem.* — Hushai's apparent adhesion to Absalom gave him high hope. Scripture narrates, without approving, Hushai's conduct. Deception is not justified by the fact of its end being a righteous one Ahithophel's atrocious counsel pandered to the passions of Absalom, and destroyed all hope of reconciliation between father and son. How accurately was Nathan's prophecy fulfilled (12:11, 12). By wisdom can no man prevail. God takes the wise in their own craftiness. Beware of that counsel which falls in with the prompting of passion. He who counsels you to do what is morally wrong can never safely guide in matters of prudence.

2 Samuel 17   A TYPE OF JUDAS

In this chapter there are many evidences that God upholds David, even while He visits him with chastisement, according to Nathan's prediction.

1-14 *The defeat of Ahithophel's counsel.* — No doubt Ahithophel's counsel was the wiser; but Absalom and his followers were blinded with passion, and were unable to discriminate, and so fell easily into the net laid by Hushai. The delay was of the utmost value to David. The descending on David as dew is very graphic — so silent, and rapid, and irresistible. The allusion to ropes is probably metaphorical. **14,** Absalom's decision was Divinely overruled, and was in answer to David's prayer. The Hebrew was accustomed to say that God did what we should say God permitted to be done (Prov. 21:30; 1 Cor. 1:19, 20).

15-22 *Tidings to David.* — Hushai was even now afraid that Ahithophel might gain his way. Hence the message to David to lose no time in placing the river between himself and his son. **17,** En-rogel was outside Jerusalem, where the valleys of Hinnom and Jehoshaphat join; and tidings were brought to them by a woman. They were, however, recognized by a lad, and would never have reached David but for a deception practiced on Absalom's servants at Bahurim, similar to that which Rahab adopted at Jericho (Josh. 2). God's purpose would doubtless have been fulfilled without this deception, which, in the sacred narrative, is not justified.

When we cease to trust God, we resort to trickery. Messages are constantly coming to us to warn us or indicate our path of duty — voices from the unseen; but we forbear to take heed. Unlike David, we make no response, and are overtaken by disaster. If only Peter had heeded his Master's sad prognostications!

23 *Ahithophel's death.* — As he had foreshadowed Judas in his treachery (Ps. 41:9), so did he in his doom (Matt. 27:5). He was prompted to it, not only by the mortification to his pride, but because he anticipated the failure of Absalom's rebellion, and feared the certain punishment David would inflict.

24-29 *David at Mahanaim.* — Amasa was Absalom's cousin (1 Chron 2:13-17). God raised up friends to minister to his servant. But nothing could compensate him for the loss of the Lord's house. The thirst of the stag in the glades of Bashan's forest was the proper emblem of his desire for the house of God. But amid all was the certainty that days of praise were coming, in which he should go again to the altar of God, his exceeding joy.

2 Samuel 18   ABSALOM'S DEATH

1-8 *The battle.* — The men of Gilead rallied around David's standard. Josephus says that he was soon at the head of four thousand soldiers. They loved their king too well to permit him to risk his life. "Worth ten thousand of us" (**3**). Thus we may address the Lord Jesus. Because of His infinite worth we are sure of our acceptance. **5,** In David's tender thought of his prodigal and rebellious son, we may clearly see God's pitiful love towards us when we go astray. We may have been thoughtless and rebellious; defied His authority, and refused to give Him His rightful place and honor; and yet He gives charge concerning us.

9-18 *The death of Absalom.* — The tree was probably a terebinth (**9**, R.V. *marg.*), for which Bashan is famous. Note that Absalom's head, rather than his hair, was caught in the fork of the branches. **11,** The girdle would be the badge of authority, the mark of an officer. Absalom met a deserved fate (Deut. 21:18, 21)

19-33 *David's lament.* — David was more of a father than a king. There were many reasons for joy — his own life was delivered, his kingdom was restored. But nothing can stay his grief that his son was dead, and in such a manner, and on account of his own sin. Those to whom public interests are committed must often subordinate themselves to their charge.

2 Samuel 19   DAVID'S TRIUMPHANT RETURN

1-8 *Joab's reproof.* — The tidings of the king's grief spread through the troops, and instead of being welcomed home, they slunk ashamed and silent into the city. Joab's sharp reproof was needed. David had every reason to be thankful for his faithfulness, though marred in the tone in which he spoke. Perhaps the father of the prodigal son filled the empty chambers of his home with words like these!

9-15 *The welcome back.* — Roused from the stupor of his grief, David began to act with his usual energy and tact. There were three parties, David's, Absalom's, and that of those who were indifferent. The king did right to await the nation's recall. This was given by Israel, but his own tribe of Judah did not speak. He made, therefore, a direct appeal to the men of Judah, which overcame the last symptoms of reluctance, and won Amasa to his side by a promise of the command of the army instead of Joab.

16-23 *Shimei.* — He had cursed David, but now took an altogether different view of matters. There is no reason to think that his repentance was sincere; but to appear repentant was his only hope. **19, 20,** These words will befit our lips. The best fitness for coming to Christ is the knowledge of sin; the best time is *first of all this day.*

24-30 *Mephibosheth.* — The Oriental is specially careful of his beard, and the neglect in this case indicated deep sorrow. David received his expressions of homage rather coldly, and decreed the division of the estate. It may be that he suspected the genuineness of the expressions employed by the son of his old friend.

31-40 *Barzillai.* — True to David in his affliction, this aged man now received his reward, even to a share in the king's palace. Even more glorious are the rewards offered by Jesus to those who suffer with him (Rom. 8:17). For Chimham's inheritance, *see* Jeremiah 41:17.

41-43 *The mutterings of the storm.* — The ten tribes were probably offended at David's having sent a special summons to his own tribe, and having awaited their reply. He appears to have not delayed for the escort of the ten tribes, but to have returned with that of Judah alone. This appearance of partiality greatly excited them.

2 Samuel 20   SHEBA'S REBELLION

1, 2 *Sheba's rebellion.* — Like Shimei, Sheba belonged to the tribe of Benjamin. The disaffection of Israel gave him his opportunity. No sooner was one rebellion quelled, and David restored to the kingdom, than another demanded his care. Thus literally was Nathan's prophecy fulfilled of the sword not departing from his house. A backslider, even when restored, tastes the bitter fruit of departure from God.

4-12 *Amasa's death.* — The appointment of Amasa as captain, and — when his delay threatened to prove fatal — of Abishai, was a terrible affront to the haughty spirit of Joab. At Gibeon, Amasa assumed his new position; and was saluted in the most friendly way by Joab. Josephus says that the old general allowed his sword to fall out on purpose, that he might have an excuse for approaching Amasa, with a naked sword in his hand.

13-22 *The pursuit and death of Sheba.* — Abelbeth-maachah was situated in the extreme north of Palestine, above Lake Merom. Joab prepared to besiege it. The intervention of this wise woman, who, probably like Deborah, was its judge and governor, prevented the siege, and saved the city from destruction. Bishop Hall says: "Spiritually, the case is ours; every man's breast is as a city enclosed; every sin is a traitor that lurks within the walls. God calls to us for our sin. If we love the head of our traitor above the life of our soul, we shall justly perish in his vengeance. We cannot be more willing to part with our sin than our merciful God is to withdraw His judgments." Probably it would be better to translate **18, 19,** freely, thus: "When the people saw thee lay siege to Abel, they said, Surely he will ask if we will have peace; for the law prescribes that he should offer peace to strangers, and much more to Israelite cities: and if he do this, we shall soon bring matters to an amicable termination, for we are a peaceable people."

2 Samuel 21   THREE YEARS' FAMINE

1-9 *The Famine.* — The time when this famine occurred cannot be fixed with certainty. "In all probability it was before Absalom's rebellion, in the account of which we may trace one, if not two allusions, to the execution of Saul's sons" (16:7, 8; 19:28) (*Cambridge Bible*). **1,** Three years passed before David took the famine seriously to heart, or realized that it might have a special cause. If God is contending with you, do not prolong your grief by delaying to inquire the cause (Job 10:2). The reason for the famine was a strange one. The Gibeonites had obtained Joshua's oath by fraud, but God regarded it as binding. Saul's violation of this oath is only referred to here. But his acts involved the whole nation (**3-9**). The remnant was in the position of the Goel, and therefore they were bound to ask for satisfaction at the hands of the representatives of the family of Saul. **6,** The fact that Saul was God's chosen monarch was cited as an aggravation of the crime. Merab (**8**) should be read for Michal (1 Sam. 18:19).

10-14 *The waiting of Rizpah.* — It was a heathen practice to expose to ridicule the malefactor's body; but the Gibeonites were not bound by the laws of Israel. Rizpah kept watch day and night, on a shadeless rock, from early spring until late into the autumn, and the falling rain proved that the famine was ended. She bore patiently the fierce heat of the sun in the Syrian summer, in the devotion of her love, which became contagious, and even stirred David to treat with similar honor the remains of Saul and Jonathan. Fire spreads itself without impoverishment, and love ignites love. Go on doing what is right at all costs; it will stir others to deeds of heroic zeal!

15-22 *The wars with the Philistines.* — This paragraph is somewhat out of chronological order. The incident is repeated in 1 Chronicles 20:4-8, as immediately following the capture of Rabbah. **17,** A beautiful figure. Monstrous sin stalked the earth in the persons of these giants. Their presence towards the close of David's life — the beginning of which was rendered memorable by the death of Goliath — reminds us that the temptations we had thought at an end will again molest us.

2 Samuel 22   A PSALM OF THANKSGIVING

This Psalm of Thanksgiving is repeated with but slight variations in Psalm 8. It was probably written, as the Cambridge Bible suggests, in the period of peace, described in 7:1. In Hebrews 2:13 and Romans 15:9, the apostle applies it to the Lord Jesus.

2-4 *David's resolution to bless God.* — "My" occurs nine times in two verses. It is thus that the heart sings to God in the day when it is delivered. And in R.V. *"even mine"* accentuates the glad sense of possession. How many-sided Christ is! The soul piles one expression on another, but they are all inadequate.

5-20 *God's delivering grace.* — The Psalm begins with a description of the depths into which David had sunk. **5, 6,** Death not only threatened, but compassed him. **7,** Yet he could cry. There is no distress so deep, no flood so high, but our cry may rise into the ear of God. **8-16,** The deliverance is sublimely described. Do not be afraid of the storm! — the dark clouds are His chariot; the thick darkness is the curtain of His pavilion; the thunder is His voice; the stormy wind His breath. He will be your stay; He will deliver; He will reward according to the righteousnes of Him in whom you stand.

21-29 *The principles of God's government.* — This was not a boast of self-righteousness before God; but of integrity in his dealings with those who persecuted him. The Psalm was evidently written before his great fall. Those who suffer wrongfully may commit their cause to Him who judgeth righteously (1 Peter 2:19-23).

30-46 *David's personal experience.* — God is extolled for His faithfulness, His exaltation of David, the destruction of His foes, and the establishment of His kingdom. Be perfect — that is, whole-hearted — towards God, and He will be whole-hearted in His love and care. His way is perfect, and He will guide your way in perfectness (**31, 33** R.V. *marg.*). What cannot that man do who is right with God, not only in the work of Jesus, but in his whole-hearted consecration! He gives power to run and leap. He is a lamp. He is a shield and a rock. And all this so gently that we are insensibly led to positions of influence and greatness, to be used for Him. And from the height we shall magnify His deliverances.

47-51 *A prophecy of the promised seed.* — The "anointed" and the "seed for evermore" anticipate a greater than David. Of Him also it shall be true that God will bring Him forth from the hate and opposition of His enemies, and lift Him on high, and give Him the heathen for His inheritance.

2 Samuel 23   DAVID'S MIGHTY MEN

1-7 *David's last words.* — These words appropriately follow the Psalm of the previous chapter. Their theme is suggested by the last verse of that thanksgiving song. **1,** His threefold designation. **2,** His consciousness of inspiration. **3,** The Rock of Israel had promised him a ruler who should rule men in the fear of God (R.V. *marg.*). The foundation of the reign of the Messiah, David's son, should be equity and righteousness. **4,** "David had been familiar with the yearly transformation of the dry and dusty downs of Bethlehem into a lovely garden of brilliant flowers; an apt emblem of the gracious influence of the perfect rule of an ideal king upon a hard and desert world" (*Cambridge Bible*). **5,** A parenthetical clause in which David explains that, so far as his own household is concerned, the dawn had been overcast, and the grass withered. But although his family history had been spotted and beclouded, yet it was a subject of deepest faith and joy to him that God would ever be mindful of the covenant into which He had entered. **6,** As thorns are uprooted from a field, so would wicked men be from the kingdom of the Messiah. **7,** Evidently then the scepter of Christ will be one of judgment as well as mercy. He will rule the nations with a rod of iron.

8-39 *David's mighty men.* — The first of these verses may be read thus: "He who sits in the seat of the Tachmonite, who was chief among the captains, was Adino." Eight hundred (**8**) is three hundred in 1 Chronicles 11:11. The great victories achieved by Eleazar and Shammah are ascribed to the Lord (**10, 12**). Even the mighty men were powerless without Him. **17,** The same principle should lead us to abstain from intoxicating drink, which is mingled with the blood of the myriads it yearly ruins. Abishai and Benaiah were probably among these three. The name of the third is unknown.

2 Samuel 24   NUMBERING THE PEOPLE

1-9 *The numbering of the people.* — God cannot tempt any man; but He is often described as doing what He permits to be done. Satan was the counsellor here (1 Chron. 21:1). **3,** Joab and others seem to have done their utmost to dissuade David, but were defeated by his strong will. So man often rushes to his destruction in spite of warning voices, which God has raised up to stay him. **5,** The census was taken first in the eastern part of the kingdom. The river of Gad is rendered "valley" in margin. **6,** Their progress was northward to Gilead, thence to Zidon, then along the western coast southwards. **9,** The total differs from 1 Chronicles 21:5 by three hundred thousand. But the bands of soldiers are not included here, whereas they are included there (1 Chron. 21:5). Pride loves to enumerate our resources, and boast of them. This is wrong and foolish. We have nothing that we have not received; and it is ours only in the sense of stewardship, to be employed for our Lord.

10-17 *Punishment.* — God forgives our sins when we confess them; but there is chastisement to be borne. **14,** It was a great strait indeed, but David chose wisely. **15,** What an agony must have filled the mind of David during those three days! How deeply humbled must he have been as he saw how easily the numbers of his people, which had caused him so much vain-glory, could melt away before the blight of the pestilence! **16,** God will not suffer us to be tempted beyond what we are able; He will bid the angels sheathe their swords, and say, "It is enough." At the threshing-floor the Lord repents; *i.e.,* He alters His procedure when we alter our behavior! He will cease threshing. **17,** A beautiful touch of self-renunciation in David, who was prepared to be sacrificed, if his people might be spared. (*Compare* Rom. 9:1, 2).

18-25 *The temple site.* — Out of this awful pestilence there came the temple-site, in the threshing-floor of Araunah, or Ornan, one of the ancient inhabitants of the land (1 Chron. 26:18; 2 Chron. 3:1). This altar was one of expiation. Jerusalem was spared because the victims suffered in the sacrificial flames. **24,** The words of this Jebusite may well shame some of our Christian giving. The sum here mentioned, about five pounds, was for floor, oxen, etc., the large sum (1 Chron. 21:25) for the whole hill. Thus a Gentile furnished the temple-site, and the materials were largely taken from Gentile nations — all emblematical of the part that Gentiles were to play in the erection of that spiritual temple, the Church.

CONTEMPORARY KINGS OF ISRAEL AND JUDAH

NOTE — The names in *italics* are the founders of the eight Dynasties of Israel

Reigned Years	Kings of Israel	Notes	Yrs. B.C.	Kings of Judah	Notes	Reigned Years
22	*Jeroboam*	Set up golden calves	975	Rehoboam	Ten tribes revolt	17
			958	Abijah, or	Continued war with Jeroboam	3
				Abijam		
			955	Asa	A foe to idolatry	41
2	Nadab	An idolater	954			
24	*Baasha*	Destroyed the house of Jeroboam	953			
2	Elah	A drunkard, killed by Zimri	930			
7 days	Zimri	Slew the house of Baasha				
12	*Omri*	Built Samaria (During the first five years, Tibni divided the throne)	929			
22	Ahab	Married Jezebel, and served Baal	918			
22		Killed in battle at Ramothgilead	914	Jehoshaphat	With Ahab when that king was slain. A good prince.	25
2	Ahaziah	Died from falling through a lattice	897			
12	Joram, or Jehoram	Killed by Jehu	896			
			888	Jehoram (For a time jointly with his father. — 2 Kings, 8:16)	Married the daughter of wicked Ahab and Jezebel.	5
			885	Ahaziah	Killed by order of Jehu, when Joram, king of Israel, was slain.	1
28	*Jehu*	Killed Jezebel, and the house of Ahab	884	Athaliah (Queen)	Murdered the seed royal: slain six years later.	6
			878	Joash	Repaired the temple: slain in a conspiracy.	40
17	Jehoahaz	Wicked: heavily oppressed by Syria.	856			
14	Jehoash	Fought against Amaziah	839	Amaziah	Slew in battle 20,000 Edomites; taken prisoner by Jehoash: killed in a conspiracy.	29
41	Jeroboam II	Recovered Damascus and Hamath from the Syrians	825			
			810	Uzziah, or Azariah	Recovered and rebuilt Elath; smitten with leprosy, and became a confirmed leper.	52
6 mths.	Zachariah	Killed by Shallum	773			
1 mth.	*Shallum*	Killed by Menahem	772			
10	*Menahem*	Committed horrible barbarities	771			
2	Pekahiah	Killed by Pekah	761			
20	*Pekah*	His kingdom invaded by Tiglath-Pileser, and a large number carried into captivity. Was killed by Hoshea	759			
			758	Jotham	Troubled by invasions from Samaria and Israel.	16
			742	Ahaz	Erected an idolatrous altar, and spoiled the temple.	16
9	*Hoshea*	The Assyrian captivity	729			
			726	Hezekiah	Miraculously saved by the destruction of Sennacherib's army; his life also miraculously lengthened	29

The First Book of Kings

INTRODUCTION

The Books of Kings were originally one book in the Hebrew Bible. They cover the whole time of the Israelitish monarchy, exclusive of the reigns of Saul and David. The Jewish tradition ascribes them to Jeremiah, and this is corroborated by internal evidence. But of course, Jeremiah, if he were the compiler, availed himself of the state records, and of all the documentary or oral sources of information within his reach. The Spirit of God was continually prompting his prophets to preserve a continuous record of the history of the chosen people; and thus abundant materials would be waiting for the author's use.

The First Book of Kings carries the story of Israel from the death of David to that of Ahab, while the record of the kingdom of Judah is carried to the death of Jehoshaphat. It is a wonderful story of the fulfilment of God's gracious promise to David, side by side with the chastisement of the people for their sins. The story of Solomon's greatness; the building of his temple; the breaking away of the ten tribes; the ministry of Elijah — are told at considerable length. This book is often quoted in the New Testament; and our Lord especially derived from it many a searching lesson, as when He spoke of the Queen of Sheba, and the widow woman of Sarepta.

1 Kings 1 SOLOMON ANOINTED KING

1-10 *Adonijah's revolt.* — Adonijah was the fourth son of David (2 Sam. 3:4), and perhaps the oldest then surviving. He was born after Absalom (**6**); and, like him, was goodly in appearance, ambitious in spirit, and spoiled by his father's indulgence (**5, 6**). This attempt on his part to usurp the kingdom was a fulfilment of Nathan's prediction in 2 Samuel 12:10, 11. To the end of his life the effects of David's sin followed him. And as Bathsheba and he met, for perhaps the last time on this dark day, each of them must have remembered the announcement which had broken in on their guilty attachment so long before. How carefully we should walk before God, trusting Him to keep us moment by moment, since one glance of the eye may lead to such disastrous results!

The revolt was abetted by Joab and Abiathar (**7**). The former had more than once crossed David's purpose, and might reasonably fear that Solomon would not favor him, while the latter was perhaps jealous of Zadok. It was a compliment to the fidelity of the others that they were not invited.

11-27 *Bathsheba's and Nathan's appeal.* — Any jealousy that might have stirred in the heart of the royal consort at seeing her place taken by another, was hushed in the presence of the supreme danger which threatened not only to engulf her hopes that Solomon should succeed to the throne, but to involve both her and him in a common death. What a noble part Nathan had played in David's life! How much we owe to a true and wise friend!

28-38 *David's decisive action.* — Though weakened in body, his mind was clear and his spirit strong and resolute. He did not forget, in those closing days of his life, the bitter adversity of his earlier years, or the redeeming mercy of God. He was equally mindful of his own solemn words of promise made in the presence of the living God: "As I sware unto thee. . . so will I do this day." His action was as prudent as it was prompt, and left no doubt as to his successor. Solomon must ride on David's own mule (**33**; Gen. 41:43;

Esther 6:8), attended by the royal body-guard (**38**), and anointed by Priest and Prophet.

39-53 *Solomon's coronation.* — The tidings of this glad event carried comfort and joy into the hearts of all loyal citizens, but dismay into the hearts of traitors. To the one a savor of life unto life, to others of death unto death. Those shouts that made the earth ring anticipated the acclamation that shall accompany the exaltation of Jesus to be King of men. Ah, happy day for His Church; but woe to them that plot against His rule! The nations rage and the peoples take counsel together; *yet* God will set His Son upon His holy hill. Let the Adonijahs and Joabs make haste to kiss Him, lest they perish from His presence.

1 Kings 2   THE DEATH OF DAVID

1-11 *David's charge and death.* — With all its faults it had been a great life. The clouds had passed away and the sun shone out as it westered. There was no faltering in the tones of the voice that gave its farewell charge. Though he was in the valley of the shadow, he feared no evil — God was with him. The dying man spoke, not only by the inspiration of God's Spirit, but as epitomizing his own experiences; and it is good to ponder these strong and noble words. To be strong in God's might; to quit oneself as a man; to keep God's charge; to walk in His ways; to keep His statutes and commandments — such is the pathway of prosperity and peace. When once God has passed His word, years may intervene; but it shall be even as He has said if only we, on our part, fulfil the conditions on which His promise is based.

At first it might appear is if David carried to the grave, feelings of bitter hatred to the men whom he named to Solomon. But we must not forget that he spoke as much as a politician as a man. He saw that they constituted a grave source of danger to the public peace, and therefore warned Solomon against them. Nor were his prognostications mistaken; for as this chapter shows, each of them was discovered in acts of treachery, for which, rather than because of David's injunctions, they suffered death. What a comment on Psalm 55:23!

12-46 *The fate of traitors.* — Adonijah, when David was dead, revived his attempt to gain the throne. To have received one of David's wives would have given him a claim for something more. The request was probably the first of a series of moves, concocted by himself and his accomplices. They made a tool of Bathsheba, who, as the king's mother, would have special weight with him. She apparently did not see through the plot; but Solomon did. And though he paid her exemplary respect (**19, 20**), he steadfastly refused her request, and proceeded to take the life of Adonijah, who had prompted it.

Abiathar's deposition, in fulfilment of an ancient prediction (1 Sam. 2:31), and the death of *Joab,* who had been guilty of atrocious murders, still further weakened the party of disaffection (**26-36**). Notice Joab's vain attempt to find safety at the altar (**28-31**). He reminds us of those who, notwithstanding their unconfessed sins, think to gain exemption from punishment by external rites. The cross itself will not save if we have not the spirit of the cross within, contrite and penitent, believing and forgiving. *Shimei* broke the condition on which his life depended, and died by the hand of Benaiah (**36-46**). (See Proverbs 25:5.)

1 Kings 3   SOLOMON'S WISDOM

1-4 *Solomon's marriage.* — More than a year before he had married Naamah, an Ammonitess, the mother of Rehoboam (2 Chron. 12:13). Shadows soon began to gather on the fair dawn. The marriage with Pharoah's daughter was not absolutely forbidden, as alliances with the Canaanites were; but it was very inopportune. Was this the theme of Psalm 45? There are two significant *onlys* in the *second* and *third* verses. But these reservations may have been due to the want of a proper temple, in which the people might observe their religious rites. Solomon's love to God, and his appropriate conduct, are delightful gleams of promise.

5-15 *Solomon's choice.* — Solomon had deeply pondered the lessons of David's life. He had seen that God's great kindness had been shown on the conditions of David's truth, righteousness, and uprightness of heart; and that God had kept His great kindness for His servant. And it was on this that he founded his own requests and trust. So may the religious life of the parent become a priceless legacy to the child. It is to those who count themselves as little children that God reveals things hidden from the wise and prudent, and shows Himself strong. Happy is the man, who, in the presence of a great responsibility, can say, "I am but a little child; I know not" (**7**).

To each of us, as we abide in Jesus, the gracious words come, "Ask what I shall give thee." (*See* 1 John 5:15). The only limitations are those imposed by our faith or our capacity to receive. Happy are we if we seek not our own, but Christ's! When we seek first the kingdom of God and His righteousness, all things else are added. When we are set on doing God's work, we may claim with confidence the special gifts needed for its effective doing; and God will bestow, not these alone, but all else we require, exceeding abundantly above all we ask or think. "No good thing will He withhold from them that walk uprightly."

16-28 *Solomon's wisdom.* — How could so difficult a case as this be decided, when no witnesses could be called on either side? The proposal to divide the child revealed the mother's heart. Better lose her babe than that it should die. It appealed to the great instincts of the human heart, and struck a responsive chord throughout all Israel, as the story of the incident spread from lip to lip. "The people feared the king, for they saw that the wisdom of God was in him" (**28**). Bishop Hall, commenting on the incident, says, "Satan, that hath no right to the heart, would be content with a piece of it; God, that made it all, will have either the whole or none."

1 Kings 4   A GLORIOUS KINGDOM

In the previous chapter an incident was given to show how

Solomon was endowed with special wisdom; here further proof is given of his unparalleled riches and honor.

1-21 *His internal administration.* — The scribes or secretaries; the recorder or annalist; the commander-in-chief; the chief of the officers; the confidential minister, adviser, or friend of the king — all are carefully enumerated. The twelve officers seem to have been charged to collect the revenues for the royal treasury, which in the East are generally paid in the produce of the soil. Each provided maintenance for the king from his district for one month in the year. It was evidently a time of great prosperity and joy **(20)**.

But from Solomon we turn to a greater than he. Who can measure the unsearchable riches of Christ! What roll-call can contain the names of those who have served Him faithfully, and are now gathered around His throne! How happy and safe are they who own Him as their King! "Eating and drinking and making merry" **(20)**. (*See* Ephesians 5:19.)

22-28 *His provision and magnificence.* — From the river Euphrates to the Philistines were the borders of the Kingdom, which at this time realized the extent predicted to Abraham (Gen. 15:18). Tiphsah was on the western bank of the Euphrates, and Azzah was Gaza on the Philistines' border. Thirty measures of fine flour would be equal to two hundred and forty bushels. Instead of forty thousand stalls (probably an error in transcription), read four thousand, as in 2 Chronicles 9:25.

So Christ shall have dominion from the river to the uttermost ends of the earth. All kings shall fall down before Him: and the uttermost parts all contribute to the magnificence of His reign (Isa. 60). All things are ours, because we are His.

29-34 *His marvellous endowments.* — What is here said of Solomon has its abundant counterpart in our blessed Lord. There is nothing in our lives, small as a hyssop, that escapes His notice. And there is no problem so perplexing that He cannot solve it. He not only speaks *of* all the abundant animal creation; but He speaks *to* each, and they serve His will. And as we read Psalm 72, we feel that its marvellous portraiture is only perfectly realized in the Prince of the kings of the earth.

1 Kings 5   HIRAM, KING OF TYRE

Before his death David made great preparations for the building of the Temple (1 Chron. 29:1-5). The time for commencing the work had at last arrived.

1-3 *Times of peace.* — David had been prevented from executing his purpose, because he was a man of war and blood (1 Chron. 22:8). But, as God had promised, "a man of rest" was now on his throne. The name Solomon means *peaceful.* God had given him rest. It is only in times of peace that the Temple of God can be built, whether in man's heart or in the world (Acts 9:31). It is the still heart that becomes the habitation of God. "This is my rest for ever, here will I dwell." Times of temptation and difficulty are needed to brace us to endure hardship; but we grow most in days of calm and loving meditation.

4-12 *Hiram.* — A lover of David; and through that love probably possessed of a faith in David's God. He was a Gentile, but he had an important function in the building of the Temple: indeed, much of its beauty and magnificence was due to him. Isaiah alludes to this as foreshadowing events still future (Isa. 60:10, 13). And our Lord Himself, of whom Solomon was a type, permits them that are "far off" to come and build in the Temple of the Lord (Zech. 6:12-15). Every believer is a living stone in the Temple, and is called to fellowship with the Lord in its erection. How careful the historian is to fall back reverently and repeatedly on the Divine promise (**12**). Amid all the splendor of Solomon's realm, we can never forget the Divine purpose and promise to which all must be counted back. My soul, boast not of aught which thou hast; thou hast nothing which thou hast not received.

Tyre gave skill and labor; Israel supplied food for the workmen as well as for Hiram's household. For twenty measures of pure oil (**11**), read twenty-thousand baths, as in 2 Chronicles 2:10.

13-18 *Solomon's levy.* — These were not Israelites, but tributary or conquered nations (9:20-22; 2 Chron. 2:17-18). This enforced service was extremely heavy and bitterly resented, as appeared afterwards (12:14, 18). According to Josephus, Solomon enlarged the area of the top of the mount by raising a wall from the valley beneath, and filling the intervening space with earth. Immense stones still attest these mighty works. Be content to hew on the mountains, or shape in the valleys; so long as thou shalt do something for the building of the Church, which is the true Temple of God, and thy work shall abide for ever.

1 Kings 6　THE ERECTED TEMPLE

1 *The time.* — Here is a chronological difficulty; there is some doubt as to the exact date (*see* Acts 13:20). The early years of Solomon's reign were spent in preparation. The kingdom needed to be settled, and the materials prepared. There must be times of subsoil work before there can be a harvest of results. Time is not wasted which is spent in preparation.

2-14 *The house.* — The Temple was twice the size of the Tabernacle, ninety feet long by thirty feet broad, and forty-five feet high; the porch fifteen feet forward along the breadth. "The walls narrowed as they ascended, by sets-off of about eleven inches on each side, which received the flooring-joists, as no cutting was permitted on the sacred building." It was built on the plan given by God to David (1 Chron. 28:11-19); and was a type, first, of the body of the believer (1 Cor. 3:16), and, lastly, of the whole Church of God (Eph. 2:21, 22). Each of these is God's dwelling-place. There is no need to seek for God in any material structure, or even in heaven — He is within.

The silence in which the Temple was reared was very significant. Like some tall palm, growing amid the silence of the desert, that wonderful building rose on the summit of Zion. The stone was made ready at the quarry. Thus all true work in the world is being done still. But how reassuring the promise which broke in on the heart of Solomon, that God would dwell there, and not forsake His people Israel.

15-38 *The furniture.* — The stone walls were lined with cedar, and this was covered with gold. The Holy of Holies — called (**16**) the oracle — was a perfect cube of thirty-five feet. The cherubim that stood erect within were seventeen feet high, made of olive wood, and covered with gold. The house was for God, and so demanded the best of everything. It took seven years to finish. Can we wonder therefore that the Church has taken so many centuries for its erection, and is not yet complete?

1 Kings 7   SOLOMON'S PALACE

1-12 *Solomon's palace.* — This building was probably called "the house of the forest of Lebanon," because of the immense amount of cedar used in its construction. It, with the house for Pharaoh's daughter, was probably one vast pile of buildings. Note the porch of pillars (**6**), the porch of judgment (**7**), his own house, with its inner porch (**8**). It may be remarked that the stonework was equally excellent on the inside, though covered with cedar, as on the outside (**9**); and in the formation, though out of sight, as in the super-structure, God sees, and our most hidden work should be done in His sight, as to Him.

13, 14 *Hiram.* — His mother probably belonged to Dan (2 Chron. 2:14), and her first husband to Naphtali (**14**). "The head of a Tyrian, and the heart of an Israelite"; God uses all.

15-22 *The brazen pillars.* — Each was twenty-seven feet high, and eighteen feet in circumference, and the capitals seven and a half feet high. Here and in Jeremiah 52:21, the height of the pillars alone is given; in 2 Chronicles 3:15, that of the pedestals on which they stood is included. They were elaborately ornamented, and stood in the temple porch. Their names spoke to every priest, as he entered on his ministry. *Jachin,* "He shall establish or prepare." *Boaz,* "In Him is strength." In worship and warfare, amid all life's changes, we need the prepared and the strong heart.

23-26 *The molten sea* was substituted for the laver. It was called a sea because of its immense size. Its contents would be equal to fourteen thousand gallons. We need not only the blood of the Altar, but the water of the Word: not only the sacrifice of the cross, but the washing of the feet — as in John 13 — from the daily defilement of the way. The same lesson is taught in *the ten lavers* used for washing the burnt-offerings (**27-40**). Our acts of consecration need cleansing; our prayers, the sweet incense of Christ's merit.

Elaborate details are given of the workmanship of the bases on which the lavers stood. They were on wheels, so as to be easily moved from one part of the ample court to the other, as required (2 Chron. 4:6). Christ comes to where we are in need of Him.

41-51 *The immeasurable weight of material.* — "The weight was not searched out" (**47**, R.V.). So is it with the unsearchable riches of Christ. Even the hinges and snuffers in Christian service should be of gold, derived from Him. You cannot weigh up God's grace; nor our hope and joy. They are unspeakable. They pass knowledge. As you leave the outer courts and go ever deeper, you find that brass is left for gold. Always from grace to grace; from strength to strength; from glory to glory.

1 Kings 8   THE TEMPLE DEDICATION

1-13 *The Temple dedicated.* — The Feast of Tabernacles, which was held in *the seventh month* (Lev. 23:34), was blended with this solemn festival: or perhaps the one feast immediately followed the other (**65**). All Israel in festive attire welcomed the ark to its abiding place, with sacrifices that could not be numbered. The *Priests* bare it; for the Levites, by whom this duty had been performed, were not permitted to enter the Holy of Holies.

There is rare joy in the heart, when He, of whom the ark was a type, with its blood-stained propitiatory, takes up His abode there. Then the glory-cloud fills the whole being, and there is no longer any part dark; but the spirit, soul, and body — the Holy of Holies, and the outer court — are all infilled. This is to be sanctified wholly. Thus the whole nature may be preserved blameless (1 Thess. 5:23).

The budding rod and the pot of manna had disappeared. They were the symbols of a life that had passed away. But the Holy Law was there. In our most rapturous experiences we shall never be able to get away from the need of loving meditation on God's Word.

14-21 *The people blessed.* — Solomon recited the chain of incidents that had conducted to that august moment. Each link is worthy of notice, especially the clause which declares that though David was not permitted to carry his pious intention into effect, it was yet accepted. "Thou didst well that it was in thine heart." There are many who desire to devote their lives to God as missionaries or ministers, but are hindered by death, or home-ties, or other considerations. But they are credited before God, not only with the desire, but with the fact. In the seed He beholds the perfected plant.

22-54 *The prayer of intercession and consecration.* — He began by standing (**22**), but in the eager pursuit of his entreaties, he found his way to his knees (**54**). Familiarity with God begets reverence (Heb. 12:28). All prayer should contain a large proportion of adoration. What scope we have for this as we meditate on God's faithfulness (**24**), and His promises (**25**)! In prayer, God's children should quote and claim the promises. Let us also be minute in prayer, passing step by step through the needs of our life, and asking appropriate help. The vindication of righteousness (**31**); defeat (**33**); drought (**35**); pestilence (**37**); the case of the stranger (**41**); captivity in a strange land (**46**) — these will suggest counterparts in all lives. But in each case there had to be confession, directed towards that place where the blood was shed and the priesthood burnt sweet incense — so in our case there is no forgiveness, save through the sacrifice and intercession of Jesus Christ. There are some notable expressions in this prayer: "The plague of the heart" (**38**), "The furnace of iron" (**51**), and so on.

55-66 *Thanksgiving and sacrifice.* — As God had not failed, so they might *reckon* on His being true. This reckoning God to be faithful to do what He has promised is the after-glow of true prayer; and then there is the obvious condition on our side of the perfect heart. In considering the great numbers of victims sacrificed, let us not forget, that though all was offered to God, only a small part was burnt on the altar; the rest was eaten. It was needful to make provision for the immense multitudes of guests.

1 Kings 9   GOD'S COVENANT WITH SOLOMON

1-9 *God's second appearance.* — It is suggested that the dedication of the Temple did not take place until Solomon had finished his own house. There was nothing then to distract his mind, and no unfinished works on the great Temple-site. This second vision was intended to assure Solomon that his prayer was heard and the new Temple hallowed; and to declare the conditions on which both king and people might be assured of permanent prosperity.

As soon as we yield ourselves to God to be only His, He enters upon a possession, guaranteeing our security. Obedience to the least prompting of the Divine Spirit is an essential condition of blessedness and prosperity. Let us watch against indolence in the self-watch. It is true that we are not under the law, but under grace; but we are under the law to Christ.

10-14 *Hiram's discontent.* — "Cabul," in the Phoenician tongue, signified *unpleasing.* It was a pity, after all their co-operation, that there was any grievance between the two. But there is no security for human friendship unless it is based on the love of God.

15-28 *Solomon's growing power.* — All great kings have been great builders. Baalath (**18**) is supposed by some to have been Baalbek, in the extreme north of Canaan; but more likely it was a town on the southern frontier. Tadma, or Tamar, is supposed to have been Palmyra, midway between Damascus and the Euphrates, forming an oasis. The remnants of the Hittites that still lived among the Israelites were reduced to bondage; but the chosen people furnished the soldiers and officers of state.

It is significant to have this mention of mercantile marine at Ezion-geber. It was a strange outburst of national life which made the Jew a sailor, willing to undertake journeys to Ophir (India). But what visions of new worlds must those voyages to the barbaric splendor of India have excited! In 2 Chronicles 8:18 the weight of gold is fixed at four-hundred and fifty talents; perhaps the thirty talents went to defray the expenses of the voyage, the balance alone being paid into the royal treasury.

In these early years Solomon's piety seemed to keep pace with his success, and we learn of his public appearance three times yearly for the purposes of sacrifice (25).

1 Kings 10   THE QUEEN OF SHEBA

1-13 *The Queen of Sheba.* — Matthew 12:42 gives the spiritual lessons of this memorable visit. She heeded the report. She came to verify it. She had many questions — questions for heart as well as head. We, too, are troubled with these; but for each of them there is a solution in Jesus, the "greater than Solomon." Too often men seem to suppose that we must stay away from Him till these questions are all answered, and only afterwards go to His feet. But at this rate we shall never go at all. We must travel to Him from the uttermost parts, and in the light of His face all mists and clouds will vanish.

This Eastern queen found that the half had not been told of Solomon"s wisdom and prosperity. So when we come to Christ, His wisdom and goodness far surpass the power of men and angels to utter. The soul exults in the golden radiance of His love and grace, which are inexpressible. We sink in our own esteem, there is no spirit left in us; while we have ever enlarging conceptions of Christ. There, however, the likeness ends. She had to leave the magnificent monarch, congratulating those who ever stood in his presence; we, on the other hand, need never pass out of the presence-chamber of our King. Fed on His provision; living on His royal bounty; and satisfied with His goodness. He also gives all our desire, and "exceeding abundantly above all that we ask or think."

14-29 *The glory of Solomon.* — The "ascent" (**5**) may have been a splendid aqueduct between Mount Zion and Mount Moriah. Almug trees, probably sandal-wood, brought from India (2 Chron. 9:10, 11). Tarshish is supposed to have been situated on the coast of Spain. The horses came up from Egypt in droves (**28**), in violation of Deuteronomy 17:16. There was a great temptation to trust in these as a means of defense rather than in Jehovah (Isa. 31:1). This magnificence furnishes materials on which the prophet constructs his conceptions of the latter-day glory of the coming King (Isa. 60).

1 Kings 11   DEATH OF SOLOMON

1-13 *Declension and sentence.* — Solomon's fall was attributable to the influence of his wives, whom, in direct defiance of God's command, he had married from surrounding nations (Deut. 7:3, 4). Strange women caused him to sin (Neh. 13:26). A wife will make or mar. How many of the greatest men have been ruined through their passions.

Temples rose in the holy city to heathen deities; and the sin was greatly aggravated in Solomon's case by the great privileges he had enjoyed. There was no help for it, but that he should be severely chastised. He had been specially pre-warned that such would be the case (2 Sam. 7:14); and the more privileged and honored we are, the more disastrous our fall, the more inevitable our sufferings. If God loved us less, He might spare us more. Because we are capable of such heights, He makes it impossible for us to rest contented in the bed of luxurious self-indulgence. He punishes us with the rod of men, and with the stripes of the children of men. All the while, however, His mercy does not depart from us;

but lingers over us, as a father will listen at the closed door of his child's chamber to detect the first symptoms of broken-hearted sorrow.

14-43 *Adversaries and death.* — Hadad was first stirred up. He was prosperous and comfortable in Egypt; but he felt that mysterious prompting to go, he knew not why or where. We know not from where these strange movings come, or where they go; but we do well to follow them. "Let me go in any wise." Then Rezon came (**23**); and lastly and most disastrously, Jeroboam (**26**). It would appear that the latter, a young man of great promise, was at the head of a large body of men, principally belonging to the tribes of Ephraim and Manasseh, and engaged on the royal works in Jerusalem.

It was thus at Ahijah, a native of Shiloh and a prophet, met him. The prophet had clothed himself with a new mantle, to give a more effective presentation of his message (**29,** R.V.). The taking away of ten tribes would leave *two* (**32**); but Simeon had by this time so lost its identity that it was practically absorbed into Judah. Solomon's attempt to murder Jeroboam (**40**) is in bitter contrast with the opening of his reign. He is said to have written the Book of Ecclesiastes after this; if this be so, we may trust that he became a penitent. But, in any case, it was a sad overcasting of a brilliant dawn.

1 Kings 12   REHOBOAM

1-15 *Rehoboam's accession.* — Solomon's reign had been splendid, but very oppressive; it was reasonable to ask for some relief. And there was much wisdom in the counsel of the *old men:* "Serve them, and they will be thy servants for ever." That is a true principle. It underlay the sacrifice of Calvary. "Thou art worthy to take the best, for Thou wast slain." It is because Jesus has girded Himself and washed our feet that we gladly bear the brand marks of His service for ever. But Rehoboam chose the counsel of the *young men,* who advised a more spirited policy. These young men had been educated with him, and were probably about the same age. He was forty. "The scorpion was a long and heavy scourge, weighted with spikes of metal."

16-24 *The revolt of the ten tribes.* — Jeroboam suddenly found himself possessor of four-fifths of the land of Canaan, together with the sovereignty of Moab (2 Kings 1:1; 3:4). A resort to arms was forbidden. The Divine purpose was being performed, though the chief agents in executing it were probably unconscious of anything more than their own ambitions and plans. God makes the wrath of man praise Him, and the remainder He restrains (see also Acts 2:23).

25-33 *The two calves.* — Jeroboam knew better than to attempt, by the setting up of the golden calves, to seduce the people from the spirituality of their worship. It was rather the worship of Jehovah under a material form as under the brow of Sinai (comp. **28** and Exod. 32:4). The introduction of new and false deities was left for Ahab's reign. But this worship of the golden calves was a distinct violation of the second commandment. Jeroboam was prompted in this matter, by distrust. Ahijah had clearly told him that, if he would be obedient, God would build him a sure house; but, not content with this, he attempted to make his position surer, and resorted to mere expediency to gain his ends. His endeavor was to make it needless for the people to go to worship at Jerusalem, by making shrines within his own territory.

Bethel was at the extreme south, Dan at the extreme north, of the new Kingdom. The Levites remained true to God (comp. **31** and 2 Chron. 11:13, 14). Jeroboam even constituted himself a priest, and changed the sacred month (**33**). These expedients to consolidate his kingdom led to its overthrow, as we shall see.

1 Kings 13   JEROBOAM

1-10 *A startling prediction.* — "A man of God"; there is no higher designation than this! He came "by the word of the Lord" to utter the Divine disapproval at Jeroboam's inauguration of the new sacred month, and of his self-consecration as priest.

This prophecy (**2**) was given three-hundred and sixty years before it was fulfilled; it indicated that the kings of Judah should be faithful to the law of God, even at that *then* remote date. It was literally realized (2 Kings 23:15). The withering of Jeroboam's arm was a token of God's preserving care over His messenger; and the rending of the altar, marked the Divine confirmation of the prophet's words. And how significant! Our strength must wither, and our religious rites be flung to the earth as contemptible, unless our hearts are right with God.

What a noble answer was that which the prophet gave, when he told the king that a bribe of half the royal house could not induce him to eat a meal therein. This faithful obedience to God's commands stood in striking contrast to the time-serving conduct of Jeroboam. It taught that there could be no fellowship between God and His erring people.

11-19 *A disastrous failure.* — This old prophet seems, like Balaam, to have had the gift of foretelling the future; but he was not a holy man. It is not easy to give reasons for his great desire to get his brother beneath his roof. Perhaps he had a vague longing for contact with one who enjoyed a fellowship with God which he had lost. But the unnamed prophet had no right to substitute the word of another, or even the voice of an angel, for the direct and authoritative message from God which had started him on his errand. When once we have heard the voice of God, we must not turn aside at the call of men who profess to be speaking under Divine influence. Each must be guided by his own revelation, and not another's.

20-34 *A terrible death.* — God does not say "yea" and "nay." In Him there is neither variableness nor shadow of turning. And they who act on the supposition that He is changeable will suffer inevitable and terrible results. The doom of the prophet must have spoken to Jeroboam's heart. For if God punished so immediately the man, who a little before had been such a resolute instrument of His will, how much more certainly would judgment descend on His people and their king!

It may be that this incident was similar to matters which are not directly told us, but which had transpired in Jeroboam's recent experience. He may have been deflected from the path of obedience by visions or voices through prophets who professed to speak by the voice of God. Hence the minuteness with which this story is told.

1 Kings 14   JUDGMENTS PREDICTED

1-6 *The sickness of Abijah* was co-incident with his father's sins (13:33). When sorrow or death invades our homes, we do well to see if the Lord may not have a controversy with us (Hos. 5:13). Trouble will often remind us of our real friends and of God's servants. Jeroboam could do well enough with Ahijah in his prosperity; but in trial he passes by the priests he had made, and goes to the man of God, to whom he owed so much (11:31). How strange was the conception which expected that the prophet could look into the future, but could not look behind the disguise assumed by a visitor! Hypocrites are stripped of their garb in the sight of God, and receive their doom: "heavy tidings."

This chapter is full of those results which disobedience and rebellion bring not to kingdoms only, but to hearts and homes. We veil ourselves under many disguises, but we do not deceive God; often we fail to deceive man. We are senseless enough to suppose that God can answer our questions and not read ourselves; can solve our problems and not understand us. But God is never mocked, and we reap as we have sown.

7-20 *The prediction of coming disaster.* — The king had thrown away marvellous opportunities. He had not only not followed in David's steps, but had misled the people by setting up the golden calves. This was intended as a clever artifice to establish his government, but it was the cause of its ruin. Vaunting ambition often over-reaches itself. To do right is the surest way to establishment (2 Chron. 16:9).

In the worst of families there is often one of God's children. Such are sometimes taken away from the evil to come. But it is a terrible thing for a home when God removes its salt and light.

It is an awful phrase which is indivisibly associated with Jeroboam's name, "He made Israel to sin" (**16**). Does it adhere to him on the other side the vail, which parts time and eternity? For certainly if Baxter was right when he expected another heaven for himself in the case of each of those who reached heaven through his means, so there will be another hell for each that has brought another toward that place. May we be preserved from laying stumbling-blocks or being such in others' ways!

21-23 *Rehoboam's reign and death.* — His mother was "Naamah" (*sweetness* or *beauty*), but she was an Ammonitess. Twice we are told this (**21, 31**), as if to emphasize and explain the disastrous influence she wielded over her son. What an awful and rapid descent from the purity and glory of the first days of Solomon! Wherefore "God gave them up" to Shishak. Sin ever weakens us, and causes God to withdraw His encircling presence.

How was the fine gold dimmed! Brass was but a poor substitute (**27**); and served as the outward evidence of the sad change for the worse in the spiritual condition of Israel. Mere traditional goodness, like that of David, cannot save us from the strong set of the current away from God; we need the mighty power of the Holy Spirit, in answer to the prayer, "Hold up my goings in Thy paths, that my footsteps slip not" (Ps. 17:5).

1 Kings 15   ASA'S GOOD REIGN

1-8 *Abijam, King of Judah.* — We have a fuller account of this reign in 2 Chronicles 13. He was not wholehearted with God; but he was maintained in his kingdom for David's sake (Ps. 132:10, 11).

How long after David's sun had set did the light of his life glimmer over his house! (**4**) God keeps His covenant and mercy unto thousands of generations. We are probably all inheriting more than we know from the prayers and tears of those who have gone before us.

What a pathetic sigh of regret that mention of Uriah is! One moment of indulged passion may cast a shadow over long years. God forgives sin, yet it grieves Him to the heart. Oh, that there may be no need for God to make such an exception in the case of any of us! And that we might never turn aside from anything He commands all the days of our life!

9-24 *Asa's good reign.* — This reign was not only good but it was also long (Ps. 91:16). A bad father may have a good son. Let no one feel that a noble life is impossible because of the difficulties of his birth or home surroundings. Through all drawbacks the true life emerges into the light; as a water lily from the muddy sediment of the pond. There were some things which might have been better even in Asa's reign (**14**), yet Asa's heart was perfect with God; from which we may infer that the perfect heart is that which lives up to the limit of its light.

He began, where we must all begin the work of reformation, by putting away evil. He first struck at immorality, then at idolatry. There must be a slaying of the members on the earth, before we put on the new nature (Col. 3:5-10). His grandmother — for such Maachah evidently was (comp. verses **2** and **10**) — was not tolerated, because she persisted in idolatry. He removed her from the court (Deut. 33:9). He brought into God's house the appointed portion from the spoils of the Ethiopians (2 Chron. 14:13). But he surely made a great mistake in seeking the help of a heathen monarch. How subtle is unbelief! How prone we are to depart from the living God!

The Book of Chronicles gives some further interesting details of Asa's life, which show the war of good and evil, and how at last he succumbed to mistrust.

25-34 *Nadab and Baasha in Israel.* — The term of Asa's reign saw six or seven different monarchs in the northern kingdom. Anarchy and misrule rode rough-shod through the land. Already the description of Isaiah's first chapter could be applied to that unhappy realm. It was a shaken reed, indeed (14:15). Men execute God's judgments on each other, as they follow their own wild will, and fall into the sins which they are raised up to punish. But God's plan moves on.

1 Kings 16   DARK DAYS IN ISRAEL

Baasha was a soldier, strong, active, daring. He waded to his throne through blood (15:29), and reigned for twenty-four years. Of Jehu we know little. The son of a prophet (2 Chron. 16:7), he continued in his office for at least thirty years (2 Chron. 19:2; 20:34); and shone as a star amid the darkness of the times.

No age has been without its prophets; no life, however abandoned, without some remonstrating voice; no soul goes over the cataract without a warning cry. And these things, answering to the voice of conscience within, reveal the merciful, pitying love of the Father, not willing that any should perish.

Baasha died in peace, and was buried in state. Men do not in this life receive the just recompense of their deeds; and herein is a strong argument for another life (Ps. 17:14).

Elah and the remainder of the royal house were cut off by Zimri (**9**). We are told explicitly that the extermination was so complete that none of his avengers were left (**11,** *marg.*). In this, God's word was literally vindicated and fulfilled; but Zimri trod in his master's footsteps, and was unwarned by his master's end. By his own hand he met a similar fate in consequence of Omri's treachery (2 Kings 9:31). In his brief reign of seven days Zimri had found time to walk in the way of Jeroboam, and in his sin. Seven days are long enough to test a man; and in that period he made manifest so great obstinacy and sin as to make longer probation needless, and all thought of reformation hopeless.

Omri (**16**) treated Zimri as he had treated Elah. For the first four years of his reign the throne was shared by Tibni (**21**), but at the death of his rival, Omri reigned alone. He built Samaria as the metropolis of his kingdom; and seems to have embodied his idolatrous statutes in a code (Micah 6:16).

Ahab succeeded him (**29-34**). He not only set aside the *second* commandment, but the *first*; and thus realized the terrible statements of verses **30** and **33**. His wife led him on — the beautiful, captivating, young idolatress, who was taught by the wily priesthood to use all her influence to bring in the idolatries of her home in Sidon.

The calf-worship at Bethel had a bad effect on its inhabitants, one of whom dared to defy the curse which Joshua had pronounced five hundred years before, and he suffered the terrible penalty of his presumption.

The inspired artist does not hesitate to paint the darkness of the times with Rembandt colors, and that the background may show up the illustrious glory of Elijah. The darkest hour is that before the dawn; desperation before the step of the Saviour over the wave; Ahab and Jezebel precede Elijah.

1 Kings 17   ELIJAH, THE TISHBITE

1-7 *A failing brook.* — God rears and trains His noblest servants in unexpected places. Gilead was far from Court and Temple. But what do they need of human help or education who bear a name like this! — "My strength is Jehovah." Elijah's nature was cast in a strong mold, suited to his great work.

The R.V. suggests that Elijah was of a pilgrim race; and certainly he learned to stand by himself in fellowship with the living God. He was ever standing in His presence-chamber; like the archangel Gabriel, who uses the same words of himself in his address to Zacharias (Luke 1:19). Oh, that we might always stand in the presence of the living God! The God of an undivided Israel — the ideal Israel.

This drought was the result of prayer (James 5:17). It was as if Elijah felt that nothing else would arrest the king and people. The man who stands before God is not afraid to stand before Ahab.

How often does God bid His servants hide themselves! (**3**). There are lessons learned in seclusion which elude us in the crowd. And, while we are in hiding, God will supply all our need by most unexpected means (Job 38:41; Ps. 147:9). But even then we must not be without trial, and it is hard to sit by a dwindling brook.

8-16 *An exhausted cruse.* — Not to Jordan, but to Zarephath (Luke 4:25, 26). God uses the weak and foolish things of the world, and those which are despised, as outside the visible Church. Yet there were noble qualities in this woman. She did not complain; she went at once to get some water, without so much as mentioning its scarceness; she was very hospitable and generous; she was willing to hear mention of Jehovah's name without resentment; and she believed unfalteringly in the Divine promise of the replenishment of her stores. "There is that scattereth, and yet increaseth." We get by giving.

17-24 *A dying child.* — Sorrow never proves that we are off the path of duty. Indeed, the way of obedience is often paved with flints; but our one aim must be to know God's plan and live on it, then no good thing can fail. Elijah found it so; but none of these things shook the heroic fortitude and courage of that noble spirit, who took each new trial as an opportunity for deriving additional grace and strength from his Almighty Friend.

1 Kings 18   THE TRIUMPH AT CARMEL

1-16 *Obadiah* was a good man, and did what he could to keep the true light from utter extinguishment (compare 2 Chron. 11:13, 14).

He was in a very abnormal position; but we must not judge him too harshly for being in Ahab's house, unless he was there at the expense of his testimony. Our loyalty to God does not involve leaving the service of men like Ahab, unless we are called upon to violate our conscience. The apostle said distinctly that we were to abide in the calling in which we were when we became Christians (1 Cor. 7:20). Still, Obadiah was doing what he could, and used his position as a means of sheltering the prophets.

17-20 *Ahab.* — How blind we are to our true interests! A sinner is strangely oblivious to the real cause of his troubles, attributing them to any other source than to his own sin. When a man forsakes God, he brings drought upon his life. Evil things multiply as noisome insects amid decay, and as false prophets did in Israel.

21-29 *The conflict with the priests.* — Baal was the sun-god; they could not resist the challenge to rely only on him. The people wavered, as they do still; they fluttered as a bird between two sprays. But a man cannot walk firmly with one foot on the curb and the other in the gutter.

30-39 *The answer by fire.* — The repaired altar was emblem of the united people; the water typified those influences which were prejudicial to the interests of vital Godliness; the fire was emblematical of the descending Spirit. Oh, to be known as God's servant, only obeying Him! (1 Thess. 2:4). Elijah had learned to reckon on God, and he could not be disappointed.

40-46 *The prayer for rain.* — The prophets must be slain before the rain can come. When God occupies His right place again, and His altar is built, the blood of Baal's priests encrimsons the brook, but the clouds cover the sky.

Our lives must be free from evil, before we can expect the showers. What a contrast between the employments of the king and the prophet! This prayer was humble, earnest, persevering. Six times the boy came back to say there was nothing. The little cloud is often detected by the servant of God before the clouds cover the heavens.

1 Kings 19   THE STILL SMALL VOICE

1-4 *Elijah's flight.* — Many causes lay at the root of his hurried departure. Perhaps the reaction from long overstrain; but especially a lapse of faith.

As long as Elijah looked at God, he was strong; but when he looked at Jezebel's threat, it seemed as if the communication of Divine strength was cut off: "when he saw *that* (when he was afraid, R.V., *marg.*) he arose and went for his life" (**3**).

It was a fatal mistake, as the movement which had been inaugurated collapsed in his absence. O man of like passions with us! We would not excuse ourselves by thy fall; but we are glad to know that your strength was not your own, for you were naturally as weak as we are, and we may be as strong as you. Let those who long to die, leave God to choose the day; else they may miss the horses and chariots of fire.

5-8 *The Divine provision.* — God might have allowed him to suffer the results of his terrible lapse. But "He knows our frame." On the desert sand the meal was lovingly spread, as afterwards on the shores of the lake (John 21). To every erring child God sends merciful help. In the wilderness the feast is spread; and instead of remonstrance, angel hands soothe the weary and despondent prophet. Our fits of depression and apparent desertion as often arise from physical as spiritual causes, and God remembers our weaknesses. In His pity the Father pays a surprise visit to His lonely and sorrowful child.

9-14 *The lesson of Horeb.* — Nature is often the vehicle of God's voice. Its storm and passion relieve us by expressing our emotion; its calm melts and soothes us. There is much of God's presence when "sounds of gentle stillness" (R.V., *marg.*) steal around. Not the storm of Sinai, but the whispers of Calvary touch and open hearts. We all need to get alone with God; our Carmels must be followed by our Horebs. There we receive fresh commissions; and there God teaches us to inspire others with the purposes with which He has filled our own hearts.

It is very beautiful to see the prophet's passionate desire for the glory of God. He had, however, thought that God's work could only be done vehemently, suddenly, and ostensibly. He was taught that God loves also to work in the still, small voice, heard only by the individual heart; and, lo, seven thousand were the result of these gentle influences stealing abroad among men. For each professing servant of God who is known, there may be thousands of secret disciples.

15-18 *Return to duty.* — This summons to anoint three successors is a little ominous. It would seem that others were to be called in to the work the prophet had left. Still there was comfort in being bidden to return. Backsliders may be encouraged by the words, "Go, return."

19-21 *The call of Elisha.* — We may expect to hear the Divine call when we are patiently plodding along the furrow of daily duty. Elisha evidently resolved to give his life to God's service. He burned his bridges behind him by sacrificing his cattle. He left all to follow, but he received more than he renounced (2 Kings 5, 6; Mark 10:30).

1 Kings 20   BEN-HADAD'S DISCOMFITURE

1-11 *Ben-hadad beseiges Samaria.* — The demand was very insolent, and the making of it proves how low Israel had sunk. Ben-hadad presumed on the cowardice which moral decrepitude always induces. There are no hours when we are tempted to such vile and abject sin as those which follow a great appeal which we have refused to heed.

Ben-hadad's boastfulness (**10**) was the forerunner of his downfall (Prov. 16:18). We always fall when we are self-confident; and our only safeguard is implicit faith in the promises and protection of God (Ps. 119:117).

We could hardly have expected that such a man as Ahab could have spoken so wisely (**11**).

12-21 *Ben-hadad's defeat.* — As in the case of Belshazzar, so here, drunkenness was predecessor of defeat. Through Obadiah's care some prophets were still left to remonstrate with Ahab, and to speak God's word even though Elijah had gone. God is not shut up to one great voice speaking like a trumpet; if that fails Him, He will call in another. His work must go on. If not by an Elijah, then by an unknown prophet.

God always chooses the weakest and most unlikely tools, as these princes (**15**) were; that the excellency of the power may be of Him, and that no flesh may glory in His presence. It seems as if God sometimes interposes, not so much for our sake as for His holy name, which had been blasphemed among the heathen (**28**; *Ezek. 36:32*).

22-30 *The second campaign.* — Thinking that he could succeed better in the valley, Ben-hadad, at the suggestion of his servants (**23**), in the next dry season returned to Samaria. Disaster again came upon them, the remnant of the fugitives from the battle being killed by a falling wall.

31-34 *Ben-hadad's deliverance.* — The servants who were the instigators of the expedition tendered the king some useful advice in his trouble. How often those who have led us into error forsake when counsel is most needed as to the way out! The mercy of the kings of Israel was proverbial, and the plea for Ahab's clemency, even after the double invasion, was not made in vain. Is it not so that the rebel sinner is encouraged by the thought of the mercy of God which is in Jesus Christ our Lord? From the throne, the Saviour stoops to call him "Brother," even after repeated transgression, so soon as he sues for pardon, girded with sackcloth and with the rope around his neck, as one who confesses that he deserves the extreme penalty of the law.

35-43 *The prophet's parable.* — The "smiting" (**35**) was against human inclination; and yet, for refusing, the man was slain by a lion. When our nature would turn us aside from "the word of the Lord," let us be careful to obey God's voice rather than our own inclinations. One point in the parable is worthy of note, "as thy servant was busy here and there, he was gone" (**40**). We may all question whether, in being busy about many petty details, we may not be missing Divinely-given opportunities. The king was self-condemned in his judgment of the prophet; so now we often find that in deciding the cases of others, we are pronouncing sentence on ourselves. May we watch each day for our Master's will, redeeming the time, because the days are few and evil.

1 Kings 21   NABOTH'S VINEYARD

1-4 *Ahab coveting Naboth's vineyard.* — The more we have the more we desire. He who possesses a kingdom is heavy at heart because he cannot have a plot of land for a kitchen garden. Naboth's refusal was probably rested upon religious grounds. He said, "The Lord forbid it me." He emphasized the fact that it had come from his fathers, according to the Divine institution. And when the king learned that it was not based on degraded and selfish reasons, he might have given way with good grace. Canaan was, in a special sense, God's land; and no Israelite might alienate his portion of it, except under very special circumstances (Lev. 25:28).

5-16 *The murder of Naboth.* — Jezebel was the king's evil genius, and Ahab must have known that she could only give him the vineyard by foul means; therefore he was as guilty as she was in her use of the power which he delegated to her. We cannot invest others with our power without being responsible for their use of it. We cannot shut our eyes to what is being done by our employees and at the same time open our hands for the gains of their misdeeds.

There could hardly be imagined a more horrible crime than this. The sanctions of religion were invoked, and a fast was instituted as if to avert some terrible judgment, caused through the special ungodliness of one of the citizens. Suspicion was directed towards Naboth, who was then assailed by bribed witnesses, and without opportunity for defense hurried away to execution. He and his whole family seem to have been involved in a common fate (2 Kings 9:26).

17-29 *Elijah's protest and prediction.* — Like an incarnate conscience he reproached the king in words remembered long after (2 Kings 9:25).

Men are blind enough, however, to count conscience their enemy, and God's prophets their foes. Yet these only tell us the natural outworking of our sins, not adding anything of their own, but indicating their inevitable result. Sold unto sin; stirred up to do evil; doing very abominably in following idols — these are the successive records of Ahab's sin; and yet because he humbled himself for a little, the love of God held back the judgment which was nevertheless certain **(29)**. "Let the wicked forsake his way," and our God will "abundantly pardon."

1 Kings 22   DEATH OF AHAB

1-4 *The compact between Jehoshaphat and Ahab.* — It seems strange that so good a man as the king of Judah should have entered into such an alliance; but he paid dearly for it, both at this time and afterwards (2 Chron. 20:37). We must not be "yoked together with unbelievers," lest we suffer their fate (Rev. 18:4). God's children will pierce themselves through with many sorrows, if they ally themselves with His foes.

5-28 *The conflict of the prophets.* — Ramoth was one of the cities of refuge in the land of Gad, across the Jordan; and the effort to regain the city from the Syrians was a natural one. It is a good thing to ask counsel of God before entering upon a new expedition; but it is not always easy or naturally pleasant to submit one's judgment and behavior absolutely to His reply. The false prophets fell in with Ahab's inclination, and advised the war, doing so in the name of Jehovah. But Jehoshaphat was not satisfied. There was something deficient in the solemn declaration of these false teachers and their object lessons (**11**).

The address of Micaiah is not a representation of things done in the heavens; but a parable, or figurative mode of expression. God cannot be tempted of evil, nor does He tempt any man (James 1:13). But He permits men to be tempted, and He overrules the working of Satan for the execution of His own purposes. Micaiah adopted an ironical method of speech, which at least suggested to the king how his prophets might claim to be God-inspired, and yet be deceiving him.

Micaiah's message was unwelcome, and was punished by imprisonment (**27**); but better a thousand times to be Micaiah, in prison and hated, yet bearing uncompromising witness against stiff-necked iniquity, than to sit beside it without rebuking it as Jehoshaphat did. In the judgment of the ages and of God, the prophets who dare to stand alone, and to endure any suffering rather than yield their countenance to the sin of high places, are they who shine like stars. The ivory house of Ahab and the cities that he built have perished, but this simple noble protest is a fountain of life and blessing. O my soul, dare to stand and live alone with God!

29-40 *The battle, and Ahab's death.* — The predictions of Micaiah had shaken Ahab, and he thought to evade their fulfilment by disguise, exposing his friend to danger. Jehoshaphat cried to God (**32**, and 2 Chron. 18:31). The arrow's flight was directed by God to execute His purpose. Our disguises cannot evade God's eye. And all our wealth will not avail to ransom our soul from death (**39**).

Do not hide from a true knowledge of yourself. Judge yourself; no, ask God to judge you, that you be not judged. Even though you can hear nothing good of yourself, but only evil, it is better so. You may yet be saved from the chariot-washing at the pool of Samaria.

41-50 *Jehoshaphat's good reign.* — Further details are given in 2 Chronicles 18—20. There was an evident effort to rid the land of the more obvious evils which had disgraced it. And God gave him rest, and victory, and prosperity. There seemed almost a gleam of the prosperity of Solomon in the revival of naval projects. The great defect of his character was the ease with which he associated himself with the kings of Israel, who wrought evil in his house (2 Kings 11).

51-53 *Ahaziah.* — This record is very terrible. The sins of the parents repeat themselves in the child, and the genealogy of his crime is traced back even to Jeroboam. The evil that men do lives after them to the third and the fourth generation. Children walk in the way of their father and mother. How great the contrast in Isaiah 59:21!

THE PROPHETS IN CHRONOLOGICAL ORDER
ACCORDING TO PREBENDARY HORNE
Other particulars are added. The reigns of the kings of Judah only are named.

Prophets	Times	Subjects	Date. B.C.
	Kings of Judah:		*Between*
JONAH	Joash,	Nineveh	860 and 784
	Amaziah, or Azariah		
AMOS	Uzziah	Syria, Philistia, Tyre, Edom, Moab, Israel's Captivity	810 and 785
HOSEA	Uzziah, Jothan, Ahaz, Hezekiah	The Jews, Messiah, Latter days	810 and 725
ISAIAH	Uzziah,	Deliverance from Captivity	800 and 700
	Jotham,	Rejection of Israel;	
	Ahaz,	Calling of Gentiles.	
	Hezekiah,	Glories of Christ's Kingdom	
	Manasseh		
JOEL	Uzziah, or Manasseh	Judah	810 and 660
MICAH	Jotham,	Judah and Israel,	758 and 699
	Ahaz,	Messiah's birthplace	
	Hezekiah		
NAHUM	Hezekiah	Downfall of Assyria	720 and 698
ZEPHANIAH	Josiah	Captivity	640 and 609
JEREMIAH	Josiah,	Desolation of Jerusalem, Judah, etc.	628 and 586
	Jehoahaz,	Captivity	
	Jehioakim,	Messiah	
	Jehoiachin		
	Zedekiah		
HABAKKUK	Jehoiakim	Destruction of Chaldean and Babylonian empire	620 and 598
DANIEL	During the Captivity	Messiah's Kingdom	606 and 534
OBADIAH	After the seige of Jerusalem by Nebuchadnezzar	Edom	588 and 583
EZEKIEL	In the Captivity	To comfort and warn the captives	595 and 536
HAGGAI	After return from Captivity	Encouraging Jews in rebuilding the temple. Christ's coming	520 and 518
ZECHARIAH	Ditto	Same as Haggai; Glory of Messiah	520 and 518
MALACHI	Days of Nehemiah	Reproving the priesthood: announcing near approach of Messiah	436 and 420

The Second Book of Kings

INTRODUCTION

This Book tells the story of the two kingdoms from the times of the deaths of Jehoshaphat, king of Judah, and Ahab, king of Israel. The occurrences recorded cover a period of about three centuries. Here are contained the narratives of the reigns of sixteen kings of Judah, and of twelve kings of Israel, amid the growing manifestations of idolatry with all its attendant evils. The shadows get darker; the apostasy more evident; the impending doom more certain; until first a portion and then the remainder of Israel is carried captive into Assyria, and Judah by the hands of Nebuchadnezzar, into Babylon.

During this period there lived the following prophets — Elijah, Elisha, Jonah, Joel, Amos, Hosea, Isaiah, Micah, Nahum, Zephaniah, Habakkuk, Daniel, Jeremiah, Ezekiel, and Obadiah. It is helpful to read the writings of these prophets side by side with the historical narrative; the history will explain many obscure allusions in the prophets, and the prophets will give many graphic touches to the histories. It is also well to read the later chapters in conjunction with the parallel chapters in the Books of Chronicles. We cannot read these books without feeling the contrast between the kings of these two earthly kingdoms and the King, and sympathizing with the eager demand of the holier men for that King who should reign in righteousness, and should realize the Divine ideal.

2 Kings 1   "FIRE FROM HEAVEN"

2 *Ahaziah's sickness* was caused by a fall through a defective lattice or fence work, which surrounded the upper stories of his house; either around the flat roof without, or enclosing one of the galleries which looked down on the open court of the palace within. There was a special instruction about this (Deut. 22:8). We should be careful of our battlements, to see that they are in good repair, and we should build them in all threatened places. The habit of abstinence from strong drink is one piece of lattice work which in these days we should very carefully maintain. If we do not fall for want of it, others may. All good habits are strong battlements.

2-14 *His mission to Baal.* — Ahaziah's messengers necessarily passed Jerusalem on their way to Ekron. It was, therefore, a direct insult to Jehovah to ask the help of the heathen oracle. As Elijah said, it was as if there were no God in Israel. See how the pride of man rages against the will and way of God! But in vain! The strongest regiments that come up against Him and His servants shall be broken in pieces. Around Elijah there was an invisible cordon of angels, as real as the soldiers of Ahaziah; and so it is with all who live by faith. These are unhurt in lions' dens; unsinged by flames; hidden in the secret of his pavillion; safe folded beneath his feathers. No weapon that is forged against them can prosper; and every tongue that rises in judgment against them they condemn.

These successive fifties perished because they shared in the contemptuous arrogance of their monarch; but as soon as one man spoke in a different tone (**13**), the awful destruction of would-be captors stayed. With the froward He shows Himself froward; with the merciful, merciful (Ps. 18:25, 26).

But how different the dispensation in which we live! Our Lord distinctly forbade His disciples attempting to imitate this episode; and in referring to it the Saviour said, "Ye know not what manner of spirit ye are of; my mission is not to destroy, but to save" (Luke 9:54, 55). We should breathe the spirit of our age — the age of the Holy Ghost, of revealed love, and of grace abounding over sin. The fire in which we must believe is that of Pentecost, which destroys not souls but sin. Oh, that we had the power of calling it from heaven, to consume sin and transform sinners!

"Thou Spirit of burning, come!"

15, 16 *Elijah before the king.* — Elijah, who had before dreaded the royal court, and fled from it, seems to have lost all fear, and goes boldly to the bedside of the dying monarch, raised on an alcove in the side of the room; and he returns unscathed, being defended by the gracious care of God (Ps. 27:1-3).

2 Kings 2   THE FIERY CHARIOT

In this chapter — one of the greatest of the Old Testament — we see how a man who one day lay on the desert sands and wished to die was translated that he should not see death. A special vehicle was sent to bring him home to his Father's palace! Oh, you who are sitting in the shadow of death, there are days of rapture and transfiguration in store for you — only be still and wait patiently. Your God will come! The waters shall part before you, and the fire shall bear you to your home. Be strong; yea, be strong!

3 *The sons of the Prophets.* — From the days of Samuel there were schools or colleges in which young men were trained for the office of teachers and prophets throughout the land. They were instructed in the law, and the principles of religion, and cultivated the art of sacred psalmody (1 Sam. 10:5, etc.). The greatest prophets were not always selected from their ranks. Elijah, notably, was not. But they seem to have given the young men the benefit of their tutelage. These sons of the prophets had been made aware of the approaching rapture of their venerated leader. Elisha was also aware of it (**3-5**).

6, 7 *They two!* — How close their kinship! Each noble, but in a different way; one supplying the other's lack. Who can estimate the blessing of such fellowship, tested and tried by repeated experiences borne in company? The older man by repeated invitations gave the younger the chance of dropping off, if he wished; and Elisha's tenacity of purpose showed the quality of his soul. Difficulties in Christian living frequently suggest our turning back. But if we comply, we miss the radiant vision and mighty enduement. Let us dare to persevere, with undeviating, unswerving faith, till we are clothed in living power.

8-12 *Elijah's last journey.* — Rivers part before men who believe in the living God. The Spirit of God can work through a flimsy cloak, as well as by an outstretched rod. The double portion (**9**) is the heritage of the eldest son and heir. Its reception in this case depended on that spiritual affinity which could behold the movements of the spiritual world. To none but the purged eyes of faith would that radiant vision have been evident. To see it was a proof of the spiritual character of Elisha's faith; and the parted river (**14**) witnessed the acquisition of his master's power. That same Spirit is for us. This is the meaning of Pentecost (Acts 2:39).

13-22 *Elisha's ministry* was sweet, beneficent, gentle. The healing of the waters at Jericho was especially significant. But there was judgment also, as his "strange work." We must not think of these children (**23**) as boys and girls. The same word is used of Joseph at 39, and of Rehoboam at 40. They were probably young men ("young lads," R.V. *marg.*) connected with the false idolatry, which had its seat in Bethel.

2 Kings 3   MOAB'S REBELLION

1-3 *Jehoram's reign* was marked by some measures of reform. He discountenanced the Baal worship, though he clave to Jeroboam's calves.

6-12 *The alliance.* — How strange it is that, after the terrible lesson received in his alliance with Ahab, Jehoshaphat drifted into an alliance with his son! The lack of water (**9**) threatened to so weaken the armies of the three kings as to make them an easy prey for Moab. It was very absurd on their part to charge the Lord with their disasters (**10**). They should have enquired of the Lord before they started; but like many others since their day, they left that for a stage of the enterprise when disaster was upon them. Experience is not enough to keep us from making fatal mistakes. Nothing but the grace of God and daily watchfulness can avail for that. But even when we have turned aside from Him, God will not desert us, and will answer our appeal for help as He did for these kings and their armies.

To pour water (**11**) on the hands of another is to act as his servant.

13-20 *Elisha's message.* — He quotes the very words of Elijah (**14**, and 1 Kings 17:1). He recognizes the presence of Jehoshaphat as a reason for clemency. The influence of music calms his agitation and predisposes him for the Divine communications. How often we have to make preparations for the advent of Divine blessing, long before we see any signs of the blessing itself! Our expectant faith is the valley full of ditches, and God is able to do exceeding abundantly above all we ask or think; but in all God's gifts there is the need for co-operation. He alone can send the water, but we must trench the ground. We must prepare the receptacles, which He alone can fill. It is for us to erect buildings, to organize the machinery, to gather meetings, to invite men to hear the Word, to prepare and deliver the message, to build up Sunday-schools, and the other associations of mission and church work; but the living water can only come by the way of the throne. Its advent is often unannounced. There is neither wind nor rain. A gracious influence suffuses the congregation. Heads are bowed, tears fall silently, lives are changed: God's heritage is refreshed, and many confess what He has done for their souls. Let us pray for this result; doing our work carefully and abundantly, not limiting time or pains in digging the ditches, assured that God will abundantly answer.

21-25 *The destruction of Moab.* — The Moabites were

deceived by the red tinge of the water caused by the rays of the rising sun; and concluding hastily that the Israelites had mutually destroyed themselves, they moved forward to a terrible defeat. Their cities were beaten down (**25**), their wells stopped, and their land invaded.

26, 27 *Mesha, king of Moab.* — This is the king who caused the celebrated "Moabite Stone" to be erected. This interesting monument, discovered in 1868, corroborates Mesha's tribute to Israel, and his revolt, as recorded in this chapter. The sacrifice of his son (**27**) was the precedent of Moabite victories over Israel and Judah in the territory occupied by them in the land of Moab.

2 Kings 4   THE SHUNAMMITE'S SON

Elisha's ministry was one of redemption. He was ever counter-working on the effects of sin and evil. In this he was a type of Jesus, who is "the universal Remedy of all evil broken forth in nature and the creature; the Destruction of misery, sin, darkness, death, and hell; the Resurrection and Life of all fallen nature; the unwearied Compassion, the long-suffering Pity, the never-ceasing Mercifulness of God to every want and infirmity of human nature" (*W. Law*).

1-7 *The widow's oil.* — God cares for the poor. How much they miss who do not go to Him about their temporal wants! "He is the God of the widow." The oil went on pouring so long as there were vessels. If only there had been more expectancy and a larger number of vessels, there would have been a more plentiful supply. Thus does Jesus fill our empty vessels with the Holy Ghost. He puts no limit on their number or size; but always stands ready to fulfil all our need, only lamenting when there is not a vessel more. God's only limitation is that which we impose by our unbelief. His oil will never cease, so long as we have empty vessels to bring.

What blessings often come to us within closed doors! (**4,** and Matt. 6:6).

8-37 *The Shunammite's son.* — A real man of God needs but little for the supply of his wants (**10,** and Phil. 4:12). How much greater joy than favor with the king was the birth of a son to an Israelite woman! (17). Sunstroke was a common cause of death (Ps. 121:6). So sure was the mother in the life-giving power of the prophet, that she needed not to tell her husband of the lad's death. Why should she grieve him, when the child would soon be again in health (Heb. 11:35)? She felt convinced that God could not mock her; and that, when he gave, it would be a gift worthy of Himself (28). How often we put the staff of doctrine and precept on the face of our beloved and unconverted children, without result! In the home and school there must be a definite contact between soul and soul, as between the body of the prophet and that of the child. Walk your house in intercessory prayer, and persevere even until seven times (35).

As the prophet in the Shunammite's house, so also does Jesus come into our hearts, when we make Him welcome; and coming, He gives life, and life more abundantly — first the life of birth, and then life through death. The law cannot revive dead souls. It lies impassive on their faces. But He communicates it, as a spark from His own body.

38-44 *The pottage and the loaves of barley.* — Miracles of benevolence and healing were akin to Elisha's gentle spirit. Is not this also the domain of the Gospel, to counterwork the ancient curse of the ground, to meet the hunger of men? The benediction of God will turn an evil into a blessing (Mark 16:18) and will multiply a little to feed many (Ps. 132:15). Jesus turns the poison into food, extracting the harm that we had carelessly gathered for ourselves; and multiplies our slender resources, so that they avail for many.

2 Kings 5   NAAMAN, THE SYRIAN

Naaman had everything that this world could give, with one sad exception — health. "*But* he was a leper." Though there is more evenness in our earthly lot than any of us realize, there is a "but" in every life, which is meant to bring us to God.

2-4 *The little maid* sought the peace of the home to which she was carried captive (Jer. 29:7). She was "the interpreter," the one of a thousand, who spoke true and health-giving words. Where she found herself, therein she abode with God (1 Cor. 7:21-23). What a blessing a Godly servant, though but a little maid, may be to a home! Let no one forsake their post in a godless household; because there may be some Naaman, whose life will be given back from death as the result of some simple testimony for God.

5-7 *The journey to Israel* was undertaken under the impression that healing might be obtained by influence and wealth at the word of a king. The lordly soldier had to learn to receive it as a gift in a humble, obedient, and believing spirit. Our physical health and other blessings may depend on the state of our hearts much more largely than we sometimes realize.

8-14 *Elisha's method of cure.* — As a first step, to teach Naaman humility, Elisha sends a message detailing the means of recovery. "But Naaman was wroth." How often do we find that the aristocratic sinner has his own notions of the treatment he merits! It hurts the pride when the officer, the nobleman, or the child of fashion is treated like any ordinary sinner. "Behold I thought" figures very largely with us all. And we must take care not to minister to that kind of pride. Elisha had a special reason in the course he adopted in dealing with this commanding nature. But where the leprosy of sin is eating out the heart and there is no other hope, humility will succeed to rage. Sorely wounded, the soul will gladly catch at any means of cure, though it be bathing in the despised Jordan.

The sevenfold dipping in the Jordan may fitly symbolize the perfect washing in the cleansing blood of Christ (Zech. 13:1). We may be young again — the pure flesh of a little child, united with the manly strength of the warrior (**14**). Naaman's bowing in the house of Rimmon may have been condoned under special circumstances which we cannot fully estimate; but it is no precedent for us.

20, 27 *Gehazi.* — What process of decay had been at work in Gehazi's mind to allow of this downfall? His sin was greed of riches, as was Achan's (Josh. 7); certainly his privilege as the prophet's servant aggravated his iniquity. What a contrast to the earnestness of the new Gentile convert! (**15**, Matt. 8:11; Luke 4:27).

2 Kings 6   ANGELIC ENVIRONMENT

1-7 *The lost axe-head.* — It was remarkable that the college became so strait in days of persecution. Yet this is the general experience of the Church (Exod. 1:12). True religion is not above personal exertion, and every man ought to take a beam (Mark 13:34). How often does the Lord step in, by a personal exercise of His power, to regain the losses caused by our blunders! If He can make dead metal float, He can surely make dead hearts live.

8-12 *The all-seeing eye.* — God knows the secret plottings of His foes, and He will either counterwork them, or deliver His own (2 Peter 2:9). The wicked may well be greatly troubled, as they learn that the whispers even of the bedroom are heard in heaven. How foolish to think that the prophet could discover plottings against the king, but not against himself!

13-18 *The surrounding Host.* — Though an host should encamp against us, our hearts need not fear. More are they for us, than those against us. This assurance made the prophet calm in the midst of danger.

Our blessed Lord was always conscious of the enveloping presence of these horses and chariots of fire. He had only to ask the Father, and He would give Him twelve legions of angels. He reminded His judge that he could have had no power at all, unless it had been given Him. And we also are ministered to. And may God give us the open eye, that we may behold the unseen, and walk as those to whom the mysteries of the eternal world are unveiled!

19-23 *The enemy foiled.* — Elisha, strong in the knowledge that God's protecting hand was over him, was able with the greatest composure to lead the army to Samaria, where he introduced them to the man whom they had come to seek, and where he "prepared great provisions for them" (Prov. 25:21, 22)

24-33 *The siege of Samaria.* — What a striking fulfilment of Deuteronomy 28:53-57! But "Dove's dung" may have been a kind of a leguminous plant. The king lamented the calamity, but did not repent of the sin which caused it. The truth which he enunciated was right, that all punishment is of the Lord; but the inference was wrong (**33**). We must learn to bow our heads to the Divine dealings, and to accept God's chastisement (Lam. 3:39, 40).

2 Kings 7   UNEXPECTED DELIVERANCE

1, 2 *The prophet's assurance.* — These were the prices of peace. The gate was the market-place. Peers are not infallible, and those who are most accustomed to rely on large material resources are sometimes least able to believe the unseen and eternal. The *poor* are rich in faith. How unwilling is man to believe that God can or will do as He says! Dare to believe even to the opening of the heavens (Mark 11:23). Unbelief shuts a man out of the enjoyment of the greatest abundance; and makes a famine amid harvest plenty.

3-11 *A welcome discovery.* — It was the extreme of misery that made these lepers count as a matter of indifference what became of them; but how soon their misery was exchanged for great joy! Such are the experiences of human lives: one day in despair, the next satisfied with all that the heart could wish. And most truly is this so with those who turn to Christ. The leper is cleansed, the hungry fed, and the impoverished soul enriched. God opens windows in heaven to supply our need. Look up beyond the mountains for His help. Nothing is impossible to Him. He turneth the shadow of death into the morning.

Indeed it is not well in a day of good tidings to hold our peace. If we do, punishment will surely overtake us. We do not become poorer when we give; and we have no right to keep to ourselves the Bread of Life, for lack of which men perish. The example of these poor men may well stimulate us, when we have discovered the unsearchable riches of Christ, to tell others the story.

12-20 *Samaria supplied.* — Though this had been predicted, it was too good to be believed. How little had Israel expected to be supplied thus! God can feed His people with the treasures of the wicked, fleeing though no man pursues. The threatenings of God are as certain as His promises. If the latter are fulfilled (**18**), so shall the former be (**20**). May we never be in this plight of seeing others included at the Divine banquet, and ourselves shut out! (Luke 13:28). Unbelief will shut us out of the enjoyment of the blessings of the Gospel. They may be all around us, so that we can see them with our eyes, and yet not eat thereof. In the day when, through the opened Heaven, God rained down the abundance of everything, he alone failed to partake who was blinded by unbelief. Beware, O Christian soul, lest thou miss aught in the day of the Lord's deliverances!

2 Kings 8   "THE MAN OF GOD WEPT"

The Shunammite, to whom Elisha was so much indebted, appears again in the sacred story (**1-6**). That kindness of hers was remembered long after.

What a blessing it is to have a man of God for a friend! There are symptoms and warnings of coming danger to which holy souls are sensitive; and we are wise to regard them, as did the woman whose son Elisha had restored to life. Enter into thy chambers, until the storm be overpast. Lives which are thus ordered by the will of God are blessed, not only spiritually, but temporally. They are guided in their going out and coming in, as this woman was, who reached the presence of the king at a moment which was specially auspicious. An hour earlier or later would have missed the mark. Her return was precisely ordered to take place at the moment when Gehazi was telling her story to the king. Commit thy ways unto the Lord, and thy works shall be established. Let God choose for thee, and life will be full of coincidences in which His handiwork is seen.

7-15 *Hazael.* — Elisha came to Damascus, evidently at the Divine bidding, just when Ben-hadad was sick. The sickness was not in itself mortal, yet he would die from another cause. Not only in the face of Hazael, the rough soldier, but in the thought of God, the prophet read his destiny, as the ruthless destroyer of the Jewish people.

Elisha's tears **(11)** resemble those of Christ. In this, as in so many other respects, he anticipated the life of our Redeemer. The unconcerned stare of men of the world; the agony of human suffering caused by sin; the declension of God's own people beneath the perverting influence of idolatry — these are themes to make our eyes fountains of tears. Oh, for fellowship with the sufferings of Christ! Would that men of God today had more of the gift of weeping over the miseries of men!

How little do we know what we shall be! None of us know the evil of our hearts. In our calmer moments we would count it impossible to do crimes which in the heat of passion we will commit tomorrow **(15)**. O my soul, walk closely with God! He only can keep you in that hour when you will be rudely disallusioned of the notions of your own goodness.

16-29 *Jehoram and Ahaziah, kings of Judah.* — Jehoram gives a terrible example of how a woman may mar a man's life. He had a good father, but a bad wife. And the latter influenced him more than the former did (2 Chron. 21). The lamp was kept burning for David's sake **(19,** and Ps. 132:17). Surely that same grace can keep the fire burning in your heart. Ahaziah, who succeeded him, was no better. Misled by his mother, he followed in the dreary steps of Ahab. The close intimacy between the two houses led to alliance in war, and to a common fate.

2 Kings 9   JEHU ANOINTED KING

1-10 *Jehu anointed king.* — The anointing of Jehu was a part of God's commission to Elijah in Horeb (1 Kings 19:16); but the ceremony was accomplished by Elisha as the prophet's successor, most probably in accordance with Elijah's expressed desire. The urgency of the nomination caused Elisha to send one of the young prophets to Ramoth-Gilead, thereby saving himself the toils of the journey. It is the province of youth to work, endure hardships, and make haste.

Jehu was appointed to the kingship for special reasons, *i.e.,* to cut off the house of Ahab, and avenge the blood of the prophets. It is a great opportunity when God lays His hand on any as chosen vessel (Acts 9:15). But it is a terrible responsibility. May He never be compelled by our sins to lay us down, as those whom He can no longer employ!

11-20 *Jehu's revolt.* — God's servants are often accounted mad (**11**); but the message which they bear is well understood by those who are ready to hear it. The situation was accepted by the soldiers under the command of Jehu; and the placing of their garments "on the bare steps" (R.V., *mar.*) was their act of homage. The measures to keep the tidings from the king's ears were taken with great precaution; and since Ramoth-Gilead was at some distance from Samaria, and no one was allowed to bear the tidings, the revolt had gained great importance, before the least suspicion reached the metropolis.

18 "Is it peace?" A question which we instinctively ask as we open the telegram, or the letter in the strange hand-writing. And they ask it with greatest alarm who know that their life is not rightly ordered. The man who is wrong with his fellowman is always expecting wrong from them. Instead of sending messenger after messenger to scout the country, it would be far better to adjust the wrongs at home. Then God becomes a sure Rock of Defense, and the soul ceases to be afraid of evil tidings, because it trusts Him.

21-37 *Jehu's punishment of Ahab's house.* — (Read also 2 Chron. 22). The meeting in "the portion of Naboth the Jezreelite" (**21**) doubtless reminded Jehu of Elijah's denunciation of Ahab upon the same ground; and after the death of Jehoram he turned to his captain with the words of the prophet, which had evidently left an ineffaceable impression upon his heart. "In some sense Ahab's blood was licked by dogs, as it flowed from the gaping wounds of his son." Long after Ahab had passed away, the curse of his life blighted other lives (Jer. 32:18). We cast shadows which reach beyond the natural term of our lives. We sow seeds, the harvest of which is reaped by our posterity. There is not one whose life is not a savior of life unto life, or of death unto death. Lamb of God, grant us thy peace, the peace of forgiveness and of a holy life; so that there may be an afterglow to our sunset, lingering with blessing.

Jezebel's heart was proud and unbroken. She thought to make the conqueror the slave of her power or charms. But she could not avert her fate. How often does truth ask: "Who is on my side?" Let us heed the summons, and dare to look out in answer (**32**). God's mills are here seen grinding, though slowly, yet to powder.

2 Kings 10   "THE HOUSE OF AHAB"

1-17 *The extermination of Ahab's family.* — This was a very terrible act of vengeance. Yet for the well-being of the race, God is sometimes obliged to cut off evil-doers, lest the plague spread with its poison, till there be no health or safety left. The brethren of Ahaziah were slain by Arabians (2 Chron. 22:1). The word *brethren* is a wide one, covering many degrees of relationship. The elders of Jezreel had been Jezebel's tools against Naboth; now they are Jehu's tools against her own house. Jehonadab was a man of unusual strength of character (1 Chron. 2:55; Jer. 35). Jehu boasted of his zeal; and such boasting generally covers insincerity. The really earnest man has no need to advertise himself. God was no party to the deceit and fraud of his behavior. Jehu might have achieved the same result by unobjectionable methods. God still cuts off the persons and families of notorious evil doers, though by more unobtrusive processes (Ps. 16:4).

The work of extermination by Jehu was very thorough: "He smote all that remained of the house of Ahab in Jezreel" —

great men, familiar friends, and priests — until none remained; and in this he set an example for us to ponder and imitate. There must be no compromise with evil in our hearts or lives. We must not spare one known wrong which rears itself against the obedience of Christ. It may seem important; it may robe itself in the garb of religion: but it must die. Oh, for that ruthless sword! that relentless vengeance.

18-32 *Jehu's decline.* — Jehu was earnest enough in uprooting all traces of Baal-worship, but his zeal against idolatry was not accompanied by personal holiness. He took no heed to walk in the law of the Lord with all his heart (**31**). When the succession to the throne had been secured by the promise of God to his fourth generation, he rapidly deteriorated, permitting the sins of Jeroboam. It is comparatively easy to denounce the sins of others, to be orthodox in our creed, and strong in our denunciation of those who are treacherous to Evangelical truth; and yet we may be permitting in our heart grievous wrongs on account of which God will have to cut us short. Judge yourselves, that ye be not judged. Take the beam out of your own eye, that you may see clearly to take it out of another's. Be careful that your own heart-life is free from the sins you are so quick to discern. Remember that conscience often drives us to find relief by venting on others the remonstrances which it denounces against the sin of the heart.

32-36 *Israel's decay.* — They were short in their duty to God, therefore God cut them short in their extent, wealth, and power. Hazael was the cause of this, fulfilling Elisha's anticipations (8:12). Those tribes suffered first whose choice had been determined by the attractions of the land. Those who choose for this life only are often the first to suffer the loss of all, as Lot did.

2 Kings 11   JOASH MADE KING

1-3 *Athaliah* well deserves the title given her in 2 Chronicles 24:7. She usurped the throne, and played the part of her mother, Jezebel, in Judah. Though Joram had been a wicked man and a bad king, he seems to have been able to recognize the value of piety in others; and so he had secured, as a husband to his daughter, the good priest, Jehoiada. The husband influenced the wife; and in the general massacre which Athaliah perpetrated, Jehosheba rescued the youngest child of Ahaziah, who was, in fact, her nephew. His nurse and he were hidden in a room where the mattresses were kept, and which was used perhaps for some sudden influx of priests at festal times. Is not this hidden prince a type of the hiding of the true Prince in the recesses of our hearts, while some Athaliah occupies too large a share of the government?

4-12 *The boy king.* — It was a joyful moment, that manifestation of the hidden prince. Many loyal hearts must have renounced all hope of such a thing as seeing again an offspring of David's line. But God kept His word. The Word of God was a befitting gift (**12**, and Deut. 17:18, 19).

There are suggestions in this chapter which may apply to our inner life as believers. There is a strong, wicked Athaliah principle in most of us, which strongly opposes all that is of God. It usurps His place, and murders His seed. And the holy but lowly Joash germ of the regenerate life is too often secreted in some remote attic of the nature for long years. Thank God it cannot be discovered or destroyed. It is hidden with Christ in God. But it is exposed to great opposition, and the conflict in the outward life is in the highest degree painful. Then there comes a moment when suddenly it breaks from its hiding-place; and, in some moment of revival or consecration, assumes its rightful position on the throne. What predominates in you — flesh or spirit, self or Christ, Athaliah or Joash?

And is not this also a type of coming events? Surely before long the Lord Jesus, who is now hidden, will be manifested (Col. 3:4), and those that have hated Him will be ashamed.

13-21 *Reformation.* — The death of Athaliah led the way to a thorough change throughout the kingdom. There was a double covenant: the demolition of the Baal-house, which had sadly profaned the holy city; and regulations for the proper performance of the worship of God. Then came joy and quiet; as there always must when evil is cast out, and the life adjusted with the holy law of the Most High.

2 Kings 12   THE TEMPLE REPAIRED

1-3 *An auspicious beginning.* — So long as the good priest lived, the young king did well. We owe more than we know to the influence of Godly men like Jehoiada; and it would be our constant prayer that God would raise up such men in these last days. Nay, let us seek to be such ourselves, acting as an antiseptic against pollution, and salt against corruption. Our speech, our behavior, our daily life, should be so healthful and wholesome as to check the growth of evil. But we should not be content with this. There is much positive good that needs doing.

4-16 *The renovation of the Temple.* — The sacred structure had suffered terribly under Athaliah (2 Chron. 24:7). The king might well take an interest in the building where he had spent his earliest years. The first attempt at raising a fund was a failure. It was in the wrong hands; surely the priests were not the proper parties to receive or collect moneys, which were dwindled away in their own maintenance. But when once an opportunity was given to the people to give their freewill offerings, the sum soon grew to a large amount, which enabled the workmen to proceed.

It was not very businesslike, perhaps, to have no contract with the men who did the work in the temple building. But the fact of it not being needed is a beautiful tribute to their faithfulness. We need more men of this stamp. They often set off in dark relief the characters of those who, like these priests, might have been expected to be the foremost in such holy work. God's noblest servants do not so often come from the classes specially trained, as from those of whom nothing was expected.

The house of God is always needing repair. Such are the breaches caused by false friends or open foes in the moral and religious life of the people, that there is ample scope for the most strenuous effort.

17-21 *Invasion and assassination* followed close on each other. Joash revolted from God, and the hand of the Lord was against him (2 Chron. 24). The reign began in sunshine, but was sadly overcast. How much we need to ask that He who has begun the good work in us may perform it to the end!

2 Kings 13   DEATH OF ELISHA

1-9 *Jehoahaz in Israel.* — At first sight there seems a discrepancy between verses **1** and **10**. We must account for the longer period by supposing that his father admitted Jehoahaz to some share of power during his lifetime. It is very interesting and pathetic to read of the compassion of Jehovah, notwithstanding the evil done in His holy sight. He heard the prayer of the king, in spite of all the evil he had done, and answered it by sending a saviour. In their distress men cry unto the Lord, and He saves them out of the stormy sea; but how often they forget Him, and repay His kindness by idolatry and neglect! "The Lord gave Israel a saviour; . . . nevertheless they departed not from the sins of Jeroboam" (**5, 6**). Oh, that the love of God, so undeserved and yet so free, might lead us to repentance!

10-19 *Jehoash.* — The grandson of Jehu, he followed in the idolatries which had become indigenous to Israel's soil. The death of Elisha was a most memorable event. It was now sixty years since he had commenced his public work as Elijah's servant. In strong contrast to the sins around him, Elisha stood as a witness for God, and much holy light shines around his closing record. The King of Israel seems to have expected to see chariots of horsemen, as in the translation of Elijah. Did Elisha expect it? This was not to be his end. But the path of his soul from his dying bed was swift and sure. It does not matter how or where we die, in any case Jesus waits to receive us to Himself.

What a model of prevailing faith and prayer Elisha's dying converse with the king affords! We do not consume our foes, because we strike only thrice and cease. We should put no limit on God by our restrained prayer and meager faith. Let us go with Him as far as we may, and only stay when He says, Ask Me no more.

20-25 *Miracle at Elisha's grave.* — The dead body was the means of giving life. Surely Elisha was living still; for God is not God of the dead, but of the living (Matt. 22:32). And is it not a parable of how the grave of Jesus is the means of life? You must die in order to live.

Mark the posthumous influence of a good man! His example, his word, his books, are full of holy power; and many a dead soul touching his remains lives. Oh, that we may live through death; and when dead, may our memory and influence still speak, and energize, and work for God.

2 Kings 14   AMAZIAH, KING OF JUDAH

1-7 *Amaziah in Judah.* — There was a gleam of better things in this reign, although not of the best (**3**). Good traits were to be found in Amaziah's character, among which was his humanity to the children of his father's murderers; the slaying of whom, although expressly forbidden (Deut. 24:16), was probably dictated as a policy by fear of their rising up to avenge their fathers' death. There was also his willingness (as recorded in 2 Chron. 25) to forego the assistance of the army of Israel, when met by the remonstrances of the man of God. He obtained a great victory over Edom (who were in a state of revolt, *see* 8:22) because he dared to trust God; but he fell a victim to the idols of Edom. "He brought the gods of the children of Seir, and set them up to be his gods, and bowed himself down before them" (2 Chron. 25:14).

7 Selah, or Petra, was largely excavated out of rock, hence its name. Oh, to live in the Rock!

8-22 *His defeat and death.* — After the idolatry which followed the campaign against Edom, it seemed as if God's Spirit left him, and gave him up to his own devices. He gave himself up to arrogance and vainglory; challenged the king of Israel to combat; and exposed himself and his people to disastrous defeat. To what lengths of folly and sin may we not go when once we get away from God!

It is always a foolish thing to run into collision with any who are willing to live peacefully with us. The beginning of strife is like the letting out of water, which may become a flood before which the instigator will be swept away. The parable was rather humbling in its comparisons, but it conveyed beneficial advice. How often are men allured to ruin by their first successes! The great enemy of souls hides the hook by the gaudy fly, the pitfall by the layer of soil. If a man persist in spite of all warnings given by friends or foes, he must bear the consequences of his own folly. We have a glimpse in the parallel record of the pride and arrogance of the king, which culminated in this disastrous challenge and overthrow (2 Chron. 25:16).

23-29 *Jeroboam II in Israel.* — This king was the fourth of Jehu's dynasty. How like God, to abundantly fulfil His promise (10:30). This was the longest reign of any of the kings in Israel. The Syrians had in past reigns cut Israel short; at Hamath in the north, and all down the Jordan to the Dead Sea. The victories which marked the reign of this intrepid soldier, and which were the means of the restoration of Israel of the lost territory, were granted by the goodness of God, who was touched by the miseries of His people, and the remembrance of His covenant. The people should have used this season for repentance; but they put this from them. Their iniquities were too deep-seated to warrant that full deliverance which God was prepared to have given them. There was some lessening of the bitter bondage, as though to show what God would have done; but not more, since they would not repent. He is long-suffering indeed, and not willing that any should perish; yet our sins seem often to compel Him to proceed to extremities, that by fire He may deliver us from all evil.

Jonah, Hosea, Joel, and Amos prophesied at this period. They foretold the earthquake which took place in this reign; the invasion of locusts and caterpillars; and the terrible dought.

2 Kings 15   ISRAEL'S DOWNFALL

1-7 *Azariah or Uzziah in Judah.* — Uzziah's reign was very splendid; fifty-two years of almost unbroken prosperity; the story of it is told in 2 Chronicles 26. The inspired historian here only emphasizes that the glory of his days went down in darkness. We learn from the other record, that at the close of his reign, being deprived of the invaluable direction of Zechariah, he sought to combine in himself the offices of priest and king, a prerogative which could only be realized in Christ (Zech. 6:13), and that for this he was branded with the awful curse of leprosy, which compelled his absence from the temple, till the day of his death.

8-31 *The last kings of Israel.* — For more than thirty years preceding its dissolution, the northern kingdom was terribly distracted. Disintegration and slavery always follow in the wake of idolatry and disobedience. So it befell in Israel. Anarchy, idolatry, high-handed wrong, and immorality, swept like a hurricane over the land. Rent with revolution, destitute of strong wise men fit to hold the helm, unable to withstand the successive invasions of Assyria, it was indeed in a pitiable plight.

32-38 *Jotham, king of Judah.* — A true conception of the state of the land may be obtained from the earlier chapters of Isaiah. Wantonness, pride, luxury, oppression, rode rough-shod over the land. Yet it was at this very crisis that the prophet saw his marvellous vision (6:1). Punishment could not be longer averted. "The Lord began to send" (**37**). These men were unrighteous and unholy; yet they are said to have been God-sent. And so always, while wicked men think only of executing their own malignant designs, they are really subserving the plans of the Most High (Acts 4:27, 28). But the full weight of this blow was averted during the comparatively good reign of Jotham, to fall with double force during that of his wicked son.

We are only safe and happy so long as we do what is right in the sight of God. Rightness is blessedness. If only we will dare to take God's faith, we shall have God's companionship;

not only as light, but as salvation. To do the will of God is the only clue to abiding for ever.

2 Kings 16   JUDAH INVADED

1-4 *Ahaz in Judah.* — He not only passed his children through lines of fire, but seems to have burnt some of them (2 Chron. 28:3). He dared to bring back the abominations of the heathen. His actions would be well-nigh incredible, did we not know something of the fickleness and evil of our own hearts. Bitter indeed was the return made to the great Vinedresser for all the care He had expended on the vine that He had planted in the very fruitful hill. Verily it brought forth wild grapes. All the abominations of Canaan were practiced by the people whom God had taken to Himself as His peculiar possession. Such a descent from the song of redemption at the Red Sea would have appeared impossible. But it came nevertheless. God foresaw it all, yet He did not relinquish His purpose. It is a great comfort to know that our God can never be surprised at any evil thing He sees in us. He loved us, notwithstanding His clear prevision of all we would cost Him. And though such love must chastise, yet it will never leave us, until it has brought us back to itself.

5-9 *The confederacy of Israel and Syria.* — Isaiah divulges their object (Isa. 7:6). It is most desirable to read Isaiah 7, 8, 9, in which the prophet calms the fear of the people, under the shadow of this great calamity. If Judah had only relied on these successive promises, and had left God to interpose on their behalf, there would have been certain deliverance and victory. But, instead of this, a bribe was offered to the king of Assyria to do what the Almighty would have done.

How great was the blunder and crime of calling in the help of Assyria to break up the confederacy! It was in the teeth of Isaiah's most eager protestations; and it was the first step towards the invasion of the land by that very nation whose help was like the broken staff, which pierces the hand of him who leans on it.

10-16 *Idolatry.* — The heavenly-designed altar was replaced by one modelled after that in Damascus, and sacrifices offered to false gods (2 Chron. 28:23). Delivered from his foes, Ahaz began to copy their idolatrous practices and to imitate the workmanship of their altars. Apparently he did not reason that the repetition of their sins would reduce him and his country to their fate. We wonder at the exchange, and yet how often do we substitute our own thoughts and plans for God's! Let us see to it that we guard our altar intact (Heb. 13:10). What a wily and unprincipled priest was here! (**16**).

17-20 *The spoiling of the Temple.* — The laver was for the ablutions of the priests. The covert for the larger congregations of the Sabbath. The entry, from the royal palace to the Temple. Evidently Assyrian influence was very much in the ascendant; and everything was done to secure a uniformity between the ritual at Jerusalem and that of their powerful neighbors. Let us turn from this sad apostasy to the predictions of our Emmanuel (Isa. 8:8).

2 Kings 17   CAPTIVITY

1-6 *Hoshea in Israel.* — The measure of their iniquities was now full. Israel in vain sought to avert its fate by appealing, not to the Lord, but to the king of Egypt. But Egypt was no match for the powerful kingdom which was arising on the banks of the Euphrates. To lean upon Pharaoh was to trust a broken reed. What agony must have been endured during the three years' siege! Shalmaneser changed the inhabitants (**6** and **24**), a policy which was continued by Esarhaddon (Ezra 4:2). The object was to keep the country tilled, and to make rebellion less likely and easy. But, after all, the Assyrian was the rod of the Divine justice (Isa. 10:5).

7-23 *The Divine indictment against Israel.* — This chapter reads like a page from the records of the great white throne. God humbles Himself to explain the reasons for His treatment of His people. He shows that it was not without cause that He dealt with them as He did. The story of Israel's sins, in spite of His earnest entreaties, the melancholy record of God-rejection and neck-hardening, of divination and enchantment, of faithlessness and disobedience, is set down without omission or compromise; and side by side is the golden tissue of goodness and mercy. It is a strange contrast. And yet if the true story of our inner experience could be written, how much there would be in common between it and this. Let us ponder those deep expressions, "they sold themselves to do evil" (**17**); "Jeroboam drove Israel from following the Lord" (**21**). Note also the expression in verse **15**, that we become like the objects we follow (Ps. 115:8). Israel was never restored; but remained dispersed among the nations, many of them being added to the Church in after days, as addressed in 1 Peter 1:1, 2 (*see* R.V.).

24-41 *The story of the new settlers.* — When Israel was taken from the land it was peopled by mongrel races from Babylon (which was already under the power of Assyria), and from other places. Every nation served its own gods, and at the same time gave some kind of allegiance to Jehovah as the local protecting deity of the land whom it was necessary to propitiate. It is a strange story; and yet there are many among us who, while really following the idols of their own evil hearts, give a nominal reverence to the name of God, partly because they think it polite, and partly because they wish to maintain a fair appearance among their fellows. They go to a place of worship with the intention of appeasing God; while they make for themselves many an idol besides (Matt. 6:24; 1 John 5:21).

2 Kings 18   SENNACHERIB

1-12 *Hezekiah.* — There was to be some hard fighting, in Hezekiah's reign, for existence and liberty. The foes of God and His people would come about them as an angry sea encircling a sand bank. The skies were dark with the gathering storm when Hezekiah ascended the throne, which his father had blackened with his crimes. It was wonderful that such a father as Ahaz should have had such a son; but he probably had a good mother (2 Chron. 29:1, 26:5). He at once commenced a course of reform; and made the best preparation possible for meeting all the contingencies of his time by putting away the evils which had alienated the Divine protection.

In the rooting out of idolatry, and in the destruction of the brazen serpent, which had become a kind of *fetish,* in the same way as the crucifix has become now, he must have raised an immense amount of opposition; but he did not swerve to the right or left. What a magnificent testimony is in verse **6**! There is no such way of meeting temptation and danger as by putting the heart right with God. Cleave to Him; depart not from following Him; keep His commandments: so shall the Lord be with you, and whithersoever you go forth, He will prosper you.

13-16 *Sennacherib.* — It must have been a vast disappointment when the Assyrian came to invade Judah. But the invasion would probably give a great assistance to the cause of reform, arresting and warning many who thought the king too particular. It was a great mistake to bribe Sennacherib; and, like so many of our expedients, it did not avail. What a lamentable pity that Hezekiah did not, from the commencement of his trouble, throw himself on the protecting care of God! If the king had only trusted this time as he did the next, there would have been no need for the bribe. God would have delivered His people.

17-37 *Rab-shakeh.* — Three years after, the generals of Sennacherib beleagured the city, in very close quarters. It is thought by some that this bold blasphemer was an apostate Jew, hence the added force of his words. He tried to prove that the Jews had forfeited Divine protection (**22**); that the Assyrians had come at the bidding of Jehovah (**25**); and that He would not be able to do more for His people than other gods (**34**).

The Jews met the taunts of Rab-shakeh in silence. It was wise policy. It is infinitely better to hand over our wrongs to God, who will avenge our cause and see that right is done, than to defend ourselves by argument and force. The only exception is when a simple explanation may relieve the cause we love from some evil imputation. Rab-shakeh could not understand the attitude of the king and people. Men of the world cannot read our secrets. God's hidden ones are as great a mystery as Christ was; but one day they will be manifested with Him.

2 Kings 19   SENNACHERIB OVERTHROWN

The lesson of this chapter needs but few words. There is no such resort for the troubled soul as God Himself. Twice did Hezekiah seek the face of the Lord.

1-7 *The royal anguish.* — In the first instance, when Hezekiah heard the blasphemous words so proudly spoken before the walls of Jerusalem, he went up into the house of the Lord, and entreated Isaiah to join him in supplication. That bowed form of Hezekiah before the altar of God, while his servants and ministers were with Isaiah, is a beautiful emblem of the true way of meeting trouble. And it is very blessed, when our cause is so identified with God's, that we can appeal for help on that account.

All through this crisis Isaiah acted the part of a patriot and hero. He poured forth words of burning eloquence and fire, denouncing the Assyrian, predicting his doom, and encouraging the people. The one figure which stands out in bold relief amid the storm is that of the intrepid prophet, who even dares to compose a funeral ode for the burial of the imperious invader. There is hardly anything in all literature so sublime as Isaiah 10, 11, 12, 13, 14.

8-34 *The blasphemous letter.* — The siege of Jerusalem was postponed till Sennacherib could undertake it in person, and the hostile forces drew off. But a letter was sent full of insult and blasphemy and proud certainty of ultimate success. For the second time, Hezekiah sought the face of the Lord, and prayed before Him. This was not the last letter which has been written with the ink of gall and bitterness, and sent to the servants of God. It is always best to lay such before God, and leave Him to answer them (**14**).

There is great beauty and earnestness in the king's prayer

(15-19). Supplications for help blend with holy argument and reasonings and allusions to the effect of the issue on the Divine glory.

In each case God sent an answer of peace through Isaiah. The second of them is a magnificent ode, full of heroic and ecstatic faith, and breathing the spirit of undaunted and unwavering trust. That was probably the sabbatic year, for the produce was promised to be sufficient for two years; but in any case, the sabbatic calm had entered the prophet's soul. They that believe enter into rest. And as in the center of the candle flame there is a vacuum of perfect safety, so amid alarm we may find in Christ's care a resting-place so happy and secure that we too may relieve ourselves of our burdens and sing triumphal odes on the very eve of the battle. There is no lack to them that trust in God.

35-37 *The enemy's destruction.* — How brief and significant the record! One of the angels was enough; how strong they must be! It is very foolish to wage war with God. Out of this memorable episode sprang Psalm 76.

2 Kings 20   HEZEKIAH'S PRAYER

1-7 *Hezekiah's sickness.* — One trouble often follows another. With Hezekiah the invasion of Assyria was followed by severe sickness. This was apparently in the same year; hence, "I will defend this city" (**6**).

Accumulated troubles present a platform for accumulated deliverance. We may understand from the prophet's announcement that the natural result of the disease would have been death. But an arrest was put on the ordinary course of things by the miraculous interposition of God, in answer to prayer.

Who does not know what it is to turn the face to the wall in unutterable anguish? We must get where God alone can read us. When we cannot be as private as we would wish, let us not discontinue our devotions, but be as private as we can. Hezekiah may have quoted the promise made to David (1 Kings 8:25), and longed for a respite; partly because life and immortality were not brought to light, and partly because he may have desired to finish his reforms. God always see our tears and hears our prayers, though He does not always answer us promptly and satisfactorily to our poor sense. The figs were, perhaps, rather the means of stimulating faith than the cause of cure.

With all our care we cannot add one cubit to our life; but God can. He assigns the number of years we have to live, and knows exactly when their number will be up. Oh, to spend each hour as being His gift as much as were the fifteen years of Hezekiah's life. God does not always prolong life in answer to prayer, and we should always leave such matters submissively with Him; because He may see reasons why it would be far better for us to be removed at once from this world of temptation and sorrow.

8-11 *The sign.* — The dial was probably a series of steps on which an upright pole cast a shadow, the hours being marked by the concurrence of the shadow with the edge of the steps. It appears that there was a partial eclipse of the sun in Jerusalem at this time, on January 11, B.C. 680, but it is not likely that this would account for this remarkable phenomenon, which was doubtless due to some Divine power which we cannot understand. But the shadow might be affected, without any necessary interference with the movements of the planetary system.

12-21 *The penalty of ostentation.* — What a lost opportunity not to show these men that the sun was, after all, but a servant in the hand of Israel's God! If Hezekiah had been taken away by early death, he would never have incurred the terrible words of verse **17**. Let us watch against the sin of show and pomp. At the best we are only caretakers and stewards. We have nothing that we have not received. But if we forget this, and yield to pride and vainglory, we are liable to forfeit all.

2 Kings 21   MANASSEH'S WICKEDNESS

1-9 *Manasseh's sins.* — Such sin is revealed in this chapter as recalls the worst abominations of the heathen; and this of the redeemed people of God, incited by the son of the good Hezekiah! A pious father cursed with a wicked son — not the last time, alas! And it is the more wonderful, as he was born after the marvellous deliverances in the State, as well as in the royal home. He carried his sacrilege into the precincts of the holy Temple, and introduced the very worst forms of idolatry. How sad the record, that they did even more evil than the nations whom the Lord destroyed before Israel!

10-16 *The predicted doom.* — There could be only one result to all this: that the Lord's help should be withdrawn, and that they should be left to reap the bitter harvest of their sins. God does not cast us off till we have cast Him off; and even then He punishes us by withdrawing to His place only till we acknowledge our offense and seek His face again. Our only defense and salvation consist in our union with God; His deliverance around us, His grace within. But directly we yield to sin, it is as if some obstruction had come into the channel of communication; and the water falls in the fountain, but not because of any failure in the cistern.

The line and plummet (**13**) were used to mark off those, in a long line of captives, who were reserved for life or condemned to death. The wiping of the dish is very expressive. The people endorsed their king in what he did, and they were therefore to share his fate. The blood of innocents (**16**) aggravated their case. The Lord was about to leave His people to suffer the results of their sins, that they might learn by contrast what an awful thing it was to forfeit His protecting care (Hosea 5:14, 15).

In this reign, Hosea, Joel, Nahum, Habakkuk, and Isaiah lived and prophesied. It is recorded by tradition that the last of these was sawn asunder (Heb. 11:37); and perhaps the blood of the other four was included in that which Manasseh shed. The more sin, the more warning voices; but the greater light, the darker sin.

17, 18 *Manasseh's death.* — We learn from 2 Chronicles 33 the story of Manasseh's repentance and acceptance with

God. In his affliction he sought the Lord. Such is the gain of pain. But his personal repentance could not obliterate the terrible results of his sins or their effect in incurring the penalty of captivity. We may be pardoned; but there is a harvest which even pardon does not avert.

19-26 *Amon's reign* was short and inglorious, and was ended by assassination (**26**). He was not stayed by the example of his father's sins or regrets from following the sinful courses to which from childhood he had been inured. "He forsook the Lord, . . . and walked not in the way of the Lord" (**22**). As the twig is bent the tree grows. Oh parents, remember that example is more decisive than words. You may adopt for yourselves, in maturer life, a holier and better course; but you can never eradicate the evil influences exerted on your children.

2 Kings 22   JOSIAH, THE BOY-KING

1-2 *Josiah's good reign.* — Aged eight on his accession to the throne, he seems from the first to have chosen the paths of goodness. In the midst of his father's court, that young life grew up as a young palm in the desert waste. Perhaps one of the prophets, or some attendant, had made him the subject of special care and love, teaching him in the ways of the Lord. In his sixteenth year, while he was still young, he began to seek God yet more earnestly; and four years after the religious life within him prompted him to begin a great work of reform (2 Chron. 34:2, 3).

3-7 *The repair of the Temple.* — Other reforms had been probably effected throughout the land; but it was not till the eighteenth year of his reign that this great work of the cleansing of the Temple, and the restoration of the holy rites, actually began. This is work to which we must all give our heedful care. The temple of the body must be kept pure for the Holy Ghost; and the inner shrine of the spirit should be maintained in perpetual repair.

The money for the Temple work seems to have been contributed voluntarily, but there was a beautiful piety in the workmen which made them deal faithfully. There is no doubt that real religion makes better masters and servants; hence so many find it worth their while to feign it.

8-14 *The discovery of the Book of the Law.* — It is at such times, when rubbish is being cleared, and breaches made good, that the Word of God is found; and it comes home to us with new freshness, and becomes first the critic, and then the joy of our hearts. This was the Temple copy, laid beside the ark in the most holy place (Deut. 31:25, 26). Some say that it had been hidden by some faithful priest during the ungodly reigns of Manasseh and Amon.

Probably Shaphan would read Deuteronomy 28, 29, 30; and there was plenty in these chapters to fill the young king with dismay, if, as was not improbable, the whole was totally new to him. Oh, to read the Bible always with a particular reference to oneself! — and then, like Josiah, to proceed at once to put its injunctions and precepts into practice. There is great encouragement here. One copy of the Scriptures, like a seed long buried, suddenly fructified, and led to a reformation. So was it when Luther began to read that copy of the Vulgate at Erfurt. One copy of the Bible is enough to upheave a nation.

14-20 *The mission to Huldah.* — Ahikam was a friend of Jeremiah (Jer. 26:24); Achbor, or Abdon, a leading courtier. Zephaniah may have been too young; Jeremiah was at Anathoth. So, as the need was urgent, they went at once to Huldah, the wife of Shallum, well known for her prophetic gifts.

There was evidently a Godly remnant in Jerusalem, who had survived the massacre of the former reigns; of these Huldah was one. Women should always live in the uplands, beholding sights and hearing voices which are hidden from the rest of us. The greatest peculiarity is a thoughtless and irreligious woman.

The college was the name, not for a school, but for a particular quarter of the city. The decree had gone forth as against Sodom; but as in the case of Lot, so here, the people of God are delivered.

2 Kings 23   RENEWING THE COVENANT

1-3 *The Law is read.* — What the king had found good for himself, he gave to his people. It is a good habit to circulate the Scriptures. And how beautiful it was that this covenant should be formed. Let us give ourselves to be only, utterly, and always for God; and then set ourselves to destroy evil, beginning with ourselves.

4-20 *Idolatry destroyed.* — It is almost incredible to find that the emblems of the most obscene idolatry had been set up in the Temple, and that the holy place had been desecrated by abominable rites. But is there not a solemn warning to us all? Baal-worship is simply the adoration of human energy, and the Asherah the license of love. May there not be more of these than we know, even in Christian hearts!

The brook Kedron runs along the east and south of the city, dry in summer, but after heavy rains a torrent bed. There the impurities of Temple and city were emptied. The grove of verse **6** was the mystic tree. Some of the levitical priests, who had fallen into the habit of officiating in high places, were degraded from their office, though still maintained from the Temple revenues. Topheth (**10**) was so called from *toph,* a drum, which was used to drown the cries of terrified children made to pass through the fire at this place. The filth of the city was collected here and burned; hence the allusion of Mark 9:44.

Not satisfied with removing every vestige of idolatry from his own dominions, Josiah made a tour of the land once inhabited by the ten tribes; and especially destroyed the ancient altar at Bethel, as had been predicted more than three hundred years before his birth (1 Kings 13:2). From that time the desolation foretold by Hosea and Amos has never been disturbed; and Bethel, *the house of God,* has literally become Bethaven, *the house of nothing.*

21-28 *The Passover observed.* — When the old leaven was cleared away, they could keep the feast. There came to it, not only Josiah's own subjects, but many of the remnant people of the ten tribes (2 Chron. 35:1-19).

When the purgation of evil is complete so far as we know, we may turn to eat the Passover; and we shall be at one with all the scattered people of God in the act of solemn commemoration.

29-37 *Josiah's death, and afterwards.* — These events are more fully related in 2 Chronicles 35:20-27. The end of Josiah was very tragic; it was the result of his own folly and presumption. A long God-fearing life may end in self-incurred disaster, unless we carefully walk with God to the very end. There is never a moment in the life of the most matured saint when he may lean to his own understanding. The defeat of Josiah at Megiddo is confirmed by Herodotus, and by sculptures on Pharaoh's tomb. Jehoahaz, a younger son, was taken prisoner by Pharaoh, and carried to Egypt, where he died (Jer. 22:10-12). Jehoiakim, notwithstanding the pressure which lay on him, did evil, and hastened his ruin.

2 Kings 24   CARRIED INTO BABYLON

1-6 *Jehoiakim's reign.* — Mark the emphatic statement of the second verse, "The Lord sent against him" bands of foes. Nebuchadnezzar now first appears upon the scene. He was then at the beginning of his reign (Jer. 25:1), and little realized that he was only an axe with which God hewed, the rod of His anger, the staff of His indignation. Ungodly men are sometimes permitted to vex God's people for their chastisement; the best way of escaping them is to turn instantly to God in confession and prayer. The Chaldees were evidently the flower of his kingdom (Dan. 2).

Note the entail of Manasseh's sin (**3**)! He had lived, been forgiven, and died years before; but Judah was irrevocably doomed for his sin. The poison had eaten so deeply into the heart of the people, that only the severest measures could eradicate its effect. "At the commandment of the Lord came this upon Judah."

"He slept with his fathers" (**6**) simply means that he died; for this king was not honored with the rites of burial (Jer. 36:30).

The battle of Carchemish, referred to in verse **7**, was one of the decisive battles of the world (see Jer. 46:2).

Note that Daniel was among the captives carried away by Nebuchadnezzar in this reign (Dan. 1:1, 2), together with a portion of the sacred vessels of the Temple.

8-16 *Jehoiachin.* — The three months' reign of this king is not inconsistent with Jeremiah's prophecy concerning Jehoiakim (Jer. 36:30). Nebuchadnezzar in person joined "his servants" in the siege of Jerusalem; and the king, the queen-mother, and the royal family "went out" (**12**), and surrendered to the Babylonian monarch. They were carried into exile, according to Jeremiah's prediction (Jer. 22:24, 25), together with "all Jerusalem, and all the princes, the mighty men of valor, and ten thousand captives, and all the craftsmen and smiths" (**14**); leaving behind only the "poorest of the people of the land."

The sacred vessels of the Temple remaining from the previous seizure were also carried away, and were put to profane uses in the land of exile (Dan. 5:2, 3); they were not returned to Jerusalem until the days of Cyrus (Ezra 1:7-11). The false prophets, who soon after the departure of the sacred vessels predicted an early return, were resisted by Jeremiah with the Divine approval; Hananiah — one of the foremost of the misleading voices — dying "in the same year" (the fourth year of the captivity, Jer. 28:1) according to the message of Jeremiah (Jer. 28:15, 16), who (chap. 29) specified seventy years as the time-limit of the captivity. The prophet Ezekiel was also among the captives at this exodus, and he dates his prophecies from this year (Ezek. 1:2; 40:1; 29:17). Kish the Benjamite, the ancestor of Mordecai, was also among the captive-band (Esther 2:6). It is very necessary to study the prophecies of Jeremiah and Ezekiel as illustrating the history of this period.

17-20 *The last of the Kings.* — Mattaniah was the uncle of the previous king, and his name was changed by Nebuchadnezzar to Zedekiah (*God's Justice*). He was young, and his heart was reckless and impenitent. Led on by ambassadors of neighboring states, he was enticed into a league with them against Babylon, in the teeth of Jeremiah's remonstrances, who wept tears of blood over the infatuation of his fellow-countrymen. Zedekiah, blinded to all warning lights as to truth and honor (Ezek. 17:15), effectually brought upon his people a yet more overwhelming destruction. How foolish and hardened is that departure of the heart from the living God which deprives it of rudder and chart, and leaves it to drift before the tide! The fear of God is the beginning of wisdom, and only those have sound understanding that keep His commandments.

2 Kings 25   DESOLATION

1-3 *Jerusalem again beseiged.* — Angered by this last traitorous revolt, the king of Babylon resolved to put an end to the separate existence of the kingdom. This was the third siege of Jerusalem. Owing to the strength of the fortifications, it lasted a year and a half, until the people were reduced to the most fearful deprivations, and perpetrated atrocities which are almost inconceivable (Lam. 2:20-22; 4:3). Jeremiah earnestly persuaded the king to surrender (Jer. 38:17); and if only the prophet had been allowed to sway the king's counsels, much of the misery of the siege would have been averted; but it seemed as if a judicial blindness had been allowed to veil his eyes, and to harden his heart to his destruction.

4-21 *The final scenes.* — Two prophecies, apparently contradictory, were fulfilled (Jer. 32:4; Ezek. 12:13). The former prophecy, where it is said the king's eyes shall behold the eyes of his captor, was true; yet only as far as the time of his surrender. Ezekiel's word that "yet shall he not see the land though he die there" foretold his dire fate in the loss of his eyesight. With Babylonian savagery Nebuchadnezzar, after slaying the king's sons before his eyes, quenched the light for ever, and the king was "bound with fetters of brass and carried to Babylon" (**7**).

The retribution was terrible: Zedekiah blinded and a

captive; the Temple, after four hundred and twenty years of varying fortunes, in ashes; the city walls and buildings razed to the ground; the remnant of the precious things carried off; the principal men put to death, while a miserable handful of eight hundred persons were driven into captivity.

22, etc. *The remnant.* — The poorest only were left, under Gedaliah, Jeremiah's friend (Jer. 26:24; 40; 41). His murder by Ishmael, who was jealous of him, was the last drop of anguish in the prophet's cup. In spite of his earnest protestations, the people deserted their own land, and settled in Egypt (Jer. 44:1), and the land was left desolate for seventy years to keep her sabbaths. Thus ended the kingdom of Judah; and thereafter the Jews became a scattered people: though destined to pass through two more extreme agonies, one of which befell them under Titus, the last awaits them still.

Such is the vengeance of God. He pleads along with man; but if he will not turn, then He whets His sword, and becomes the terrible avenger of sin. Such a story as this makes it possible to understand the anguish of the Hereafter, where men receive the reward of bad things done in the body. But, amid all, we recall the tears of the Book of Lamentations, like the tears of the Son of God. There is that in God which weeps while He chastises, which cries, "How shall I make thee as Admah and set thee as Zeboim?" Nor are tears all. He is the Redeemer. He gathers again the outcasts of Israel. There will be a return from the captivity, because "He delighteth in mercy."

KINGS OF JUDAH — AFTER ISRAEL'S CAPTIVITY

Yrs. B.C.	Kings	Notes
698	Manasseh 55 yrs.	Idolater: afterwards penitent
643	Amon 2 Yrs.	Did wickedly, slain by his servants
641	Josiah 31 yrs.	Caused Law to be read, killed in battle
610	Jehoahaz 3 mths.	Dethroned by Pharoah-nechoh
609	Jehoiakim 11 yrs.	Subdued by Nebuchadnezzar
599	Jehoiachin 3½ mths.	Carried into captivity
598	Zedekiah 11 mths.	JERUSALEM DESTROYED

THE KINGDOM OF ISRAEL continued from the revolt of the ten tribes 254 years; THE KINGDOM OF JUDAH 387 years. Chronologers disagree, and make up their discrepancies with the total by several interregna.

INDEX

Abdon 41, 207
Abiathar 127, 147, 149
Abigail 109
Abijah 163
Abijam 164-165
Abimelech 41, 53-54
Abinadab 87, 123
Abishai 110, 126, 143
Abner 116, 119-120
Absalom 132, 136; death 137-138; rebellion 133-135
Achan, sin of 18, 19-20, 129
Achish 112-113
Achor, Valley of 20
Achsah's request 29-30
Adonijah's revolt 147-148
Adullam, cave of 105-106
Agag 98
Ahab 167, 169, 173-173; death 174-175; family destroyed 189-190; house of 190-191
Ahaz 176, 198-199
Ahaziah, King of Israel 175, 178
Ahaziah, King of Judah 188
Ahijah 160
Ahikam 207
Ahimelech 104, 127
Ahithophel 134-137
Ai taken 20-21
Altar of Witness 35-36
Altar on Mount Ebal 21
Amalekites 97, 113-114
Amasa, death of 139
Amaziah, King of Judah 176, 195-196
Ammonites 56, 128-129
Amnon 70, 132
Amon 206-207, 213
Amos 176, 196, 208
Anakim 25
Angelic environment 185-186

Apostasy and failure 44-45
Ark, in Dagon's Temple 85-86; in Zion 122-124; sent back 85-87; taken 84-85
Araunah, threshing floor of 144
Asa 164-166
Asahel 120
Ashdod 30
Assyrian invasion 202
Astaroth 46
Athaliah 191-192
Axe-head, lost 185
Azariah 176, 197

Baal, sun god 51, 169, 178; altars destroyed 50-51, 191, 208
Baalath (Baalbek) 157
Babylonian captivity 209-211
Balaam 27, 162
Barak 41, 47-48
Barzillai 138-139
Bathsheba 134, 147
Beersheba 33
Benaiah 143
Ben-hadad 171-172, 188
Benjamin 67-69; Israel's lamentation for 68; portion of 32; punishment 67
Bethel 167, 208
Bethlehem 73, 99
Beth-shemesh, catastrophe at 86-87
Boaz 74-78, 154-155
"Bow, song of the" 117-118
Brazen serpent destroyed 201
Brotherhood, memorable 100

Canaan, as divided among the tribes (map) 39
Canaan; alarm of 22; terror of 17
Canaanite Kings combine 23

Caleb, portion of 28-29, 42-43
Calves, two golden 167
"Captain of the Lord's host"
    17-18
Captivity of Israel 199-200
Carchemish, Battle of 210
Carmel, triumph at 168-169
Chariot, fiery 179-180
Chilion 72
Cherethites 127
Cherubim 154
"Choose ye this Day" 38-39
Circumcision renewed 17-18
Cities; of the Levites 34-35; of
    Refuge 33-34
"Cleave unto the Lord" 37-38
Confederation, defeat of the
    Northern 24
Confession and forgiveness
    130-131
Contemporary Kings of Judah
    and Israel 145
Covenant; brotherly 103-104; the
    New 38; renewing the 208-209
Crime, a terrible 66-67
Cush, the Benjamite 110

Dagon 85
Dan 33, 49, 64-65
Daniel 176, 210
David and Achish 112-113
David and Jonathan 101-102, 107
David; anointed 98-99; crowned
    king 118-119; death of
    148-149; flight from Absalom
    134; at Gath 104-105; God's
    promises to 124-125; city of
    121-122; communion with
    God 125; lament over Ab-
    salom 137-138; last words
    142-143; mighty men of

142-143; personal experience
    142; reconciliation with Saul
    107-108; resolution to bless
    God 141; sin confessed
    129-130; slays Goliath 100;
    triumphant return 138-139
Deborah 41, 46, 47-49
Delilah 62-63
Deliverance, from danger
    102-103; great 106-107; unex-
    pected 186-187
Division of the country 26-27
Doeg 106

Ebal and Gerizim 21
Eben-ezer 83, 87-88
Edom 126
"Egypt to the Euphrates, from"
    125-127
Ehud 41, 46
Ekron, plague at 85-86
Elah 166
Eli; flight and return 169-170;
    judge of Israel 41; priest
    82-82; and his sons, 82, 84
Elijah, prayer for rain 167; pro-
    test and prediction 173;
    translation 179-180, 194
Elimelech 72
Elisha 180, 185, 187-188; call of
    171; death of 194-195;
    message of 181; method of
    cure 184; miracle at grave
    195; prophecy of plenty 186
Elkanah 80
Elon 41
Endor, witch of 111-112
Enemies cast out 42-43
En-gedi 107
Environing Host, the 185-186
Ephods 53, 64

Ephraim, tribe of 30-31
Esdraelon 114-115
Ezekiel 176, 211
Ezion-geber 158
Ezra 11

Failure, cause of 43
Failure to occupy the land 26-27
Famine, three years of 140-141
Fate of traitors 149
Feast of Tabernacles 155
Fiery Chariot 179-180
"Fire from Heaven" 178-179
Fire, answer by 169
Friendship of David and Jonathan 103-104

Gaal 54
Gaza 30
Gedaliah 212
Gehazi 184-185
Gezer 30
Giants of life 100
Gibeon, league with 22-23, 140
Gideon 41, 50-53
Gilboa 117
Gilgal 12, 16, 92, 94
God's government, principles of 141
Goliath of Gath 100-101
Grace; God's delivering 141; prevenient 102

Habakkuk 176, 205
Hadad 160
Hadarezer 128
Haggai 176
Hailstones 23
Hamath 126
Hananiah 210
Hannah 80-82
Hanun, insult to David 128

Hazael 188, 191
Hazor 25
Hebron 28-29, 134
Hewers of wood and drawers of water 22-23
Hezekiah 176, 200-201; prayer of 203-204
Hiel, the Bethelite 19
Hiram, King of Tyre 152-154, 157
Holy of Holies 154, 156
Horeb, Elijah at 170
Hosea 176, 196, 205, 208
Hoshea 199
Huldah 207
Hushai 136

Ibzan 41
"Ichabod" 84-85
Idolatry in Judah 198-199
Idols, destruction of 50-51, 208
Idol making 63-64
Isaiah 176, 205
Ish-bosheth 118-119; murder of 120
Israel and Syria, confederation of 198
Israel, captivity of 199-200; dark days in 166, 167; decay 191; distress of 48-49; divine indictment against 199-200; downfall 197-198; judges of 41; last kings of 197; victories 26
Ittai 134

Jabesh-Gilead, 68-69, 94, 115
Jabin, King of Hazor 47-48; his confederates 24
Jachin and Boaz 154-155
Jael 48
Jair 41, 54

"Jawbone of an ass" 60-62
Jedidiah 131
Jehoahaz, King of Israel 194
Jehoahaz, King of Judah 176, 209, 213
Jehoash 194-195
Jehoiachin 176, 210, 213
Jehoiada 192
Jehoiakim 176, 209-210, 213
Jehonadab 190
Jehoram, King of Israel 180
Jehoram, King of Judah 188
Jehoshaphat 174-175
Jehosheba 192
Jehu, King of Israel 188-190
Jehu, the prophet 166
Jephthah 41, 55-56
Jeremiah 176, 210, 212
Jericho, capture of 18-19; healing of the waters at 180
Jeroboam, son of Nebat 161-163
Jeroboam II 196
Jerusalem 121, 176, 202, 211, 213
Jezebel 167, 169, 173, 190-191
Joab 119, 128, 133, 138, 147
Joash 176, 191-194
Joel 176, 196, 205
Jonah 176, 196
Jonathan; intercession for David 102; interview with David 107; valor of 95-97
Jordan; Elijah and Elisha at the 180; memorial 15-16; passage of the 14-15
Joseph; bones buried 39; complaint of the children of 31-32
Joshua, Book of 11-39
Joshua; death of 39, 44; inheritance of 33; solicitude for the people 37-39

Josiah 176, 206-207, 209
Jotham, King of Judah 176, 197
Jotham, parable of 54
Judah, tribe of 29-30
Judah; invaded 198-199
Judah, kings of; chart 213
Judas, type of 136-137
Judges, Book of 40-69
Judges of Israel; chart of 41; the first 45-47
Judgments predicted 128, 163-164

Kedron, Brook 208
Keilites, treachery of the 107
Kingdom; glorious 150-152; renewed 92-93
King; request for a 89; description of 89
Kings; battle with five 23; last of Israel 197; of Judah 210, 213; thirty-one 26
Kings, First Book of 146-175
Kings, Second Book of 177-213
Kinsman, a near 75-76
Kirjath-Jearim 29, 87, 123
Kirjath-Sepher 29, 42
Kish, the Benjamite 210

Laish 33; capture of 65
Lamentation, a Song of 117-118
Lavers, the ten 155
Law, the 12 21; Book of the 207; court 77
Levi, cities of 34-35; tribe of 27
Lot, choosing by 28, 34

Mahlon 72
Maid, little 183-184
Makkedah, cave of 24
Malachi 176

Manasseh, King of Israel 204-206, 209, 213
Manasseh, tribe of 30, 31-32
Manoah, prayer of 58
Mattaniah 210
Medeba, battle at 128
Megiddo, battle of 209
Memorial, twofold 15-16
Mephibosheth 120, 127-128, 138
Mesha, King of Moab 182
Micah 176; idols of 63-64, 65
Micaiah 174
Michal 120, 124
Midianites 50, 52
Mizpeh 25, 67, 87, 91
Moab 125-126, 70, 181-182; rebellion of 180-182; return from 72-74
Molten sea 155
Moses 11-12, 27, 30, 35

Naamah 149, 164
Naaman 183-185
Nabal, folly of 108-109
Naboth 172-173, 189
Nadab 165-166
Nahash, the Ammonite 92, 128
Nahum 176, 205
Naioth 102
Naomi 72, 75
Nathan 116, 135-136, 147; parable of 130; prophecy of, fulfilled 135, 147
National indignation 67-68
Nebuchadnezzar 210-211, 213
Nethinim 22
Nob 104
Numbering the people 143-144
North, conquest of the 24-25
Obadiah 168, 171, 176
Obed-Edom 87, 123

"Old Prophet, the" 162
Omri 166-167
Oreb and Zeeb 52
Ostentation, penalty of 204
Othniel 29, 41-42, 46
Og 26

Paran, Wilderness of 109
Passover observed, the 17, 208-209
Petra 195
Philistia 26, 70, 85, 125
Philistine wars 65, 83, 87, 95, 100, 106, 115, 122, 125, 140-141
Phinehas 67
Pillars, brazen 154-155
Pottage healed at Gilgal 183
Prediction of coming disaster 163-164
Priest making 64
Promised Seed, prophecy of the 142
Prophecies concerning Israel's oppression 70
Prophets; conflict of the 174-175; in chronological order 176; schools of the 102-103, 179, 185; sons of the 179
Psalm of Thanksgiving 141-142

Rabbah 131, 141
Rab-shakeh 201-202
Rahab, faith of 13-14, 18
Rain, prayer for 169
Ramah 88
"Rebellious and brought low" 54-55
Refuge, cities of 33-34
Rehoboam 160-161, 164
Repentence, times of 55

"Reproach of Egypt, the" 17
Revolt of the ten tribes 161
Rezon 160
Riddles 60
Rizpah 140
"Rule Thou over us" 52-53
Ruth, the Book of 71-78
Ruth, bride of Boaz 77; the gleaner 74-75

Samaria, sieges of 171, 186-187
Samson, judge of Israel 41; birth of 57-58; marriage feast of 59-60
Samuel, First Book of 79-115
Samuel, Second Book of 116-144
Samuel; birth of 80-81; call of 82-83; death of 108; message of 97-98; reproof of the people 93-94; remorse of 98; revelations to 83; sons of 88
Saul; among the Prophets 103; anointed king 90-92; death of 114-115, 117; rash folly of 94-95; rejected 97-98
Saul and David 99, 102
Saul and Jonathan, burial of 90
Scarlet line, the 13-14
Sennacherib 200-203
Shalmaneser 199
Shamgar 41, 46-47
Shaphan 207
Sheba 139-140; Queen of 146, 158-159
Shechem 54
"Shibboleth" 56-57
Shiloh, journey to 80; scheme at the dances at 69; tabernacle at 32
Shimei 135-136, 138

Shishak 164
Shunammite widow, 182, 187-188; sons of 182-183
Sihon and Og 26
Simeon 42
Sin and sorrow 44, 131-132
Sin and suffering 55
Sisera 47-48
Solomon; anointed king 147-148; death of 159-160; God's covenant with 157-158; glory of 159; growing power of 158-158; marriage of 149; palace of 154-155; wisdom of 149-150
Spies, hiding of the 13
"Still small voice, the" 169-171
Stone of witness, 39
Strife, fracticidal 56-57
Sun and Moon stand still 23-24
Sun's shadow recedes 204
Syria, war with 126

Tabernacle at Shiloh 32
Tadma (Tadmar) 157
Tamar 132
Tekoah, woman of 132-133
Temple; David's desire to build 124; David's preparations 152-153; dedication 155-157; destroyed 212; erected 153-154; prayer of intercession 156; repaired by Joash 193-194; repaired by Josiah 206-207; site of 145-145; spoiling of 199
Tibni 166
Tola 41, 54
Topheth 208
Tribes; failure of 43; ten 161; two and a half 13, 36; nine and a half 28

"Trumpets and pitchers" 51-52
Tyre 152, 122

Uriah 129-130
Uzzah 123
Uzziah 176, 197-198

Vessels of the Temple in
    Babylon 210
Victory, source of 126-127

War, rest from 25
Waters of Merom 24
Wiles of the Gibeonites 22
Witchcraft 112

Zarephath, widow of 168
Zadok 82
Zechariah 176
Zedekiah 176, 210-211, 213
Zelophehad, daughters of 31
Zephaniah 176, 207
Ziba 128, 135
Zimri 166
Ziphites, treachery of the 107,
    109
Zobah, war against 126, 128

F.B. MEYER MEMORIAL LIBRARY

Devotional Commentary on Exodus

This descriptive, directive and devotional work will be a special help to the hungry soul, the busy pastor, the pressured evangelist, the weighted missionary, and the searching scholar. 476 pages.

Choice Notes on Joshua—2 Kings

F.B. Meyer designed the book to record understandable, accessible notes on the books of Joshua through 2 Kings. The reader will gain new insight and challenge for today from these Old Testament books. 208 pages.

Choice Notes on the Psalms

This chapter-by-chapter commentary examines the Psalms from three perspectives: the historical setting, featuring the inner struggle of David; the prophetical references to Christ; and the practical applications. 192 pages.

Devotional Commentary on Philippians

The compressed and profound teaching of Philippians is X-rayed in this verse-by-verse commentary. This popular devotional is characterized by loyalty to the Scriptures and applications to the needs of today's believer. 262 pages.